THE HIDDEN WEALTH OF NATIONS

THE HIDDEN WEALTH OF NATIONS

David Halpern

polity

First published in 2010 by Polity Press

Polity Press
65 Bridge Street
Cambridge CB2 1UR, UK

Polity Press
350 Main Street
Malden, MA 02148, USA

ISBN-13: 978-0-7456-4801-9
ISBN-13: 978-0-7456-4802-6(pb)

A catalogue record for this book is available from the British Library.

Typeset in 10 on 12 pt Palatino
by Toppan Best-set Premedia Limited
Printed and bound in Great Britain by MPG Books Group Limited, Bodmin, Cornwall

The publisher has used its best endeavours to ensure that the URLs for external websites referred to in this book are correct and active at the time of going to press. However, the publisher has no responsibility for the websites and can make no guarantee that a site will remain live or that the content is or will remain appropriate.

Every effort has been made to trace all copyright holders, but if any have been inadvertently overlooked the publisher will be pleased to include any necessary credits in any subsequent reprint or edition.

For further information on Polity, visit our website: www.politybooks.com

Contents

Preface

I started writing this book in the Spring of 2007. The original intent was to write a series of short articles to update and pull together conclusions from papers I had worked on while at the UK's Prime Minister's Strategy Unit (PMSU), including those on life satisfaction, social capital, public service improvement, personal responsibility and behaviour change. I had spent from 2001 until Spring 2007 in the PMSU, mainly as the Chief Analyst, working on almost every area of domestic policy including leading our 'Strategic Audits'; the Respect campaign of 2005; setting up the Social Exclusion Task Force in 2006; and Policy Review before Blair handed over to Brown in 2007.

It has been a difficult but interesting period to write a book. This isn't a 'kiss and tell' history of my time in Government – that would have been much easier. Rather it is a book that draws heavily on empirical, cross-national material about how societies work and are changing, and the implications for policy. But the world doesn't stay still, and particularly over this last two years. The credit crunch and subsequent recession have wiped trillions of dollars off the world economy, leading to rapidly rising unemployment and changing public concerns, and have challenged and humbled the assumptions of many of my economist colleagues.

Many now see this as an important pivot point in global history. This is certainly the view of the current British Prime Minister, whose relatively optimistic take is that this is the moment at which the world has finally come to terms with the reality of the profound interconnection of the modern economy and the necessity for nations to work together to solve our common challenges. These challenges are not only about the operation of a global finance system, but also the protection of the environment; global health; and global poverty.

At the very least, the current situation has led economists to dust off their models of long economic cycles and ask whether the world is now entering a 15 to 20-year economic winter of a Kondratiev cycle.[1] I am not really an economist myself, though I did spend three years at Nuffield College, Oxford – the self-styled bastion of hard-nosed empirical economics and sociology in the UK – as a young Research Fellow. My own disciplinary roots lie more in social psychology, which is what I lectured on at Cambridge for seven years. In this sense, I suppose I am apt to look through the ups and downs of particular economic cycles and events to the continuities of human striving that run through them. The recession will come and go, and through it all we will argue and make up; laugh and cry; endure our private tragedies and successes – the flow of life will carry on.

I hope that this book taps into some of these deeper issues, relevant both in times of recession and beyond. Many countries now face a difficult fiscal environment for the next five years or more, with big rises in national debt that will seem to greatly limit the scope of policymakers and societies. But societies have far more assets than are captured by the tally of national debt and expenditure. For imaginative communities and policymakers, especially for those with the insight and daring to tap into societies' hidden wealth, the coming decades can be golden ones.

This book is about some of the big challenges that face advanced industrialized nations at the start of the twenty-first century, and how policymakers and citizens could respond to them. History tells us that many seemingly intractable problems of the day go on to be addressed, though often taking a generation to do so. From the 'great stink' of London's sewage in the nineteenth century, to the inflation and labour unrest of the 1970s, many seemingly intractable problems have gone on to be solved. Similarly, unrelenting negative trends, from rising crime to rising smoking, have been replaced with equally dramatic declines through a mutually reinforcing combination of changing public mood and government action. There is no reason why the challenges of today cannot be overcome, especially if citizens and governments work together.

Acknowledgements

I need to say thank you to a number of people. This book was written in fragments of time between my main activities of the last two years, and I thank those involved for enduring my periodic absences to work on the book or some obscure analysis connected with it. In this respect, particular thanks go to Lord Sainsbury with whom it has been the utmost pleasure to work with so closely in the creation of the Institute for Government. Anyone who spends a long time working in government – or perhaps in any institution – ends up sure that it could work better. The Institute, through a combination of research and development for top policymakers, should help make this a reality. It has already helped shape my own thinking about how governments and societies can improve their own working. A very special thanks is also due to my fine young research team at the Institute who came up with the title for this book, in particular Simon Parker and Tom Gash. Well done guys!

Other thanks are due to the large numbers of people involved in the Options for a New Britain project, which I edited over the same period. Though much more focused on the nuts and bolts of UK policy, I'm sure that some of my conclusions in this book have borrowed from ideas or analysis that was generated within Options. At the very least, the clear thinking of people like Steve Nickell and Tim Leunig on policy options around the planning system, or Peter Kenway's sober assessment of the Labour Government's attempts to reduce poverty over the last decade, provided a powerful sounding board for many of my own thoughts.

I am grateful to many conversations and reflections that I have had over the content and drafts of this book. These include with Lord Richard Wilson, Dan Corry, Michael Bichard, Bob Putnam, Simon

Szreter, Mike Woolcock, Peter Gooby-Taylor, Geoff Mulgan, Matthew Taylor, Lord Richard Lugard, Avner Offer, Richard Reeves, Edgar Cahn, Susan Hitch, two anonymous reviewers and various past and present members of the PMSU, including Stephen Aldridge, Gareth Davies, Julian McCrae, Nick Canning, Jonathan Brearley, Harvey Redgrave and Jacob West. I am also grateful to those at Polity who have helped navigate this book through to completion, and particularly John Thompson, Sarah Lambert, and Susan Beer.

Most of all, of course, go thanks to my family – my partner Jen and our two wonderful boys, Aaron and Isaac – and to Michael and Amy and my American relatives who forgave me the antisocial few days. I needed to work through the proofs, including to Eleanor for her sharp-eyed corrections. I know it's not quite the same, but books do seem a bit like pregnancy – very painful and you'll swear you'll never do it again, until the next time.

The publishers are grateful to the following for permission to reproduce copyright material:

Figure 1.2 'The relationship between life satisfaction and commuting time' from the work of Bruno Frey, source SOEP, copyright © Deutsches Institut für Wirtschaftsforschung; Figure 1.4 'Changing satisfactions with age' (UK data, 2007); Figure 4.3 'Satisfaction with different domains of life by social class' (UK data, 2007), source: Defra. Figure 5.6 'The characteristics of world class public service', source: Cabinet Office, 2008. Crown © copyright © 2009. Crown Copyright material is reproduced with permission under the terms of the Click-Use License; Figure 4.7 'Educational Inequality and Intergenerational Mobility' from *What's the Good of Education?* By Stephen Machin, Princeton University Press. Reprinted by permission of Princeton University Press; Figure 4.9 from 'Poverty and Inequality in the UK: 2008' (IFS Commentary 105), by Mike Brewer, Alastair Muriel, David Phillips and Luke Sibieta copyright © The Institute for Fiscal Studies; Figure 5.4 'The UK government's model of 'self-improving' public sector reform', Prime Minister's Strategy Unit (PMSU) copyright © 2006; Figure 5.5 'Key drivers of satisfaction with public services' from *Citizens First Survey* by George Spears and Kasia Seydegart, Erin Research Inc, for the Public Sector Service Delivery Council and The Institute of Public Administration of Canada copyright © The Institute of Public Administration of Canada; and Figure 5.7 'Rates of obesity across the world: Prevalence of obesity, males, aged 30+, 2005' World Health Organisation, http://apps.who.int/infobase/publicfiles/Obesity_Male_2005.png, copyright © World Health Organisation, 2005.

Introduction

You can't see the wood for the trees

Common expression

Humans notice change. When someone comes in the office with a new hair cut, everyone comments. If there's a movement in the corner of the room while you're watching TV, it will catch your eye. If the extractor fan in your bathroom that you'd forgotten was even there changes its tone, it will suddenly seem very loud.

On the other hand, things that don't change, or change very slowly, almost disappear from our consciousness. We don't notice the feeling of our toes in our shoes, unless we focus on them. The blind spot in our eyes (where our optic nerve leaves a hole in our retina) is undetectable to us unless we shut one eye and look in just the right place. And for most of us, even if we try our hardest, we can't hear the pounding of our hearts in our ears.

We see changes, contrasts, the edges of things. Fashioned by the hand of evolution, this overwhelming bias in our perception works well in most of life. But it gives us a rather odd viewpoint on the society and economy around us. It's not just citizens: even the sharpest of analysts and policymakers see the world this way too. Our attention is drawn to the latest crisis, the latest technological development, or the latest change in our output, tax take or poll. At the same time we are prone to under-attend to the great mass of things that don't change much. We see only the 'tip of the iceberg', and are shocked by the result when we hit it. Governments find that their policies often don't have the effect they thought they would. Corporations find that the merger that looked sensible on paper proves much more difficult in practice. And individuals find that what really matters in their lives isn't always the things they thought.

For those in a hurry, the basic argument is set out below.

Hidden Wealth: The Argument

This book is about the parallel world of relationships and habits that forms the backdrop to much of the chatter of contemporary politics. My argument is simple: it's this stuff that, for most part, makes our societies and economies work. If we try to estimate its value even in the crudest way, such as the economic value of all the time we spend supporting our friends and family, it is more than GDP. But of course, the monetary valuation alone doesn't really do it justice. It's the hidden wealth of nations.

This hidden wealth helps explain perhaps the biggest puzzle of contemporary economics: that richer nations are happier, yet economic growth within nations seems to have little impact on our happiness (the Easterlin paradox – see Chapter 1). Our ability to get on with our fellow citizens oils the working of markets, lowering the costs of transactions and speeding the flow of information on which economies rely. But it also affects our well-being more fundamentally. Our relationships to those around us – not just family but strangers too – have big impacts on our psychological and physical wellbeing. A society of trustworthy citizens is a platform for both economic growth and well-being.

But there are cracks in this hidden wealth. By the mid 2000s, public concerns in a number of nations – such as Britain, Spain and Denmark – had become dominated by a fear of other people. The top public concerns had become crime, immigration and terrorism – not a fear of distant others, but those in their midst. This was especially striking in Denmark, a nation otherwise long noted in social surveys as having the happiest citizens in Europe. Perhaps the most striking finding is the sheer gap between public concerns and the objective risks. Chapter 2 examines the underlying causes of these concerns, and what evidence-based policies might look like to do something about them. In many areas, the evidence base takes us in a very different direction from current policies, particularly in the Anglo-Saxon nations.

The onset of the global recession in 2008-9 has pushed some of these fears underground, with public attention shifting to unemployment and the state of the economy. But the same fears remain just beneath the surface. They colour the reaction to the recession, such as in protests against foreign workers; stories that crime will surge; or nervousness that the social order could break down within a country. Yet once again, the resilience of a community or nation to survive through economically difficult times rests heavily on its hidden wealth – not the money that its citizens have squirreled away under their mattresses, but the preparedness of citizens to help each other.

Chapter 3 shifts attention directly onto what the nature of this hidden, soft 'economy' is – such as our common values, the way we look after our children and elderly, or whether we trust and help strangers. The chapter examines how values have changed over the last 30 years, and how in some respects they appear not to have changed at all. Contrary to popular belief – and the widespread expectation of social commentators – religious beliefs appear to have changed very little. However, these beliefs have become less consequential for what else people believe, with the notable exception of North America. Across Europe, religious beliefs have become hollowed out. But this has not been associated with a general 'moral decline' – though people have become more relaxed about personal-sexual behaviour, they have become less tolerant in relation to many acts of self-interest.

A common belief of leading politicians is that globalization is leading the values of nations to become more similar, while at home nations are becoming more diverse as a result of immigration and marketization. There can be no doubt that nations share some common challenges, such as the risks and benefits of integrated financial markets on the one hand or of global warming on the other. But analysis shows that in terms of values, this common belief is wrong. Nations are actually becoming less similar in terms of values, with value divergence even within the OECD. Yet within nations, the most common pattern is value convergence. This remarkable result suggests that despite the power of globalization, there remains a dynamic within nations that is even more powerful in the moulding of our common values. The winds of globalization may be driving nations in the same general direction, but we are at the same time also drifting apart.

Another important but subtle change in Western societies is that, although the market economy may have become more dominant in our minds and our political narratives, we are spending less and less time in paid work. As the great economist Keynes predicted – and even despite the current recession – economic growth is gradually setting us free to do other things with our time. Much of this time is spent in the 'economy of regard' – a world of friendship, care and gift-based exchanges over which conventional economics has little to say but that for most people is what makes life worth living. In this sense, there is something fundamentally wrong with the dominant gestalt of our economics and politics – its foreground is the citizen's background. Is there anything the state can do to support this alternative world of relationships and exchange? I think the answer is yes – if we want it to. Chapter 3 starts to explore what kind of policies this might lead to, such as the support of 'complementary currencies' to oil the works of the economy of regard in much the same way as conventional currencies oil the 'real' economy.

Any account of contemporary society is not complete without a consideration of inequality and fairness. This is examined in Chapter 4. Globally, inequality has risen over the last 150 years, but mainly because inequality between countries has become larger. But there is also great variation in levels of inequality between countries, from the yawning gulfs between rich and poor in South America to the relatively narrow gaps within the Scandinavian nations. In respect of inequality, hidden wealth takes on a darker tone. It is argued that one of the reasons that policy efforts to reduce inequality and increase social mobility tend to under-deliver is because efforts focus on inequalities in relation to the conventional economy, such as income or qualifications. Policymakers have been far less successful at addressing the other kinds of capitals that explain persistent inequalities in society. These include inequalities in financial capital, soft skills, social networks and cultural capital. At the same time, public support for addressing inequality and fairness through conventional means, such as through further income support, is close to its limit in many countries.

We need to find ways of addressing inequalities and fairness that tap into these hidden forms of wealth, rather than fight against them. The laissez-faire approaches of the traditional right will clearly make the problem worse. The rational 'Weberian' welfare state, as favoured by the traditional left, faces the dual challenge of lack of public support and a failure to get to the deeper dynamics that underlie inequality. The alternative of 'affiliative welfare' is instead explored. This involves strengthening our support of those that we have some relationship to and stretching it to reach a little further than it might otherwise do. The model leads to some surprising policy conclusions. If we do it right, this approach can also change how we feel about the society around us, and help build the reservoirs of our collective hidden wealth. Perhaps the biggest driver of inequality within countries is the acceptability of income and other differences. Interestingly, recessions change these attitudes, leading to greater sympathy for the disadvantaged and more intolerance for the excesses of the very rich. These value changes can in turn have substantial and lasting impacts.

The changing role of government is considered in Chapter 5. It is examined from three different viewpoints: the division of power (the classic state); the provision of public goods (the practical state); and the guiding of citizen behaviour (the paternalistic state).

In terms of power, a number of common beliefs are debunked, such as the idea that there has been a collapse in trust in politicians, political engagement and political interest. But other concerns are identified, such as the growing dominance of more affluent and advantaged citizens in the arena of alternative political activity and the falling salience of politics compared with other domains of life. The case is examined for the greater use of new forms of democratic engagement, such as citizens' juries and forums. These mechanisms offer ways of addressing the social skew in engagement while respecting the desire of most citizens not to spend their lives engaged in politics.

The expansion of the state into the provision of public services has been one of the great innovations of the post-war period. The discussion reflects on what we have learnt about how public services can be not just 'delivered' but 'co-produced' with citizens. It examines the implications for how we measure, incentivize, and empower through public service provision.

The state has also become re-engaged in the shaping of citizen behaviour, not only in relation to where our behaviour affects others (such as anti-social behaviour or the environment) but where the costs fall mainly on ourselves (such as obesity). The insights of behavioural economists have changed the policy landscape, illustrating the vulnerability of citizens to 'behavioural predators' and giving powerful new tools to policymakers. But policymakers need the permission of citizens to use such tools, powerfully reinforcing the case for the wider use of new democratic innovations.

The state, in partnership with citizens, has the ability to greatly improve the quality of our lives. But its effectiveness also rests substantially on the hidden wealth of nations – the character of its citizens and their relationships to each other – and states neglect this at their peril.

In the final concluding chapter, a shortlist of some of the most promising policy ideas for the next decade is identified. This includes a mix of ideas, some specifically aimed at boosting and building on the hidden wealth of nations, others which are just sensible ideas whose time has come.

1

Prosperity and Well-being

> ... for the first time since his creation man will be faced with his real, his permanent problem – how to use his freedom from pressing economic cares, how to occupy the leisure, which science and compound interest will have won for him, to live wisely and agreeably and well.
>
> Keynes, *Economic Possibilities for our Grandchildren* (1930)

I hate the 7.45a.m. train from Cambridge to London. It's a good train in principle. I can see the kids at breakfast, and get into Whitehall a minute or two after 9a.m. But it's a good time for everybody else as well, so unless you get to the station very early and stand in just the right spot, you won't get a seat.[1]

It's not just that you have to stand for an hour that makes it mildly unpleasant, it's that it makes my fellow travellers sources of inconvenience and hassle. As the incoming train draws into the platform, we all huddle forward, bunched around where the doors will come to rest. Some will have misjudged their spot to stand, their closeness to the platform edge rendered worthless by the twenty other people that stand between them and the train doors. Meanwhile, ranged opposite us are the people in the train ready to get out. The two packs silently size each other up, like two rugby scrums about to engage. The doors open and we're off! Thank god we're English. Against all the odds, the cold but focused commuters hold back, parted like the Dead Sea to let the arrivals off. But at a certain moment the discipline will break – especially if one of the arrivals dare dawdle – and we surge forward to get on. If the discipline breaks early – perhaps we have a tourist in our midst – there will be 'tusking' and shaking of heads, but it will be everyone for themselves.

I have a double disadvantage. I am carrying a fold-up bike and, even worse, am prone to be over-polite, the mixed blessing of a minor public school education. But I am also a reasonably old hand, and do sometimes get a seat, albeit with guilt. Still, best to take the 6.45, though even that's getting pretty tight now too.

Of course, crowded commuting is not unique to the UK. Commuters in the wealthy cities of New York and Tokyo have long endured their crowded subways, a pattern that economic growth often brings. In the booming city of Mumbai, Indian officials now refer to 'super-dense crush load' to refer to times when commuters now regularly exceed train capacities by two and a half (compared with the UK's peak excess of a mere 1.76).

Markets and Well-being

Well-being is not the only justification that can be used for wanting economic prosperity, but it's a pretty good start. This chapter looks at this relationship, and also offers some thoughts about what we might do to boost economic prosperity in its own right.

At the time of writing, there are grave concerns about the economy. Across the world, the credit-crunch induced recession has led public concerns about the economy to move back to centre stage. 'The economy' was a record-breaking top concern of 70% of the British public by early 2009, up from just 20% at the start of 2008.[2] The worry of losing jobs and houses became something extra for the crowded Cambridge–London commuters to think about. But for some city workers, offered generous redundancy packages, the crunch turned into an opportunity of sorts. Some took their money and went off travelling, or took a step down to a quieter life, and at least escaped the wretched train.

The crowded 7.45 is an everyday example of what Fred Hirsch, more than thirty years ago, called the 'social limits to growth'.[3] Cambridge is a great place to live, especially with kids, and the 7.45 should be the ideal train to take. But as more and more people reach the same conclusion and buy themselves a place there, the train gets busier and busier, and the comfort and convenience seems to melt away. Yet for all these concerns, people who live in richer nations do seem to be happier, and there seems little surprise that for most people recessions are an unwelcome reversal in their growing fortunes (see Figure 1.1).

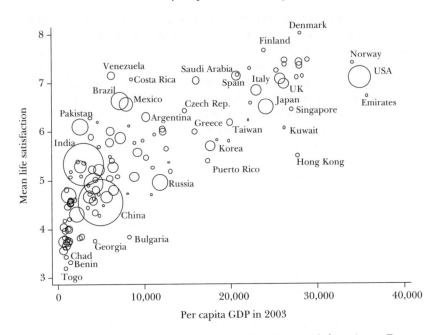

Figure 1.1 *Life satisfaction across nations (Gallup data; graph from Angus Deaton, Harvard). The size of the circles corresponds to population size.*

In December 2002, we published a Prime Minister's Strategy Unit paper on life satisfaction, updating the work of Hirsch and reflecting on what the policy implications might be.[4] A number of people within No. 10 thought it a rather odd and potentially inappropriate issue for us to be meddling with, and it had taken more than a year for the workstream to be approved. When the paper did go out, just to be doubly sure there was no confusion, every page had printed at the top 'This is not a statement of government policy'. We were putting our toes in what then seemed rather uncertain political and analytical waters.

Since 2002, subjective well-being has moved steadily from the fringe towards the mainstream both in academia and, albeit more tentatively, in policy. Figures such as the economist Richard Layard raised its profile among the academic community, while commentators such as Polly Toynbee began to pick up on its implications for a wider audience. In the political arena, Labour Ministers began to cautiously explore the idea. A further big leap in profile came from David Cameron, the Opposition leader, who flagged that we should consider following Bhutan's lead and start talking about 'Gross National Happiness' instead of just wealth.

The 2002 paper reflected the body of evidence that had been built up by psychologists and economists in the twenty-five years after Hirsch wrote his book, including the impact on subjective well-being of everyday phenomena such as work, income, leisure and relationships – and even commuting. Classically, economists argued that commuters like me were making a perfectly sensible trade-off: getting on the 7.45 not only allowed me to sleep an extra half hour in the morning, but also meant that I got to live in a slightly bigger and nicer house than I could have got in London, perhaps with schools I liked better, and a more accessible town centre. The net effect is that I and my family made an overall choice that made us happier.

In fact, it turns out that we tend to get it wrong about commuting (see Figure 1.2). The longer you commute, the less happy you are, despite the fact that you might be earning more and living in a nicer place. It also makes your partner less happy – what economists call a 'negative externality' – it looks like we'd have been better off in the smaller house with the smaller commute after all.[5]

'Of course,' you say, 'we just need longer trains.' Alternatively, the operator can just keep putting the price up until enough people give up on the 7.45 for the remainder to all get seats again. No doubt pricing and new trains can help, but Hirsch's point is that this kind

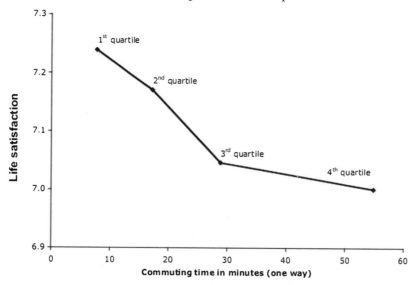

Commuting time and average reported satisfaction with life, Germany 1985–1998

Data source: GSOEP.

Figure 1.2 *The relationship between life satisfaction and commuting time (from the work of Bruno Frey).*

of 'crunch' is an inevitable dynamic that will tend to repeat. It's also quite difficult for me as an individual commuter – or even as an operator – to get the trains to double in size, such as because of the limited capacity of the network or stations run by someone else.

Writing at a similar period to Hirsch, Tibor Scitovsky also described how efficient markets will often fail to increase our well-being, a very troubling line of reasoning for economists who otherwise assume that if two people freely enter into a transaction it ought to be because it is increasing the well-being, or utility, of both. But it often doesn't work like that for lots of reasons. To take an example, imagine that you are a skilled craftsman making beautiful, but expensive furniture. But then along comes Ikea. Though we all liked the old furniture, the Ikea stuff is so much cheaper and still kind of funky, so that lots of us go and buy that instead. So now the old guy who makes the hand-made furniture is out of business, and we can't buy that furniture anymore. So he's obviously less happy and, more controversially, we might not be that much happier either. The point is that individuals each rationally seeking to maximize their own well-being don't always maximize the well-being of society, despite Adam Smith. This may help to explain why it is that decades of unprecedented economic growth have had such little impact on life satisfaction in industrialized nations such as the USA, UK and most of Europe.

A younger generation of economists continues to detail the circumstances under which efficient markets tend to increase well-being, or utility, and when they fail to do so. Much of this new generation of work draws on our growing understanding of behavioural economics – the mental shortcuts that we all use to reach decisions. It turns out that we're not very good 'utility maximizers', at least when we're in a hurry. Our predictions about what will make us happy in the future are strongly distorted by our mood and desires in the present; by a strong discounting of the future that we often come to regret; and by errors in remembering what made us happy in the past (see also Chapter 5). For example, consumers buy far more items that weren't on their shopping lists and pick more unhealthy foods if shopping when hungry. Discounting of the future makes us commit to deferred payment mortgages we often regret, and we repeat activities and obligations that we didn't enjoy, but thought that we did.

One important argument is that markets can sort out some of the errors that we are prone to. David Laibson, a professor of economics at Harvard, has explored how we make choices about investment decisions, including when markets 'save us from ourselves' but also when they amplify our proneness to error. For example, he gives the hypothetical example of someone who decided that an apple was worth millions, but who would be saved from this misjudgement by the fact that the marketplace would sell him one for 20 pence/40 cents just the same as everyone else. However, markets don't always interact so helpfully with our departures from rationality. For example, our tendency to discount future gains relative to the hassle of making a decision today leads us to procrastinate perpetually– we end up, quite sincerely, always intending to sort out our pension, or other investments, tomorrow.

An everyday example that Laibson gives is banking. The average American pays $90 per year in add-on charges, against the banks' costs of providing an account of $40. Customers are drawn to such accounts through freebies such as free toasters or cash gifts. Of course, a minority of savvy customers avoid paying the add-ons through managing their accounts and thereby get cross-subsidied by those who are less careful. The economics textbook, and classic libertarian, would point out that this leaves a market opportunity for a new bank to come along and offer a good straightforward service that dispenses with the gifts and the sneaky add-on charges, and just offers a good service for which you will pay, say, $50 per year. But as Laibson points out, with a good smattering of equations, this strategy is doomed to fail. If you are a savvy customer, you definitely want to stay with the old bank where your less savvy fellow customers will continue to sub-sidize you. If you're a normal un-savvy customer, then you don't get the point – and without a $50 gift you're not going to move anyway. An interesting group are those customers who wise up and *become* savvy customers. But wait – now they're savvy, they realize that they should stay where they are and just manage their accounts a bit better! So the net result is that few customers will move over to the new bank. Existing banks will lose a bit of profit to the unsuccessful newcomer, but not much. It turned out that it was in no banks' interest to rock the boat after all.

Laibson and his colleagues aren't against markets, and indeed high-light many examples where competitive markets will work to increase our total utility. But what his work does show, like that of his pre-decessors, is that in a significant number of areas markets won't act to maximize our well-being even if they are highly competitive and efficient. This is a particular problem where the attributes of goods or choices are somewhat 'shrouded' or where our own mental shortcuts are prone to certain systematic biases.

The work of Laibson suggests a key role of government policy to overcome these types of subtle, systematic failures that arise between our cognition and efficient markets. But he is still left with the puzzle of what it is that government should be trying to maximize. Behavioural economics takes away the prop that economists used to rely on: that what people would freely choose was what they wanted.

Returning to the example of commuting, not all is lost. There are a couple of ways of reducing the problem apart from indefinitely expanding the rail network for rush hours. We can, as individuals, simply learn to adjust our habits – in this case to get an earlier or later train, or perhaps arrange to work at home more often. There is clear evidence that we do learn. Again, Laibson *et al.* have shown this in relation to many commercial activities, such as how people learn over several years to avoid charges on credit cards or avoid high interest rates on home loans. Typically around a third of credit card users pay late fees when they first get their card, but this drops rapidly over the first two years of using the card.

But, if Hirsch is right, economic growth will continue to create 'limits to growth' problems like the rush hour. Where this happens, and especially where the resources concerned have a natural limit, the social norms and habits that let us coordinate and get along with others become critical. These prosaic habits of everyday life tend not to get much attention, but they do much of the heavy lifting in both our economy and our society. Basically, they are what make modern life liveable, and will be a major theme through this book, including how they are built and can be strengthened by both state and citizens.

Can Well-being be Measured?

There is a popular argument that you can't measure happiness. Empirically, this appears nonsense. Though some might wrinkle their noses a little, people across the world seem to have little trouble answering the question 'Are you happy?' or its more reflective cousin, 'Thinking about your life as a whole, would you say you were very satisfied, fairly satisfied, not very satisfied or not at all satisfied?'

How people answer these questions is highly correlated with pretty much any other measure you can think of, such as the answer your friends would give about you; the answer a stranger would give if observing you; the answers you would give to a much more elaborate set of questions about your mood or your mental health; and even evidence from brain scans.

Similarly, it is sometimes said that the big cross-national differences in satisfaction and happiness that are found (see Figure 1.1, p. 8) really just reflect differences in language. However, the evidence is strongly against this hypothesis. In countries where more than one language is spoken, such as Switzerland or Belgium, it is the nation that you are

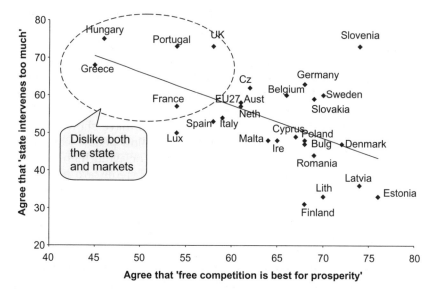

Figure 1.3 *Cross-national differences in public opinion that 'free competition is best for prosperity' versus agreement that 'the state intervenes too much' (data from Eurobarometer 69, 2008). A clear majority in most European countries now sees free market competition as the best route to prosperity, but those nations that have least confidence in competition are also most suspicious of the state too – including Greece, Hungary, Portugal and the UK.*

in that seems to shape your answer, not the language you speak. For example, German and French speakers in Switzerland are both much happier than their cousins in Germany and France – it's living in Switzerland that makes you happy, not some artefact of the language you speak. Second, as we shall see, the cross-national differences seem to be highly related to a host of plausible variables, not the random mess that you would expect if the answers people gave were just an artefact of the language they spoke.

This is not to say that there are no language effects. For example, the Nigerians seem oddly happy for a nation in pretty tough circumstances, and some linguists think there is a particular problem with the translation of the word in this case. Similarly, some Danes – who appear to be a particularly happy lot – say that they really mean something more like 'contentment'. But even for the Danes, this doesn't explain why they seem to have got happier over the last three decades – unless we also posit that the meaning of the word has also changed.

This isn't to say that there aren't some important controversies about the differences between different measures. Layard has championed the idea that there is only one basic dimension of happiness, echoing the tentative line we took in the PMSU paper that preceded his book. However, leading researchers, including the Noble Prize winner Danny Kahneman, have generally been moving to the conclusion that there are at least two different measures or dimensions of happiness, both of which are important and that are driven by different factors. The first dimension concerns how you feel, almost moment by moment. This can be measured by 'experiential sampling' – where you carry a bleeper and have to write down how you are feeling when it goes off, but also to some extent by simple survey questions asking about whether you feel happy. The second concerns more cognitive or reflective appraisals of how your life is going, such as the Gallup 'ladder of life' question or the life satisfaction question quoted above. A key difference is that people often, on reflection, appear to 'misremember' how happy they were. Hence, you might remember your holiday as having been wonderful, whereas if we look at what you said moment by moment it might not look so good.[6]

These differences have implications both for the decisions that we make as individuals and for policymakers, some of which are picked up below. But these difference of view shouldn't obscure the fact that, in general, it's pretty easy to find out if people are, broadly speaking, happy or not.[7]

Is Well-being Important?

Most people think that happiness, life satisfaction or well-being is a good thing, both for themselves and for society.[8] Some go one step further to say that it is not only a good thing, but is our ultimate objective as humans – a hard-wired gold-standard of success. This leads to the argument that maximizing happiness should therefore be the objective of government. We will return to this fundamental question at the end of the chapter. But even if you were sceptical about happiness as an objective in itself, a fairly robust case can be made why happiness is good for other reasons.

For a start, happy and upbeat people live longer. This was famously shown by a study of the longevity of nuns.[9] Danner *et al.* retrospectively analysed the written statements of young nuns and compared these to how long the nuns lived for. They found that, on average, the happy young nuns went on to live for more than a decade longer than their less happy colleagues despite the fact that they were otherwise living in exactly the same conditions. Hence, by age 85, only a third of the least happy quarter of nuns were still alive, while nine out of ten of the happier quartile were still alive.

Happy people tend to have more successful relationships, which is one of the reasons why marriage and well-being are so strongly associated (see below). An elegant illustration of this effect is that researchers have found that graduates who have a real, 'Duchene' smile in their college photographs – about 1 in 3 – are significantly more likely to go on and have successful and lasting marriages in the decades following. Sorry guys, those fake smiles that a further 1 in 3 have for the photo didn't make the cut – you're just as well looking miserable.

Happy people also end up earning more. Ed Diener and his colleagues found that cheerful college students at entry gained a 30% boost to their earnings relative to their peers 19 years later.[10] To put that in perspective, if you wanted to boost your earnings and could choose between being cheerful and going to a top university, choose being cheerful. The cheerful college entry students also ended up with more friends, being more trusted by their neighbours, more liked by their supervisors and workers, and in better health.

There is also growing interest in the relationship between positive mood and productivity at work. When researchers studied work back in the 1960s and 1970s, they generally concluded that there wasn't much of a relationship between work satisfaction and productivity – in other words, happy workers didn't seem to work harder than miserable ones. But in the last decade, views have shifted quite dramatically. Now many researchers have found that happiness, or more specifically workers in a positive mood, tend to be more productive, creative in their thinking and reach accurate conclusions faster.[11] For example, simply giving a doctor a sweet to put them in a good mood before asking them to make a tricky diagnosis, made them reach the diagnosis faster and more accurately than a control group given the same clinical information.[12]

One of the reasons that this literature has turned around is probably because the nature of work has itself changed. If you are working on a factory line, being bored or happy may not have much impact on the quality or rate of your work. If employers want their line worker to work harder, a few 'extrinsic' rewards – i.e. money – will probably do the trick. But for workers who are doing more conceptual and creative work – work which has become more dominant in our economy – positive mood seems to matter. Positive mood also helps in face-to-face interactions, i.e. service industries: for example, it's no great surprise that waiting staff get bigger tips if they are in a positive mood, or that the satisfaction of a bank's customers is strongly affected by the mood of the bank's tellers.

An interesting aside is whether you can be *too* happy. Psychologist Ed Diener argues that you really want to be an '8' or a '9' on a 10-point scale. There seem to be some downsides to being too happy, at least all the time. It may be an indication of being unrealistic, or it may be linked to irrational optimism that could get you into trouble in a world where not all investments will turn out as successes and where sometimes a bad feeling is telling you something important.

Finally, it's worth asking what are we are trying to maximize if it's *not* well-being. Various candidates have been proposed, such as freedom (maximize people's choices, and let them decide if they want happiness or something else), justice, meaning and so on. But, as Layard has argued, when pressed on these other alternatives, people tend to refer back to some notion of increasing well-being as a major part of the justification for their alternative objective, even if is not reducible to it. What we surely all can agree on, is that if we could increase subjective well-being with other things remaining constant – such as freedom – then we should.

The Drivers of Well-being

Even if you buy the argument that happiness and life-satisfaction is a good thing, it doesn't mean that anything can be done about it, let alone whether government could do anything. For a start, you need to figure out what affects happiness, and assess whether any of these drivers might be amenable to change. Research has focused on four broad drivers of well-being:

- Personality and individual factors
- Money
- How you spend your time: work, leisure and relationships
- Wider context

The section below provides a brief overview of the literature to date. An excellent and more detailed summary can be found in reviews by Paul Dolan, or in more accessible forms by Ed Diener, Marty Seligman or Richard Layard.[13]

Personality and individual factors

There is no doubt that some people are constitutionally more inclined to be happy than others. How happy you are today is a pretty good indication of how happy you will be in 15 or 20 years' time, and this is thought to at least partly reflect your underlying orientation in life.[14]

Twin studies have suggested that genetics may explain the majority of the individual variability in expressed well-being, at least within a given country and region. However, these studies almost certainly overestimate the overall impact of genes, since the adoption studies on which they are heavily based compare people from within a country, and from very similar settings and families. There is no evidence, for example, that the substantial cross-national differences are explained by genes. National changes over a few decades – such as the rising happiness of the Danes – are even harder to explain in terms of genes.

Women tend to report slightly higher subjective well-being, but also report more negative feelings raising the possibility that women are more open to, or likely to report, their feelings. There is some evidence that the subjective well-being of women has fallen slightly over recent decades, such as in the USA, while that of men has increased. This may reflect the fact that while women have entered the labour market, men still haven't picked up the household chores, despite the claims. Attractive women and taller men are a little happier than their peers, though the effects are modest. These effects seem to vary between countries, suggesting a role for culture too (see context below).

There are some age effects. People seem happier in their early twenties, are a little less happy in middle age, then a little happier again by the time they reach retirement. This is often interpreted in terms of how people's aspirations relative to achievements change over the life span, though there is some evidence that it's partly the hard emotional work of raising children (especially in the teenage years). Although satisfaction with health falls with age, this seems to be more than offset by increasing satisfaction with community and with financial security. If you are a healthy and just-retired 65 year old, statistically this is as happy as you'll get. However, these patterns do vary across countries, and the detail of the measure. For example, measures of vitality tend to fall with age but sense of belonging to a community rises. One recent study found that well-being didn't vary much by age in Scandinavian countries, rose with age in the UK and Ireland, but fell marked with age in Southern and Eastern Europe, the latter perhaps reflecting generational differences in reactions to the emergence of market capitalism in those countries.[15]

Ethnicity is known to have some associations with well-being. American blacks have been repeatedly found to have lower life satisfaction than whites, for example, whereas Hispanics, controlling for income, have been found to have higher satisfaction. Similarly, minorities in a number of countries have been found to have poorer life satisfaction and mental health. Many of these ethnic differences reflect social and

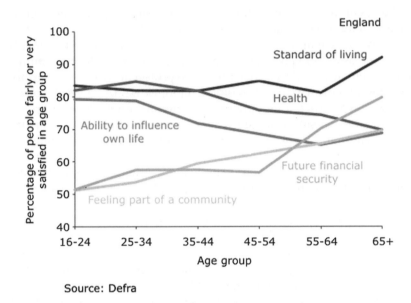

Source: Defra

Figure 1.4 *Changing satisfactions with age (UK data, 2007).*

economic factors of the populations, as well as some selection effects
in the characteristics of the population who migrated.

There are some individual differences that we acquire through the
course of life, sometimes called socially developed characteristics, such
as our state of health, our education and, to some extent, our beliefs.
These also affect our subjective well-being.

Being healthy is associated with higher subjective well-being, and
self-reported health is strongly associated with feeling happy, though
this may be as much a symptom as a cause. Acquiring a disability
has strong and sustained negative impact on life satisfaction, contrary
to the claims of some early researchers. True, the life satisfaction of
someone who becomes disabled is not as bad as an able-bodied person
thinks it will be – we overestimate how bad it will be because when
we answer the question the disability is uppermost in our mind and
we forget all the other satisfactions that will remain. But disability still
leads to a very substantial hit on life satisfaction that shows no sign of
falling over the years following.

Being better educated is also associated with higher life satisfaction
and happiness, though it seems largely attributable to the better health
and higher earnings associated with more education. Some of the positive effects of education may also be relative – higher educational
attainment gives us status – but educational attainment may also relate
to 'flourishing', that is, allowing us to reach our potential.

Personal beliefs have impacts. For example, people who believe in God tend to be happier. In fact, more or less no matter what your religion, being religious seems to benefit your well-being. The positive effect seems to stem partly from belief *per se*, and partly through buffering the impacts of certain negative life events, such as loss of income or unemployment (see also relationships below). In contrast, college students who place a high value on materialism tend to end up less happy. Unsurprisingly, there is also an interaction between your personal beliefs and the impact of *other* variables on your well-being. For example, politically left-leaning Europeans are made more unhappy by higher inequality than are right-leaning Americans, and the happiness of those with more material orientations are more affected by future income.

One of the main factors behind individual variations in well-being is cognitive style, or how you interpret the world. If you are a person who tends to interpret bad events as due to your own clumsiness or lack of ability (a tendency to make negative, general, internal attributions) then the chances are you will end up miserable. But the good news is that psychologists have shown that you can help people change this style of thought, in particular to help prevent subsequent depression, but also to help brighten the outlook of the everyday grump.

Money, income and wealth

The study of the relationship between income and well-being has probably been the single greatest focus of the well-being literature. At its heart is a profound puzzle, often known as the 'Easterlin paradox' after the person who first called wider attention to it. The essence of the puzzle is that people in richer countries are much happier than in poorer ones (see Figure 1.1), and yet within wealthy countries, such as the USA and UK, decades of economic growth have led to little or no increases in happiness. As we shall see, money does make you happier, but not much.

Both across and within nations, wealth *is* strongly associated with happiness and life satisfaction. Indeed, across a large sample of nations, the correlation between income and life satisfaction is 0.82 (where '1' would be a perfect straight line) – this is a very strong relationship in social science terms, suggesting a two-thirds overlap of variability between cross-national income and life satisfaction. Similarly, within nations there is a robust relationship between income and life satisfaction, with richer people tending to be significantly happier.

Both within and across nations, the relationship is curvilinear – i.e. at lower levels of income, small increases in income are associated with large increases in satisfaction, but at higher levels of income, increases have much less impact. Roughly speaking, once a country's GDP per capita passes about $10,000 – a point the UK passed back in the 1950s – the relationship between income and satisfaction seems to weaken.[16] Similarly, increases in wealth in poorer nations are associated with increases in life satisfaction.[17] But for wealthy nations such as the USA, UK and Japan, the last thirty to fifty years of growth seem to have had little or no overall impact on satisfaction. So, what is the causal relationship between money and subjective well-being?

A good test of causality is provided by lottery winners. An early American study that interviewed people who had won substantial sums on the lottery in the last year, found – much to everyone's surprise – that the lottery winners were not much happier than anyone else.[18] One of the arguments that followed was that maybe people who entered the lottery were a particularly unhappy lot, but more recent studies that have compared US state lottery winners who won millions with those who merely won smaller amounts found much the same result – those who won millions were marginally, but not statistically significantly, happier than those who had smaller wins.[19] Similarly, a study of lottery winners in Norway concluded that the net result was 'moderate happiness and relief'.[20]

An alternative approach is to look at lottery winners in longitudinal surveys, where it is possible to compare the individual's subjective well-being before and after. Of course, the downside is that in a sample of 10,000 people, there are only a few such winners, and their winnings tend to be relatively modest. Such longitudinal studies have concluded that winnings, or other windfalls, tend to make people a little happier, but the effect is modest. Curiously, a recent study by Oswald appears to show that the positive effect became slightly stronger by two years than the initial effect, at least on a composite measure of mental health.[21]

Just to be clear, winning the lottery did have effects on people, just not much on their subjective well-being. For example, Green *et al.* found that among their American lottery winners, having controlled for various factors and as you might expect, the more money that people had won the less in favour they were for redistribution; the more they supported the Republican party; and more in favour they became for the repeal of death duties. Among those who had won less than $100,000, around 45% supported repeal of inheritance tax and most supported the Democrats; but among those who won more than $4 million, 76% supported repeal and they supported Republicans by a ratio of 2:1. They just didn't seem to be much happier.

Interestingly, Green *et al.* did find that those who won more on the lottery tended to live longer, which fits with Oswald's finding that GHQ scores were markedly better two years after winning. This raises the intriguing possibility that suddenly becoming richer improves your health and longevity, even if it doesn't have quite the impact on your long-term subjective well-being that most of us assume that it will.

Wealth – that is how much money you have in the bank and so on – also has an impact on well-being. Indeed, the impact of wealth in longitudinal panel surveys seems to be quite a bit larger than the interest you get paid from it (see further discussion on capital inequalities in Chapter 4).[22] In contrast, people who find themselves with unsecured debt, such as on credit cards or unpaid bills, end up much less happy, though secured debt such as a mortgage doesn't seem to be a problem.[23]

One contributory factor to explain the relationship between income and happiness within countries could be that happier people end up richer, noting that the evidence from college students supports this. Indeed, some analyses have found that happy populations are predictive of economic growth at the national level.[24]

Another factor widely thought to be important is not income *per se*, but the position that income gives you relative to others. Humans are very status conscious creatures and this, combined with the greater control that people on top have, does help to account for within country differences by income. A number of analyses have shown that your income relative to that of others in your neighbourhood or city has a significant effect on your well-being (see also context below). Some studies have concluded that the key comparison seem to be upwards to the fifth who earn the most, whereas we get relatively little comfort from the knowledge that others earn less than us.[25] Similarly, there is evidence that countries that grow at a faster rate than their neighbours, or whose GDP growth rates accelerate relative to their past trend rates, do show increases in life satisfaction.[26]

However, the effects of relative income seem to vary according to the exact measure of well-being used (see discussion on measurement above). This has led to considerable controversy and confusion between researchers about relative income effects. More conceptual or reflective measures of well-being, such as the 'ladder' measure of well-being used by Gallup, tend to show strong relative income effects – people living with richer neighbours on reflection rate their lives as less good. But more affective measures, that focus on your mood and feelings, don't show them. This is the kind of evidence that has led Kahneman to conclude that there are two different 'types' of well-being.

Importantly, people *think* that if they were to become richer, such as by winning the lottery, then they would be much happier. I have to confess, even knowing the literature, I still can't help feeling that if I won the lottery I'd handle it very well and would end up happier. The chances are, you feel much the same. But there seem to be two powerful reasons why increases in income have a more modest effect on subjective well-being that we might expect – particularly on the more reflective measures. First, we rapidly adapt to increases in income and to the extra material goods that this brings. In short, we soon learn that the shiny new Porsche has to sit in traffic just the same as our old car, and the novelty of racing down our road a few seconds faster soon wears off. To take a more everyday example, if you ask people to list what they consider the necessities of life, they more-or-less list items that they already have, not noticing that the dishwasher and high-definition plasma TV seemed like luxuries before we got them. Second, much of our consumption has negative effects on other people (negative externalities). Hence the shiny Porsche on your driveway makes your neighbours feel less happy with the not-so-shiny Fords and BMWs on theirs.

Economists have ball-parked that about two-thirds of our additional income gets wiped out by these two effects.[27] This has led to a second line of research as to why we get our personal predictions so wrong about the happiness that extra car or bigger house will bring. Indeed, we may find more clues to our personal happiness in these psychological processes than in the standard regression equations of economists. As Diener puts it, 'happiness is not a desirable set of life circumstances. It's a way of travelling.'[28]

So how do we explain the Easterlin paradox – that richer countries *are* much happier, yet that economic growth within them has *not* been associated with increases in happiness? Relative income effects between countries – the citizens in one country comparing their lot to those in others – may help to explain it. There is evidence that people's self-ratings of wealth in poorer countries make at least some reference to international comparisons (certainly for the more conceptual measures of well-being). However, an additional explanation, for the more effective measures of well-being, is that there are a number of societal and institutional factors that independently explain *both* national differences in economic growth and well-being. These are factors that have deep cultural roots such as freedom, political stability, prevalent levels of trust, and well-functioning state and welfare institutions. These relatively stable factors help to explain why some countries are able to take the economic opportunities from new developments in technology, trade or institutional design while others trail behind.

It is these same factors that help to explain why economic 'catch-up variables' – i.e. poor countries catching-up on richer ones simply by imitation – are relatively modest. In my view, this 'hidden wealth' helps to explain national differences in happiness and the Easterlin paradox itself.

Let me use a metaphor to explain how this could work. Imagine a round-the-world race between a set of very differently designed boats. They all set off at the same time, but within a relatively short period of time, some of the boats are pulling ahead, while others are foundering. We might think of the distance travelled by the boats as economic growth – all are making progress, but some are becoming quite a long way ahead of others. Now let's suppose that we compare the levels of sea-sickness on the various boats (a metaphor for happiness). As the boats enter various storms, levels of sickness would go up and down. But we would also find that, while the crews of the more stable ships hardly ever got sick, those on the less stable ships felt pretty queasy much of the time. Now let's look at the relationship between progress in the race and feeling well. When we look cross-sectionally comparing all the ships, i.e. at one point in time, we find a strong association between progress and feeling well. But when we look longitudinally, i.e. over time, we find no simple relationship between the progress travelled by an individual ship and feeling well, though we might notice the graph of 'feeling well' going up and down (as the ship went in and out of storms). It looks just like the Easterlin paradox. There's a strong relationship between progress and feeling well at any point of time (i.e. cross-sectionally), and yet little relationship between progress and feeling well over time at the level of the individual ship (i.e. longitudinally). Of course, the reason for the 'Halpern shipping paradox' is that the faster ships that are well-suited to cutting through the ocean waters also turn out to be the ones that are relatively stable (in this hypothetical example).

I think something similar is happening with economic growth and well-being. For example, nations differ greatly in their degree of 'social trust' – the extent to which relative strangers trust each other. In Scandinavian countries, 60 to 70% of people think that most other people can be trusted and treat them accordingly, whereas in Brazil it is less than 10%.[29] Furthermore, we know that this cultural habit is very robust over time. For example, we find that the variation in levels of trust across US states can be predicted by the countries from which their populations emigrated from four or five generations before. Hence we find that Minnesota, the US state where levels of trust are highest in the USA today, is full of people whose great-great grandparents were – you guessed it – Scandinavians. It also turns out that high levels of social trust are a very powerful catalyst of economic growth. It means that you trust strangers to work in your firm; to buy goods from that will do what they say they're supposed to; to lend money because they'll give it back, and so on.[30] In economic terms, social trust oils the workings of an economy by lowering 'transaction costs' (i.e. you don't have to get a lawyer in every time you make a transaction) and by helping information flow. But it also turns out that social trust is strongly predictive of your subjective well-being, both individually and cross-nationally (see below).

A final empirical illustration of how the social and cultural characteristics of an area can independently affect growth and well-being is provided in a case study by Helliwell and Putnam. In his classic study of Italy, Bob Putnam had already shown that regional variations in levels of social capital – informal social networks and trust – substantially explained regional differences in multiple outcomes in Italy. The economist John Helliwell extended this finding by examining how the introduction of enhanced regional government in Italy in the 1970s affected regional growth rates, and how this interacted with levels of social capital. Helliwell found that, following the creation of the new institutional framework, the growth rates of the high social capital regions, principally in the North, shot ahead of the low social capital Southern regions. This was especially striking since the Southern regions started with lower rates of GDP per capita and therefore were predicted to catch up. It seemed that the regions with higher levels of social capital were able to take better advantage of the new institutional arrangements. In other words, latent and largely unchanging social and cultural characteristics helped give those regions the edge in taking advantage of new opportunities, as well as providing other well-being benefits through more positive social relationships in society.

How you spend your time: work, leisure and relationships

A popular assumption is that we should all work less and play more – what's normally labelled as getting a better work-life balance. While it's true that spending more time in the garden or playing sports is associated with higher life satisfaction, it is not true that there is any simple relationship between the number of hours worked and how happy you are. Indeed, being unemployed is one of the highest risk factors for low life satisfaction.

The negative impacts of being unemployed are far greater than would be expected from the loss of income. This echoes work going right back to the 1930s which documented that the psychological importance of work extends far beyond the pay it generates. In crude terms, statistical models suggest that you'd have to pay someone £23,000 per month – or £250,000 per year – to compensate for the loss of happiness from being unemployed, far short of even the most generous benefit system.[31]

For most people, work is not just a source of income, but also status, challenge and social contact. Furthermore, the negative impacts of unemployment don't seem to decay much over time. The negative impact on subjective well-being, if anything, gets worse over time, being larger at 3 years after losing your job than at 1 year. There is also evidence that men suffer worse from the impact of unemployment than women, partly because it hits their personal sense of status harder. Insecure employment also has negative impacts.[32]

For those in work, there is only a modest relationship between hours worked and life satisfaction. Some researchers have found a modest inverted-U relationship between hours worked and life satisfaction – those who work very long hours, or very few, are slightly less happy.[33] What complicates the relationship is that many people who work long hours – especially professionals – enjoy their jobs.

A similar story is true for 'informal' or household work – it's not the hours *per se*, but how you feel about it that counts. For example, the more hours spent doing housework, the greater the reduction in well-being – but only for those who say they hate housework! Informal care is associated with marked reductions in well-being, though it is difficult to separate this negative effect from the worry and concern about the loved-one who is being cared for.

In both leisure and work, a key determinant of well-being is the match between the challenge of the activity and our own ability. In short, we get great satisfaction from tasks that present us with interesting challenges that we are able to master. The term 'flow' is sometimes used to describe this state of active engagement in a challenge – it is when absorbed in such flow that we feel most satisfied.[34] Mihaly Csikszentmihalyi, who is most linked to the idea, describes it as:

> . . . being completely involved in an activity for its own sake. The ego falls away. Time flies. Every action, movement and thought follows inevitably from the previous one, like playing jazz. Your whole being is involved, and you're using your skills to the utmost.[35]

The concept of flow helps to explain why there is no simple linear relationship between subjects' reports of stress, at work or play, and their life satisfaction. If anything, more stress is generally associated with *more* satisfaction, not less, at least up to quite a high level.

The other activity on, and in which, we spend our time is our relationships. One of the most consistent results of the life satisfaction literature is that relationships matter greatly. The headline result that is often quoted is the happiness boost from being married, in contrast to the deficit in well-being associated with being single or divorced.

Easterlin contrasted the way in which people habituated to material goods and increased incomes – hence why economic growth rates weren't associated with increases in national well-being – whereas the effects of relationships such as being married did not decay. Oswald calculated the monetary value equivalent of being married (versus single) as £6,000 per month, or £72,000 per year – a figure quoted eagerly by both the tabloids and long-married partners.

Longitudinal analysis has shown that these cross-sectional calculations may have overstated the scale of the effect, but that the effect is real nonetheless. Those who get married tend to start happier, and sadly, the positive effects of marriage on well-being tend to decay after a few years. But a substantial 5 year boost to your well-being is still worth having.

What seems to be key, just as in work and leisure, is the quality and stability of the relationship. Relationship conflict and break-up has very powerful negative effects, including on the next generation, whereas partnerships where people support and care for each other have very powerful positive effects. One stable relationship beats a string of short-term relationships in happiness terms – the optimum number of sexual partners in the last year is one, by a long shot.

These positive effects of supportive relationships affect not only subjective well-being, but 'hard' outcomes too, such as longevity, physical illness and the functioning of the immune system.[36] Your best protection from the common cold, it turns out, is being able to say that there's someone who loves you. It seems that we derive both material and emotional sustenance from our personal relationships. Relationships help to insulate you from the shocks of the world. When you're sick, your partner brings you soup. A partnership allows for economic division of labour. And partners can make you feel better about yourself by seeing the best in you, emphasizing your qualities and strengths rather than your weaknesses and shortcomings.[37]

Similarly, having children *per se* seems to have no overall effects on well-being, but is conditional on the quality of the relationship. For example, one of the classic risk factors for depression in mothers is having three or more children under the age of fourteen, but the mental health outcomes are much worse if your partner is not supportive.[38] On the other hand, our children, and grandchildren, can be the greatest source of satisfaction in our lives. This 'mixed blessing' of relationships may also help to explain the paradoxical result that overall, women report both higher happiness and higher rates of depression – it

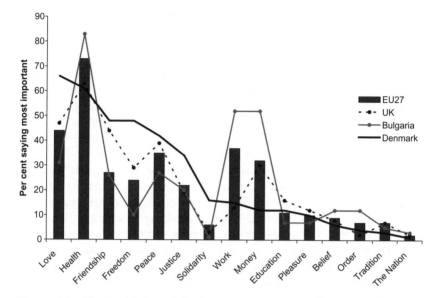

Figure 1.5 *The Danish formula for happiness: factors that the public feel are most important to their happiness (solid bars). The views of the Danes – the happiest nation in the EU, and that has also seen marked increases in life satisfaction over the past 30 years – are shown in the solid black line, and have been used to rank the factors. The grey line shows the Bulgarians – least happy nation in the EU. Note the high emphasis the Danes put on relationships and values associated with getting along with other people, while the Bulgarians remain much more focused on work and money. The British are generally somewhere in between.*

is women who take on more of both the burden and satisfactions of maintaining relationships, harvesting a corresponding mix of mutual support and obligation.

The character of relationships in the wider community also seems to have an impact. If you live in an area or country where most people agree with the statement 'most people can be trusted' then your life satisfaction is increased. Importantly, this positive effect works its magic even if you personally don't report particularly high levels of trust (a positive externality).[39]

Another activity that is known to boost well-being is religion (see also above). Which religion, generally doesn't seem to matter. For example, both Christian evangelists and ultra-orthodox Jews have been found to have higher levels of happiness than their less evangelical peers. The main cause of the positive effect of religion on well-being seems to come from attending church, temple or mosque – in other words, the main benefit comes from contact with the community, though holding religious beliefs and the act of praying also make a contribution. As with other relationships, being part of a religious community helps to buffer people against the shocks of life, such as unemployment and having a lower income.

Looking across activities – work, leisure and relationships – a number of common patterns can be seen. It's quality rather than quantity that generally matters. Psychologists have found, both in workplace relationships and in marriage, there seems to be a 'magic ratio' of positive to negative comments that is predictive of success or failure. Roughly speaking, if you want your marriage to survive, there needs to be about three or more positive comments made about your partner for every negative one (and vice versa). If you consistently drop below this ratio, then a visit to a divorce lawyer is probably heading your way. A similar ratio operates in workplaces, where dropping below the 3 to 1 ratio is predictive of teams that spiral into negativity, low productivity and break-up. So next time that critical comment about your partner or work colleague slips out, remember you need to rattle off three positive things to say to compensate. We've all been there, but now at least we know the quantum.

Issues of flow, control, personal meaning, interpersonal dynamics and, of course, tangible reward matter across all domains of our lives. For example, it is not surprising that half of the ten most satisfying jobs have a strong managerial component, compared with none of the bottom ten, given that managerial jobs generally involve a lot of human contact, a high degree of challenge combined with a high degree of control. But less conventional activities also make it into the top ten, such as hairdressing (with its high degree of social contact and immediate satisfaction) and artistic and literary occupations (challenging, creative and satisfied – despite the stereotype of the miserable but creative soul). In contrast, the bottom ten occupations are far more skewed to repetitive and manual occupations. Interestingly, high paying occupations such as IT workers and lawyers don't fare very well in such rankings, despite their relatively generous pay. The pay doesn't seem to make up for the lack of human contact (IT at 66th) or the conflict (lawyers at 44th), whereas teachers do relatively well (at 11th) as do health professionals of various kinds (13th, 17th, 18th and 20th).

Finally, we might note that the all-time lowest life satisfaction for any group so far recorded in the life satisfaction literature was for an occupational group – prostitutes in a US sample. These women had lower life satisfaction scores than hospitalized, depressed patients, or even than slum dwellers in Calcutta.[40] Once again, we see that money doesn't seem to make up for the other satisfactions, or dissatisfactions, of life.

Highest job satisfaction	Lowest job satisfaction
1. Corporate managers and senior officials	81. Assemblers and routine operatives
2. Hairdressers and related occupations	80. Metal forming, welding and related trades
3. Health and social service managers	79. Elementary admin occupations
4. Personal services occupations	78. Customer service occupations
5. Managers in distribution, storage and retail	77. Textiles and garments trades
6. Production managers	76. Admin occupations (government and related)
7. Managers and proprietors (other serviced industries)	75. Process operatives
8. Sports and fitness occupations	74. Draughtspersons and building inspectors
9. Functional managers	73. Skilled trades
10. Artistic and literary occupations	72. Plant and machinery operatives

Figure 1.6 *Job satisfaction by UK occupational groupings (top and bottom).*[41]

Wider context

We have already noted quite a number of context effects on subjective well-being, both positive and negative. Having neighbours who earn more than you depresses your well-being, regardless of your absolute income. In contrast, having neighbours who say 'others can be trusted' boosts your well-being, regardless of your own level of trust.

Recent reanalysis of the long-running Framingham study, which has now tracked the health and well-being of a community over several generations, has revealed the remarkable influence of the well-being of those in our extended social networks on our own well-being. For example, the researchers found that not only was an individual's happiness strongly affected by the happiness of their friends living close by and next door neighbour, but that it was also being affected by the happiness of their *friends'* next door neighbours and friends, and even by the friends of their neighbour. And the effects are quite large. The researchers found that:

> A friend who lives within a mile (about 1.6 km) and who becomes happy increases the probability that a person is happy by 25% (95% confidence interval 1% to 57%). Similar effects are seen in co-resident spouses (8%, 0.2% to 16%), siblings who live within a mile (14%, 1% to 28%), and next door neighbours (34%, 7% to 70%).[42]

It is these second and third degree effects that have led some to describe happiness as contagious, and to suggest that if you want to be happy, choose happy friends. Interestingly, the rippling of happiness through social networks over time seems to happen primarily through same sex relationships, and decays away sharply with geographical distance. Co-workers seem to have relatively little effect.

What other people around you think is important matters too, and this conditions many of the effects described earlier. For example, having a high body mass index is associated with reduced subjective well-being in Anglo-Saxon countries, but not in Sweden. Similarly, belief in God is associated with a substantial boost to well-being in the relatively religious USA, but has a much more modest effect in relatively secular Britain.

Both natural hazards, such as violent climatic events, and human hazards, such as living in a high crime area, affect well-being. At the national level, higher rates of inflation, unemployment and political instability all are associated with lower levels of life satisfaction.

But many national and democratic institutions are designed to reduce, or attenuate the impact of, such events. Sure enough, nations with more extensive welfare states and nations with greater political freedoms are associated with higher rates of life satisfaction.[43] Similarly, higher trust in a country's key institutions is associated with higher life satisfaction. Putting this in reverse, feeling that your institutions cannot be trusted, or that other people cannot be trusted and are all cheating on their taxes, has a big negative impact on your subjective well-being. More controversially, there is evidence that the opportunity to vote is associated with a boost to life satisfaction, which fits with the micro-level evidence that control is very important to subjective well-being.[44]

One difficulty with interpreting these relationships, especially at cross-national level, is that many of these variables are compounded with each other. Wealthier nations tend to have more generous welfare systems; longer life expectancy; greater political stability; higher trust between people; and so on. However, controlling for cross-national differences in GDP per capita, there is still significant variability explained by these other types of cross-national variables, especially in wealthy nations, and it is likely that these variables in turn help explain the powerful association between GDP and life satisfaction. In other words, it turns out that many of the conditions that generally foster economic growth – such as political freedoms, effective welfare states, and high trust between members of a society – also turn out to be conducive to subjective well-being.

Is Subjective Well-being the Business of Government?

Now that we have a sense of the web of causal factors that lie behind an individual's or nation's happiness, we can revisit the question of whether the state could, or should, do anything about it. It turns out that there are powerful arguments to suggest that the state, and policy-makers, should take subjective well-being seriously.

- **Most people think it's important**. The public consistently rate 'happiness' as more important than wealth, and more than four in five people think that the goal of governments should be the 'greatest happiness' rather than the 'greatest wealth'.[45] And where there's no major trade-off, it is surely a 'no-brainer' that government should be in the business of increasing well-being.
- **It's democratic**. Unlike most government or service provider objectives, the beauty of a subjective well-being objective is that it is profoundly democratic – it makes providers focus on what the public want and aspire to, not what some official thinks the public should want.
- **A focus on well-being may change priorities.** A policy programme aimed at increasing life satisfaction may imply different actions than one based on, say, increasing GDP per capita – though in some areas of policy it may imply no changes at all.
- **Many of the causes of subjective well-being 'spill-over' onto others**. In economic terms, the drivers of well-being are characterized by significant externalities – if I buy a fancy new car, I feel a bit better, but my neighbour feels a bit worse (a negative externality). If I do something to increase trust between people where I live, I benefit, but so does everyone else. Such externalities suggest systematic problems such as free-riding and underinvestment (why bother to invest in my neighbourhood since I benefit anyway). It is precisely these kinds of problems that governments were invented to correct, such as funding education and training rather than leaving it to firms (that would otherwise under-invest because of free-riding).
- **Collective action problems.** Many of the issues that affect well-being are beyond the control of the individual. For example, even if I know that commuting isn't great for my well-being, it's quite difficult for me as an individual to reorganize the whole geography of the South East, or the way that large organizations work, to reduce the need for such long journey times.
- **We're prone to systematic errors about what will make us happy**. This is essentially a paternalistic argument that we look to institu-

tions to guide markets, and ourselves, to make decisions in our best interests. This is perhaps the most controversial argument linked with the well-being agenda, and one we shall return to in later chapters.

- **It can help in marginal decision-making**. Mild sounding though it is, this is arguably the most powerful argument that draws the policy-maker to look closely at the well-being literature. Policy-makers often have to make decisions between completely different kinds of goods, like shall we spend more on health or education? Even within areas, the decisions can be very difficult to call – how should we decide between one form of social care or another? Traditionally we use cost-benefit analysis, but what is the 'benefit'? It may be several things, but an important one is surely: will it make the citizen and community happier?

There are also a number of arguments *against* the use of subjective well-being that are important to think about:

- **Which aspect of subjective well-being are we trying to maximize?** Though measures of well-being are generally highly correlated, they are not the same, and this raises the question of which one should we be trying to maximize. For example, more cognitive versus affective measures would lead to different conclusions about what we might do about wealth and inequality. Which do we go for? This is a genuinely intriguing puzzle which remains far from resolved.
- **The distribution of well-being**. This concern comes in various forms. One is the belief that justice is a more important objective than well-being. However, it is worth noting that most people believe that one of the reasons why justice is good is because it promotes the well-being of all (and it is difficult to argue the reverse). A second argument, most closely associated with Sen, is that well-being underplays inequality (implying a kind of false consciousness of the poor and disadvantaged). This is again a particular problem with more reflective well-being questions, such as the ladder of life (see above). Despite this, most measures still show massive and consistent differences between classes and countries and, as we shall see, the corresponding implications are generally viewed as highly progressive. Finally, there is the most basic, but difficult question over the trade-off between promoting the well-being of one person or group over that of another. In particular, there is no easy answer that can be drawn within the life satisfaction literature about whether it would be justified to increase the well-being of the average if that meant a reduction in the well-being of a

minority. For example, in one recent analysis Austria was found to have marginally higher well-being than Norway and Finland, but much higher inequality in well-being – which is to be preferred?[46] This seems unavoidably a value-based question, though it is eased by the assumption that, generally speaking, people don't find satisfaction in the misery of others, and that some countries such as Switzerland manage to achieve both high well-being and low inequality in well-being.

- **Can government do anything?** In my view, it is this practical question that really drives hesitation on the part of policymakers. Imagine, for a moment, that the time series of happiness and life satisfaction for countries such as the USA or UK was not essentially flat but a steady rise. Politicians and media would be crawling over it, arguing over who managed the largest increases and what could be done to increase happiness still further. I'm sure that those who instigated the collection of this data had this picture in mind. But the fact that average happiness – at least in the USA and UK – has hardly moved when so much else has happened suggests either that it doesn't tell us anything or that we can't do anything about it. What sane politician is going to campaign on the promise of making us happier or more satisfied with life, when history tells them they are doomed to fail?

At the very least, we are now at the point where politicians and policy-makers are at least thinking about subjective well-being, even if they are not quite sure what to do about it. This is already quite an advance on when we published the Prime Minister's Strategy Unit life satisfaction paper in 2002, when even talking about it seemed radical.

What are the Implications for Policy?

Faced with the literature on the drivers of subjective well-being, there are two easy ways for policymakers to respond, and one that is more difficult.

First, the policymaker may seek to dismiss the literature or its relevance to policy, such as by highlighting problems around measurement or ridiculing the neo-Benthamites more naïve proposals. In my experience, this is the standard response of the young, bright Minister who doesn't want to go out on too much of a limb.

The second 'easy' response is to highlight how the literature confirms that what we are already doing is the right thing to do after all. For example, the well-being evidence strongly supports Anglo-

Saxon and Scandinavian welfare-to-work approaches that prioritize getting people back to work rather than seeking to negate the effect of unemployment through more generous benefits. Politicians in these countries can readily cite the well-being literature in favour of their welfare-to-work programmes over the seemingly more generous Germanic and French systems. Similarly, those on the left might highlight how the evidence supports poverty reduction and redistribution, while those on the right might highlight the well-being benefits of freedom or the necessity to crack down on crime, given its corrosive effects on well-being.

But the difficult response is to acknowledge that, at least in some areas, the well-being evidence suggests that policy isn't quite right. For example, a number of academics including Richard Layard, Nick Humphries and others have put together a shortlist of policy 'do's and don'ts', some of which are clearly contrary to recent policy while others are compatible but imply a marked shift in effort and resources. Let us have a look at some of the ideas.

The usual suspects . . .

Radically expand provision for those suffering from mental illness. Richard Layard has argued that the most unhappy people in society are those suffering from mental illness, and that if reducing unhappiness is our objective, then we should make this group a higher priority. Practical implications are the expansion of clinical provision and a greater focus on the underlying causes of mental illness in both research and policy.

Supporters of greater investment in mental health provision often point to the astonishing increase in levels of medication for depression – in the UK, prescriptions of anti-depressants rose 500% in the 1990s, with a 2000% increase in associated costs. However, since underlying prevalence rates don't seem to have moved much, this increase seems mainly due to increased willingness to medicate (plus the increased costs of new drugs), and could therefore be seen as a good thing. Critics can also point out that there is something slightly tautological in the observation that the mentally ill are unhappy, since this is often built into the clinical judgement.

Nonetheless, there is a strong 'well-being' case that we should further expand well-evidenced 'talking cures' such as cognitive behavioural therapy. There are also substantial gaps in many countries between adult and child mental health services; between housing and social care provision; and between mental health services and the criminal justice system, with very large numbers of people with mental health problems being swept into our prisons.[47] We might also push harder on supporting more people with mental health problems back to work. It is striking that during the decade of rising employment in the UK from the mid 1990s, those with mental health problems were one of the only groups to experience a rise in unemployment (along with those without qualifications) despite the evidence that work normally helps the conditions, and that mental health issues have become the number one reason for Incapacity Benefit claims.

Conclusion: the SWB literature suggests that the mentally ill are the 'well-being poor' and merit a higher priority.

Teach children resilience skills. There is great interest in whether children can be given the mental skills or 'resilience' to better weather the challenges of life, and thereby improve their long-term subjective well-being. One can think of this as a sort of 'inoculation' against later mental health problems, but it also seems to have other benefits, such as fostering the kinds of social skills that are increasingly important in the modern labour market (see also Chapter 3).

A number of trials, such of the Pennsylvania programme developed by the American psychologist Marty Seligman, have suggested that such resilience can be taught, leading to lower levels of teenage depression and improved behaviour. It is too early to know whether the positive effects of such programmes will persist into adulthood, with some evidence that a 'booster' programme may be needed to maintain the positive effects.

Conclusion: giving children the mental skills and insight into the drivers of well-being – 'a user-guide to their own minds' as the headmaster of Welling-ton, Anthony Sheldon puts it – is arguably the 'no-brainer' of a well-being agenda, subject to confirmation that the programmes really do work.

Avoid performance-related pay. The argument here is that individual level performance-related pay reduces life and work satisfaction, but without much benefit to performance. The classic illustration of these negative effects goes right back to studies of military personnel in the 1940s and 1950s. It was found, much to the researchers' surprise, that satisfaction was lowest in branches of the military where promotion was fastest (such as parts of the air force) and satisfaction was highest in areas of slow promotion (such as the military police).

Certain forms of group or organization-based performance-related pay can increase cooperation between fellow workers, and could incentivize performance without undermining satisfaction. Ironically, the wider use of individual-level performance related pay has come into fashion in the public sector of a number of countries just as it has gone out of fashion in the private sector.

Conclusion: crude individual-level performance pay systems tend to have negative impacts on well-being and anyway, intrinsic rewards are generally more effective motivators of performance in relation to high skill, knowledge economy work than extrinsic (money) rewards.

Ban advertising for children. One of the key objectives of advertising is to make us want things we don't have, and is therefore an obvious source of dissatisfaction. While it is generally felt that adults should make their own minds up, a number of writers have suggested that it is reasonable to protect children from the 'hedonic treadmill' of consumer society. Studies have shown that, courtesy mainly of television advertising, toddlers recognize well-known brands by the age of two, and express overt preferences for them long before they reach school at age five.

Some countries have already moved against advertising aimed at children, and in the UK a ban was recently introduced against food advertising between children's shows. Bans present a major practical challenge for commercial television, particularly for the funding of children's television programmes, and are complicated by the rise of the internet. Bans therefore require a wider settlement on public service broadcasting, whether through a traditional provider such as the BBC or PBS, or via subsidies to, or regulation of, commercial broadcasters. We also await evidence that advertising bans have the promised impact on well-being.

Conclusion: there will be growing calls for restrictions on advertising, which in turn raise wider questions about the funding and nature of public sector broadcasting.

Increase redistribution to the poor (but strengthen welfare to work). Despite the concerns of Sen, a headline conclusion of the well-being literature is that a marginal pound will have a greater impact on lifting the well-being of someone who is poor than someone who is rich.[48] We have also seen that getting people into work is a clear and strong conclusion of the well-being literature. Finally, in as far as redistribution reduces inequalities in income and wealth, it may also reduce comparison effects, though the evidence suggests that the main effect would be on affective measures of well-being, not more cognitive measures.

Of course, arguments about redistribution run deep, both around the politics and the purported effects on the economy (see Chapter 4). Some argue that since the absolute impacts of income on well-being are small, greater equality should trump growth (in as far as there is a trade-off). However, we know that people find the experience of losses very unpleasant, so redistribution out of existing income rather than future growth will be especially painful.

The strong, curvilinear relationship between national incomes and well-being can be used to support expansions in the aid budget, since this relationship suggests that marginal increases in the incomes of poor countries will have much bigger impacts on well-being than similar increases in affluent countries. This seems an intuitive proposition, but is complicated by two observations. First, there is the practical question of how best such aid might be provided, noting the mixed successes of historic aid programmes. It may be that simple income transfers are not the best, or sufficient, manner in which to boost the income of poorer countries. Second, as noted in the discussion of the Easterlin paradox above, cross-sectional data may overstate the scale of the benefit that would flow to cross-national income transfers. We also do not know what the well-being impact would be on the populations of richer nations if we were to succeed in raising the incomes of the poorest nations. Again, the evidence suggests that while affective measures would not fall, more cognitive measures would.

Conclusion: net (affective) well-being would probably be increased faster by disproportionately using future growth to raise the incomes and wealth of the less affluent within and between countries.

Discourage gambling. Layard and others have argued that gambling causes great misery without any real benefit. Opponents might argue that gamblers do get some utility from the dream that they might be rich. I'm not sure whether the evidence is strong enough either way, but it should be testable.

Conclusion: more research needed.

Discourage commuting. A number of researchers have now found evidence that commuting is bad for our well-being, and that the benefits of extra income and bigger houses do not make up for the negative effects of commuting. But the question arises about what government can usefully do. Decades of experience has taught us that building more roads and railways generally just increases commuting still further. The issue is complicated further by the complex web of taxes and subsidies that exist in most countries between different modes of transport, though the well-being literature has yet to tell us whether mass or private transport is to be preferred (leaving aside environmental issues).

It's one of those issues where the more you dig, the less obvious it becomes what you should do. You could crank up the cost of travel, and reduce the cost of moving (such as by reducing taxes on the buying and selling of houses, e.g. stamp duty in the UK). This should reduce commuting by increasing geographical mobility – people would move homes instead – but you would then have to offset the negative impacts on both movers and neighbours of this higher mobility society. It may be that technology will help us out, with tele-working increasing year-on-year, albeit from a low base. Perhaps the best we can do is to make better informed choices as individuals. A typical error that we are prone to, in well-being terms, is to think that we will be happier jumping from the small pool in which we are a big fish, to a big pool (typically in the big city) in which we will be a small fish. We make this error because we think of how impressed our present friends and work-mates will be by the move, but after we make it, of course, we don't see those friends so much and they aren't our work-mates.[49] If we do commute, perhaps the best we can do is be more social commuters: travel with your friends, or make friends with your fellow travellers.

Conclusion: we would be wise to reduce commuting where we can, but perhaps the best the state and operators can do – apart from adding a few extra carriages and encouraging employers to be flexible – is to help us be more aware of the well-being impacts of our own choices.

Encourage residential stability. Residential mobility tends to disrupt both our social networks and that of those around us. Rather like commuting, we often seem to misjudge the SWB costs and benefits. A well-known empirical example is how many people think that they would be happier living in a warmer climate, such as California, but the evidence clearly shows that it would make no difference.[50] On the other hand, residential mobility may be too low for certain groups, such as the long-term unemployed.

In fact, the typical mobility pattern for most people, with the possible exception of the USA, is that people generally don't move very far during their lives (and especially those from lower socio-economic groups) and the vast majority of people live within eight miles of where they were born. The most educated often make one large geographical move in their lives, but then they too tend to settle.

Conclusion: there is no clear-cut position from the well-being literature on geographical mobility. It looks like the unemployed should move a bit more, and the most frenetic corporate movers might be better settling down, but beyond that the conclusion is unclear.

Work-life balance. The well-being literature is often linked to the argument that we should work less and play more. However, as we have seen above, for most people work is a source of considerable satisfaction and well-being. The key seems to be quality rather than quantity.

One of the surprises of recent years has been the rise in work satisfaction in the UK in the 2000s, in contrast to the falls through the 1990s. This is unlikely to have been the result of rather timid government and union campaigns to encourage a better work-life balance. More likely it resulted from employers having to compete with each other over work quality in the face of increasingly tight labour markets (it is noteworthy that the UK improvement has not been seen across the EU). We also know from other evidence that the quality of people's leisure depends on having 'someone to play with' – in other words, why bother to stay at home if everyone else is at work. It may be therefore that the best thing government can do is to facilitate workers' rights to take flexible leave, so they can choose what they want to do, but otherwise simply keep the labour market as tight but flexible as possible – though a case can also be made for more common national holidays.

Conclusion: the best that government and unions can do is to facilitate individuals' choices and maintain the conditions under which employers have to compete over the quality of work. This could include encouraging the publication of firm-specific employee satisfaction tables such as extending the 'best employer' league tables as published by The Times.

Expand consumption taxes. One of the hottest arguments of the well-being literature, most closely linked with the economist Robert Frank, is whether governments should use taxes to shift activity towards activities that increase SWB, and away from those that reduce well-being. Layard used a variant of this argument to defend the efficiency of progressive income taxes, suggesting that higher income taxes usefully discourage people from working too much to gain income that has much less impact on their well-being than they think it will.

Others have argued that the problem is more specifically related to 'conspicuous consumption'. It is argued that it is buying 'positional goods' that causes most of the negative externalities: my shiny new Porsche making my neighbours feel bad about their old Ford. But there are also arguments against over-taxing positional goods – goods whose value comes from their high price. These include the practical difficulty of judging what is, or is not, a positional good; the argument that positional goods represent the cutting edge of innovation in the economy; and that ironically, taxing positional goods just makes them even more exclusive and divisive.

Frank's proposition is more focused than a general tax, but arguably more practical than a positional goods tax. He says that one can broadly divide how we use our income into two categories: investment and consumption. He argues that there don't seem to be any SWB problems with people investing in pensions or savings for their children, but that one could apply a graduated tax on the consumption element of our spending. Hence instead of having an income tax, we would have a graduated tax payable on our income less our savings or investment. So the person who builds a £300,000 extension to their house might end up paying 50% tax on it, while the person building a £10,000 extension might only pay 10%.

Conclusion: if we could make it work, there is a theoretical argument for shifting taxes onto well-being 'bads' and away from less differentiated taxes – but that remains a big practical and political 'if'.

What else . . .

There are a number of other policy implications and developments that follow from the well-being literature that are important but have tended to attract less attention. Some of these are listed below.

Measure it. It might seem a little dull, but one of the most important policy developments in relation to well-being is the decision to routinely measure it. I remember the to-be Cabinet Minister David Blunkett saying to me back in the mid 1990s how governments can shape what is, or isn't, a policy issue by what is measured. He was right.

Of course, happiness and life satisfaction has been measured at a headline level since the 1940s in the USA, and since the 1970s in Europe. But to be of real use, we need measures at a level below this so that the data can start to inform the day-to-day choices of policymakers and citizens alike. Generally speaking, the choice is not 'Shall we be Sweden or the UK?' Rather, it is 'Shall I live in Cambridge or London?'; 'Shall we run schools like this or like that?'; or 'Shall we spend more on hospitals or on the police?'

Canada was an early mover in incorporating well-being measures into its national surveys. The UK too has now added well-being to its bundle of regular 'sustainability' indicators, securing its place in routine national indicators. This is an important development as it creates the foundation, and a stream of data, to start asking the really interesting questions about what kind of spending and interventions are most cost effective at boosting well-being. Led by economists such as Paul Dolan and Andrew Oswald, people are now starting to empirically evaluate the subjective well-being impact of specific areas of public spending, such as art galleries, regeneration, or wind-farms. I predict that within five years, and certainly within a decade, large areas of government policy will be routinely subject to a subjective well-being cost-benefit analysis, just as within health policy today different treatments are evaluated according to how many 'quality years of life' they can add per pound, euro or dollar. This type of metric is likely to get a further boost from the courts, which will increasingly use the same kind of analysis to calculate the SWB impacts from the loss of a job, a limb or a loved one.

Conclusion: the decision of national governments to routinely measure SWB will gradually put in the hands of policy-makers, citizens and lawyers the data needed to construct detailed cost-benefit analyses of interventions to increase well-being, and it will become an increasingly familiar part of the discourse around key policy decisions.

Use subjective measures as performance targets. If the idea of policy-makers routinely using well-being measures as a yard-stick by which to judge policy seems a bit of a stretch, just look at the quiet revolution that is being driven by the use of more domain-specific satisfaction measures in public and private services (see also Chapter 5).

Around 1995, the Canadians made a commitment to increase public satisfaction with public-facing services by 10% within a decade. Outside Canada, I don't think many people noticed this pledge, and those who did mostly didn't think it credible. The main tool the Canadians used was a survey under the brand 'Citizens First', which measured citizen satisfaction with different parts of the public sector. Public sector professionals helpfully felt ownership of the survey, further aided by the early finding that the public were at least, if not more, satisfied with most public services as with private sector services. The survey created a direct feedback loop to professionals, not only telling public sector services how well they were doing but also pinpointing the key drivers of satisfaction (or dissatisfaction) so that service providers could do something about them. And the result? Satisfaction with public services rose and the 10% target was reached. Not only that, but satisfaction with local, regional and national government was also pulled up in the process.

It is important to understand why, and how, satisfaction surveys work their magic. Let's take a UK example. A few years ago, Merseyside police started gathering regular data not just on crimes committed or clear-up rates, but on whether the public were satisfied with their contact with the police. As in Canada, the real power of the data are that it highlighted the drivers of satisfaction, and it turned out that these drivers weren't quite what the police thought they were. For example, when someone called in a burglary, the presumption was that it was response time that was key to public satisfaction – in other words, the police should get there as fast as they could. But it turned out this was wrong. What was much more important was that the police showed up when they said they would. Residents weren't really bothered whether it took two or three hours to turn up, as long as they turned up at 4pm, or whatever, like they said they would. The police were then able to use this insight to change their operational behaviour, and in so doing increase both efficiency and public satisfaction.

There are now measures of satisfaction with the police across the country, and satisfaction measures are being introduced for many other public services too. In each case, focusing on public satisfaction can significantly change the behaviour and priorities of the provider. For example, it has been found that by far the most powerful predictor of satisfaction with health services is 'being treated with respect and dignity', not the clinical outcome *per se*. This can generate real tension. As a clinician, the priority is normally taken to be getting the patient better, whereas the satisfaction data instead highlights a respectful and considerate bedside manner. But the tension is not really that deep – most clinicians don't set out to be rude and insensitive, but they may not realize the impact they are having. Chances are, they can adjust their behaviour without impacting on 'hard' clinical outcomes, and anyway, most clinicians would rather be focusing on the sensitivities of the patient than a set of targets set from on high.

There is a further benefit of using satisfaction measures in the public sector, and that is that they can help drive up the satisfaction of the staff too. A primary driver of satisfaction in public sector workers is the feeling that you are focused on the patient or citizen in front of you, and you feel you are helping them.[51] Satisfaction measures allow the interests of citizen, public servant and government to be aligned behind the same objective, and also enable the removal of other kinds of traditional outcome targets, and the pre-judgements that they contain.

The last point is illustrated in the recent reforms to local government in the UK. Essentially, the deal at the heart of the 2006 reforms was that central government would radically reduce the number of specific outcome targets that local government had to deliver, provided that satisfaction surveys of local government and its services were put in place – a form of what is sometimes known as 'double devolution'.

So the increasing use of domain-specific satisfaction measures is leading to important, qualitative changes in the character of public service delivery. Just as we have seen with overall satisfaction measures, domain-specific measures tend to increase the focus on relational aspects of services and away from 'hard' conventional outcome measures. But it also primes the next step – once it is decided that the subjective experience of the citizen matters within healthcare, policing or local government – to start asking questions about 'what then will increase satisfaction in general?'

Conclusion: the use of satisfaction measures in services like health and policing, is leading a quiet revolution in the delivery of public services, qualitatively changing what and how they deliver, and laying the ground for the use of more holistic measures of SWB.

Building social capital. Social capital refers to social networks and the norms, or everyday habits, that oil the workings of everyday life, and particularly social trust. In my experience, all the key researchers on social capital eventually get interested in SWB (such as Bob Putnam and John Helliwell), and similarly, most researchers into the determinants of SWB end up interested in social capital (like Easterlin or Offer). The reason is simple enough – relationships have a big impact on well-being.

It is unsurprising, then, that many of the policy implications of the well-being literature are the same as those of the social capital literature, as the causal pathways overlap so heavily. For example in US data, for every extra ten minutes of commuting, involvement in social and community groups falls by 10% – a negative and robust effect much like that on SWB. This issue is returned to in later chapters (notably Chapter 3), and I have also written about it elsewhere, so let me just draw out some policy headlines here.

Social capital can be built at the individual, community, and at the national level. At the individual level, it can be built through mentoring; volunteering programmes; and through strengthening the skills of parents, such as through parenting classes. At the community level, it can be built through physical environments that make it easy for people to interact with each other but that do not force them together; using ICT to lower the barriers to interaction and informing others of mutual interests; and creating situations that encourage mixing between people from different social and ethnic groups. At the national level, it can be built through service learning programmes in schools; through national community service schemes; and through vibrant democratic and media spheres that enable people to negotiate and develop shared social norms and habits (see later chapters).

Conclusion: social capital is a major determinant of individual and national SWB, and can be strengthened through policy intervention. It is discussed in more detail in the later chapters.

Encourage religion? One of the findings of the SWB literature is that religion, at least at the individual level, makes people happier. But it's almost never mentioned as a policy conclusion, whereas other policy suggestions with much thinner evidence often are proposed, such as banning gambling.

Of course, within the UK and other countries, there is a long tradition of not mixing religion and politics. There is also a credible argument that even if religion makes people happier at the individual level, it might reduce overall SWB by encouraging conflict between groups. But let's face it, the main reason that encouraging religion doesn't make the cut is that it feels like a very odd thing to propose in a secular system of government. But an interesting question, that we shall return to in Chapter 3, is whether there are secular equivalents to religion that it is appropriate for policymakers to promote.

Conclusion: an area policymakers should stay away from?

Well-being Doesn't Mean Abandoning the Economy

Wealth gives us choices: what we do with those choices – individually and collectively – does have impacts on our well-being. The unfolding world recession of 2009 prompted some commentators to urge people to turn their backs on economic growth and instead focus on other satisfactions. My own view is that, though I think we should use well-being as one of our key objectives, I don't think we should, or need to be, anti-growth.

The comments that follow are not a comprehensive economic policy, but highlight a few areas where we might be able to make further, or faster advances.

Technology and investment

Technological innovation is a, if not the, key driver of economic growth. A common pattern across the OECD is a falling contribution of low-tech manufacturing as a percentage of gross national value-added. This has been particularly marked in the UK, falling from 12.3% to 9% between 1993 and 2002, compared with a fall from 11.5 to 10.5 in France; 11.7 to 10.4 in Germany; and 9.4 to 8.1% in the USA.

Over the same period, the percentage of gross-value-added from knowledge services, such as the now-bemoaned financial services, rose in the UK from 28.4 to 34.3%, rising to match that of the USA (31.4 to 34.3%), and substantially exceeding that of France (28.4 rising to 30.8%) or Germany (29.1 to 31.2%). This was illustrated by the dramatic increase in the value of the UK's business service exports. In the decade 1995 to 2005, the value of UK exports increased three-fold in legal services, advertising and market research; increased four-fold in R & D; and increased five-fold in accounting and in business management. On the other hand, countries such as Germany and France were more successful than the UK over the period in growing their high-tech manufacturing bases – though the UK was not without successes, notably in strong growth in chemicals; transport equipment and electrical and optical equipment.[52]

The classic contribution that the state can make is through investment in education, training and research. These activities have both public and private good elements to them. Firms and individuals can gain market advantages through investment in training and research, but since many of the benefits are uncertain and imperfectly captured, firms and individuals will tend to invest below the optimum level.

OECD models have consistently found that marginal increases in spending on Higher Education and research are associated with significant boosts to economic growth (with the exception of defence spending). A major part of this benefit is that it increases a nation's 'absorptive capacity' to take advantage of the huge amount of research and advances that are occurring in other countries. Britain, like other nations, has sought to boost long-range growth through such investments, such as through spending on HE and tax-credits for firms conducting research. Other countries have been even bolder, such as Finland and Sweden which have raised research spending to around 4% of GDP – but interestingly, with a high proportion of that coming from the private sector. It is this spending, including on new 'disruptive technologies', that is thought to help explain Finland's successful bounce out of the last recession, and is now being much studied by other countries in the current context.

This is all pretty much conventional wisdom these days. But there are three areas that merit further attention, particularly for the UK:

- How to support service industry
- Valley of death and the problem of 'uninventive consumption'
- The market in education and training

The first issue is how we might support research in the service industries – arguably the UK's greatest success story, though in the current recession sometimes regarded as its curse too. Many of the basic skill sets, such as the importance of maths, are just as important to service as to other knowledge intensive industries (such as high-tech manufacturing), reinforcing the case for supporting these skills in schools and HE. But there is a danger that our R & D models and targets remain too rooted in a traditional manufacturing and industry model.

Canny venture capitalists, and service industry leaders, know that a key site for innovation is around failures – as one put it to me 'a service failure is an opportunity'. Given that this is the case, it may be that a key point of public and industry investment might be around systematically identifying failures, or consumer disappointments, in services. This isn't just about during recessions – it is at all times. The pure science equivalent for services might lie in future developments in behavioural economics, around both consumer and market behaviours, and in supporting the development of the complex maths behind current financial models. It does not seem that our research councils, or our research communities, have moved very far into populating such new research worlds.

Second, there are perennial issues around the so-called 'valley of death' between pure research and market application, and especially in the UK. Germany famously has its Fraunhofer Institutes for applied research, while Sweden and Finland seem to be more successful at bridging the gap through a contemporary version of corporatism – a strong partnership between industry and government to coordinate investment. One of the more interesting arguments is that the UK's difficulty has been less institutional, and more cultural – that we're not very innovative consumers. To put this another way, the British don't really like to use a new product or service until it has been around for a few years (with the possible ironic exception of financial products). In contrast, it is argued, consumers in countries such as the USA and Japan can't wait to try a new product, and will want to start using it even before all its glitches are ironed out.

I have a hypothesis, and it is only that, that one of the most useful things that the UK state could do is to foster the spirit of adventure in us consumers. I think it could do this through a radical expansion in consumer association activity, most popularly embodied in 'Which?' This idea is explored in further detail below.

Third, I think we have further to go to help the 'education and training' market work better. A striking contrast is often made between the increasingly market sensitive and successful UK HE sector, and its poor relative, the Further Education (FE) sector. The wind of reform is starting to blow through the FE sector, moving it slowly towards a system within which money follows student interest and away from the top-down, block provision that traditionally characterized the sector. There are also strong grounds for more personalization, and money following student interest, in the school system in the years to come too. This is not just about a blind belief in consumer choice, but because younger generations are often more tuned into the power of disruptive technologies than the older generations that drive top-down labour market and educational policies.

Yet these shifts to more student-based preferences, or bottom-up systems, are premised on students and adult learners making well-informed choices. The evidence is that these choices are often poorly informed: from students giving up maths and stats much too early for the good of their long-term earnings, to the taking of vocational qualifications that have no impact on their earnings at all. Once again, one of the key gaps appears to be information. A fourteen year old, 18 year old or 30 year old ought to be able to find out not just what their educational and training choices are, but what impact they are likely to have on their opportunities, earnings and – of course – their life satisfaction.

Curiously, governments often already fund large-scale surveys that could be adapted to provide this kind of highly personalized information. For example, in the UK every university graduate is asked to participate in the First Destination Survey (FDS) six months after they have left. Unfortunately, the FDS is conducted too soon after leaving and, in my view, doesn't ask the right questions. Whilst catching students six months on ensures a good response rate, it is too early to know the impact of the degree on their life chances. The successful Oxbridge student might be taking a year to travel around the world before they enter the city, while another might be employed, but in a dead-end job at McDonald's. But if we followed them up three or five years later, it would be much clearer what is going on. If we then asked 'How much are you earning?'; 'Would you say the knowledge you learnt at college was useful?' and 'Are you satisfied with your work and your life?' we'd get some fantastically valuable information to guide the choices of those that follow.

Finally, also on education, there is a strong argument that the economic premium and importance of soft skills is likely to rise in the coming years. This is particularly true in strongly service-based economies like the UK. As noted above, there are also well-being grounds to put more emphasis in this area and, as we shall see in later chapters, reasons rooted in addressing other big policy challenges that we face, such as crime and anti-social behaviour.

Information as a public good

The reader will gather that I have come to think that information is a very important public good, and one that has been relatively neglected.

In fact, let me put it more strongly. Perhaps the single biggest marginal impact that government could have on boosting economic growth, and on the performance of the public sector, is fostering an expansion in citizen-consumer information. This doesn't necessarily mean that government should gather or disseminate the information, but it may mean a role for government in ensuring that the information is gathered and accessible.

What kind of information do I mean? Imagine that you need a builder, a solicitor or a medical specialist. For the former, you might go to the Yellow Pages, and for the latter, your GP might give you a list. But how do you choose between them? Most of us might ask a few friends or relatives for recommendations, but otherwise we stick in a pin and hope for the best. At the end of the process, we'll probably have some idea whether we chose well or not, but by then it's a bit late.

Contrast this to how an innovation like 'trip adviser' is changing how most of us book our holidays, or how reputations on ebay are changing how we buy goods from small traders. We can look at what other people thought, and whether they were satisfied or not. Poor quality or unreliable traders get squeezed out, while good value and reliable traders prosper.

One could argue that eventually the market will deliver a trip adviser equivalent for everything, however, there is reason to doubt this. Information has strong public good characteristics: providing considered feedback is a cost to the individual, and there is a strong temptation to free-ride on the feed-back provided by others. The value of information also grows the more comprehensive it becomes. The public good issue is illustrated by the consumer publication 'Which?' – most people don't want to join, but try and get a copy off someone else when they need to buy a particular good. But this means that it never quite reaches the critical mass it needs, so that the reviews tend to be of a relatively narrow range of products, creating a vicious circle against scale rather than for it.

The benefits to the economy, as well as to the individual consumer, would be considerable of enhanced citizen-generated and utilized information. The use of high quality consumer information squeezes out inefficient or weaker suppliers, reducing consumer detriments and creating a hot-house to catalyse the development of services and products. Firms exposed to such feedback loops would evolve faster, and this would also give them a competitive advantage where they trade overseas.

Similar general arguments apply for public services, with league tables being just the very beginning of this journey. In twenty years time, who can doubt that individual teachers, doctors, policemen – as well as schools, hospitals and police Basic Command Units (BCUs) – will have online reputations that will grow and change over time, providing detailed feedback to service deliverers, purchasers and citizens alike. The real question is whether this information will be fair and trustworthy, or fragmented and unreliable. In this context, it is important to realize that what we have traditionally called public services – especially health and education – are almost certainly going to be ever larger parts of our economy going forward. The more we can drive up their quality and efficiency, the more not only will we benefit directly as citizens and taxpayers, but the more people from other countries will also come to use these services and boost our economy (or else we will go to theirs).

How will this evolve? A good place to start is with the regulators. Much of the information they hold and gather could seed this public space. Ironically, it could also mean a lighter regulatory touch, as problematic providers would be put out of business long before illegal behaviour brought a regulator to act. The state, and regulators, would seek to ensure that every sector had such information flowing, though generally simply by applying pressure on the relevant trade organization to ensure a suitable framework existed. Such enhanced information flows won't entirely put the regulators out of business, especially in areas of the economy or public services that are characterized by strong asymmetries of expertise (e.g. a financial-adviser–consumer relationship, or doctor–patient relationship) or where delivery strongly favours local monopolies, such as in transport or certain utilities. If you want a 'post-bureaucratic state', enhancing the flow of citizen-generated, consumer-used, but state facilitated information is a pretty good place to start.[53]

Incentives

I don't think you can have a serious discussion about prosperity and well-being without at least mentioning incentives. Of course, part of the argument of this chapter has been that a combination of the incentives presented in a market economy and the heuristics in our heads don't always maximize our well-being. But that doesn't mean that incentives don't work, and particularly financial incentives.

Being a lawyer by training, in common with many politicians, Tony Blair tended to reach for legislation and laws as his preferred instrument of change. But there are plenty of other incentives and sanctions that affect our behaviour (see also Chapter 5).

There is no doubt, for example, that the structuring of the benefits system does affect behaviour, which in turn affects the whole economy. Layard's work, before he got into well-being, showed us this, and how welfare systems affected the underlying, or 'natural' rate of unemployment. If I was chronically unemployed in the UK of the last decade, I would surely want to get myself onto Incapacity Benefit (IB) and off much less generous unemployment benefit, and then I'd be pretty worried about getting a job that might be short-term and would ruin my chances of getting back on IB. I'm not the only one to think this. In areas of high unemployment, IB claims are also high, but the real telltale is that IB claims are also massively inflated for younger people in those same areas. Hotspots of chronic illness often develop around specific industries, such as the old coal industry, but it is much more difficult to attribute the high IB claims of those workers' children and grandchildren to the pits they never worked in. More plausible is that the community has rationally learnt its way around the best way of using the benefit system.

Benefit reforms are always tough, because it's right to be careful about the obvious hardships that we want our welfare system to protect people from. But you've also got to look at the incentives that are built within them and seek to ensure that work really does pay – both on grounds of prosperity and well-being. There are also important questions about the relationship between taxes and incentives to work at the *top* end of the income distribution. We will return to both issues in the chapter on fairness (Chapter 4).

There is one other idea I want to mention, and that is the concept of the 'economy of regard'.[54] This refers to a different kind of incentive that is 'non-fungible', or non-exchangeable, with the conventional economy and money. The key point is that much of what incentivizes and drives our behaviour both in the 'real' economy and in our private lives is not money, but what other people think of us, and what we think of them in return.

Some economists have argued that a huge swath of economic activity is inefficient precisely because it is distorted by regard-based relationships – we buy things from people that we know, rather than going out and getting the best product or service for the price. However, going back to Adam Smith and beyond, scholars have recognized that this cuts two ways. On the one hand, networks and relationships can be used in ways that slow the economy and work against the interests of the public, such as when merchants form a cartel to artificially inflate prices. On the other hand, we also know that trustworthy relationships can oil the workings of the economy to the benefit of both traders and citizens, easing the flow of information and reducing the need for expensive contractual relationships.

The economy of regard is interesting in that it has massive impact on both the 'real' economy, therefore on prosperity conventionally defined, and also on our subjective well-being. In fact, as we shall explore further in later chapters, far from being a marginal issue that occasionally distorts the normal incentives of the 'real' economy, it is often the dominant force affecting both our prosperity and our well-being. The economy of regard, I will argue, is like the dark matter of the universe – you can't make any sense of what we see without it, yet we hardly notice that it's there.

The environment

In the twenty-first century, you cannot have a serious or complete discussion of prosperity without highlighting the link to the physical environment. While Hirsch's discussion of the 'social limits to growth' talked of environmental limits thirty years ago, these are today obvious in a way that cannot be ignored, be it on news bulletins of melting ice sheets or policy talk of the jobs to be created in the 'low carbon economy'.

There are so many books and policy reports in this area, I will limit myself to a few comments only. First, for all the profile given to the issue, there is strong evidence that we – the public and policymakers – are 'cheap talk environmentalists'.[55] When the public are asked a direct question about how important is the environment, they invariably express high concern. Yet on the standard trackers of public concerns, where concern about the environment is offered alongside other public concerns such as unemployment, healthcare or crime, the environment rarely makes the cut. Even in environmentally 'concerned' Europe – and this is before the current recession – not a single European country had the environment as one of the top three concerns of the public.

We do care about the environment, but just not that much. It's a problem that is always psychologically, and therefore politically, a long way off. Our psychological discounting of the future, of problems that emerge slowly rather than dramatically, and our self-serving attributional biases, all work strongly against us taking the issue seriously, or at least until it is too late. We see it as a problem for others, not for our behaviour now. I think two firm conclusions can be drawn from this. First, if ever there was an area for governments and political parties to take a lead, it is this. Don't expect to win elections over it, but just do it. Second, if you are pinning your hopes on radical, self-motivated behavioural change, as so many environmentalists seem to, then we're doomed. People aren't going to give up their cars, but they will substitute to green alternatives that work just as well – at least with the pull of price signals and the occasional push of regulation. Don't hope to try and get everyone in tiny electric cars that struggle to do 30 miles an hour – get them into electric Teslas and its cousins that can do 0–60 in a few seconds or next generation SUVs that can run off the ten thousandth of incident sunlight that we need to collect.

We can augment the change with a bit of clever behavioural economics – higher tax at the point of purchase of high carbon vehicles rather than spreading it on duties after the key decision is made, and so on (see Chapter 5) – but the heavy lifting will be done by technology and incentives.

Similarly, we know that systems and industries don't vote for their own downfall. It will take heavy state action, and quite a bit of pain, to transfer to the long-promised low carbon economy. It is a curious irony that the current economic crisis might just turn out to be what saves the world. There are real synergies and economic opportunities that can be exploited. Electric vehicles can charge overnight on the otherwise unused excesses generated by renewables (that you can't switch off, unlike a coal power station). Power companies can be made to charge some version of 'negawatts', charging us for outcomes like heat rather than power consumed and changing their incentives to want to insulate our homes and businesses rather than just encourage our consumption.

Finally, though I am broadly upbeat about the prospects for international trading in carbon and so on, I do think we'd better have a plan B. The combination of our psychological discounting of the problem and the temptation for individual nations to default does not look like a solid foundation for our future. So whether it is paying farmers to turn organic waste into charcoal, or seeding clouds from commercial airlines to enhance global dimming, we'd better have a few tricks up our sleeve for 'just in case'. Global prosperity will look pretty thin when we're sliding into a re-run of the great Permian extinction.[56]

Conclusion

The relationship between economic growth, or prosperity, and subjective well-being is empirically strong, yet causally subtle. In wealthy countries, prosperity and subjective well-being appear to be orthogonal objectives – that is, they are not incompatible, but point in different directions so that it is possible to achieve one without the other. The chapter has argued that a key explanation for the 'Easterlin paradox' – the puzzling fact that there is a strong correlation between countries GDP and well-being at any given time yet little relationship between the economic growth of rich countries and well-being over time – is at least partly due to cultural and social factors that change little over time that tend to determine both a country's relative well-being and its capacity to take advantage of technological and institutional opportunities for growth. We might think of these common causal factors as a nation's 'hidden wealth'.

In my view, many of the leading 'happiness gurus' both overstate the paradigm-changing nature of the well-being literature, while understating its potentially radical impact at the level of everyday policy analysis and changes.

The implications for policy are not that we should all retire to the country to grow our own vegetables – the 'good life' – for humans seem to thrive on stress and challenge. Indeed, in many policy areas, the well-being literature reinforces existing policy priorities, such as helping people back into work, reducing crime and fear, and reducing inequalities between and within countries. The hard work of delivering on such priorities remains just the same.

But a focus on well-being does change priorities in a number of areas. Perhaps the most striking change is that an emphasis on subjective well-being greatly raises the profile and importance of relationships in policy, and in our own lives. At the same time, it suggests that we, both as citizens and as a community, are prone to systematic misjudgements about what will maximize our well-being. Hence we tend to end up commuting a lot to earn extra money to buy things that we're a bit disappointed with, when we might have been better off just seeing our friends or families a little bit more.

One of the most promising developments is the use of both general and service-specific satisfaction measures as a tool to shape the character and shape of service delivery. The use of satisfaction measures encourages providers to focus on the aspects of service delivery that are important to citizens without having to specify in advance what these are, such as treating people with respect and dignity (versus reducing infection rates). As our knowledge builds up, I am convinced that this data will increasingly be used to help policy-makers and citizens make difficult marginal decisions about how and where to spend time and money.

Having concluded that well-being and economic growth are neither mortal enemies nor causally linked at the hip, we briefly noted some of the key policies that might be used to drive up both prosperity and well-being. These included upping our investment in information as a public good (see also Chapter 5); in the broadening of our conception of skills required to be a successful and fulfilled citizen (see also Chapter 4); and support for the 'dark matter' of our economy and society – the economy of regard (see also Chapter 3). Economic incentives shaped by the state remain important too, such as around the unintended incentives to remain on benefits. Finally, we acknowledged the necessary, if not sufficient, role played by the environment and sustainability in our well-being, though also the sobering evidence that both policy-makers and the public have a poor record on the issue to date, and that prudent policy-makers had better not rely on goodwill and human nature to save the world.

In sum, the insights from the well-being literature provide an important re-tuning of both personal and societal objectives – a sort of health-check on how we are spending our time and our money. I feel less Hirsch's despair at the social limits to growth, and more room for Keynes's tempered optimism (Box 1.1). We are, of course, Keynes's grandchildren and we live with the wealth he predicted. It is right that we wrestle with the dilemma that he predicted too, though with an eye on the hidden wealth of society too.

How struck he would have been by the findings of the last thirty years of time budget studies that have shown, across countries, that the wealthy are choosing to work more, while the 'working class' are choosing to work less.[57] We are making choices all the time, many of which economic growth make possible. It is for us to make sure, individually and collectively, that they're the ones we really want.

Box 1.1   *Extract from John Maynard Keynes,* Economic Possibilities for our Grandchildren *(1930).*[58]

Now for my conclusion, which you will find, I think, to become more and more startling to the imagination the longer you think about it.

I draw the conclusion that, assuming no important wars and no important increase in population, the *economic problem* may be solved, or be at least within sight of solution, within a hundred years. This means that the economic problem is not – if we look into the future – *the permanent problem of the human race.*

Why, you may ask, is this so startling? It is startling because – if, instead of looking into the future, we look into the past – we find that the economic problem, the struggle for subsistence, always has been hitherto the primary, most pressing problem of the human race – not only of the human race, but of the whole of the biological kingdom from the beginnings of life in its most primitive forms.

. . . Thus for the first time since his creation man will be faced with his real, his permanent problem – how to use his freedom from pressing economic cares, how to occupy the leisure, which science and compound interest will have won for him, to live wisely and agreeably and well.

The strenuous purposeful money-makers may carry all of us along with them into the lap of economic abundance. But it will be those peoples, who can keep alive, and cultivate into a fuller perfection, the art of life itself and do not sell themselves for the means of life, who will be able to enjoy the abundance when it comes.

Yet there is no country and no people, I think, who can look forward to the age of leisure and of abundance without a dread. For we have been trained too long to strive and not to enjoy. It is a fearful problem for the ordinary person, with no special talents, to occupy himself, especially if he no longer has roots in the soil or in custom or in the beloved conventions of a traditional society. To judge from the behaviour and the achievements of the wealthy classes today in any quarter of the world, the outlook is very depressing! For these are, so to speak, our advance guard – those who are spying out the promised land for the rest of us and pitching their camp there. For they have most of them failed disastrously, so it seems to me – those who have an independent income but no associations or duties or ties – to solve the problem which has been set them.

I feel sure that with a little more experience we shall use the new-found bounty of nature quite differently from the way in which the rich use it today, and will map out for ourselves a plan of life quite otherwise than theirs.

2

Not Getting Along

Don't you think it's interesting that in the most modern of ages, the biggest problem is the oldest problem of human society – the fear of the other . . .

It's great that your kids will live to be ninety years old but I don't want it to be behind barbed wire. It's great that we're gonna have all these benefits of the modern world, but I don't want you to feel like you're emotional prisoners. And I don't want you to look at people who look different from you and see a potential enemy instead of a fellow travel-ler. We can make the world of our dreams for our children, but since it's a world without walls, it will have to be a home for all our children.

Bill Clinton, Dimbleby Lecture, December 2001

People's worries have changed over the decades. In the war and post-war period, concerns were dominated by the need to survive. In the 1970s, concerns about inflation and industrial conflicts dominated con-cerns in Britain, while internationally the long shadow of the cold war and nuclear conflict hung over us. As these concerns eased, they were overtaken by concerns about unemployment in the 1980s and then public services in the 1990s and early 2000s.

The dominant concerns have varied between countries. Hence while the British public had stopped worrying about unemployment by the mid 2000s, it remained the top concern of over half of all European countries in 2007 – even pre-credit-crunch – just as it dominated the concerns of the British public through the 1980s to mid 1990s.

By early 2009, public concerns across the world were increasingly dominated by the latest recession. The exact expression of these concerns was tinted by national context. In Britain, it was expressed as a concern about 'the economy' in general. In the USA it was about the economy and jobs. In parts of Southern Europe, it was tinted with resentment about rising prices linked to euro-membership. In France, the mass protests were driven by a perception of unfairness that bankers were protected while the common worker was not. In general, despite the ubiquitous nature of the emerging global recession, there has not been a great sense of 'solidarity'. Rather there has often been a sense, both within and between nations, of 'every man for himself', not least in the rising calls for protectionism and hostility to foreign workers and goods.

This 'meaner' side of the reaction to the economic crisis can be seen to have had its roots in the concerns of national publics even before the crisis began. The top public concerns across EU nations in 2007 – after unemployment – were crime and immigration. This pattern was particularly clear in Britain, where unemployment was much less pronounced as a concern. By 2007–8, the dominant concerns in the UK had become, in order: crime, immigration and terrorism. At the local level, Britons are also fearful, with worries about 'gangs of teenagers hanging

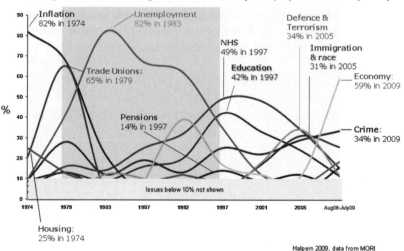

Figure 2.1 *Public concerns in the UK in the year preceding each election since 1974. Note how dramatically dominant public concerns have changed over time. The last data point shows public concerns for the last 6 months of 2008.*

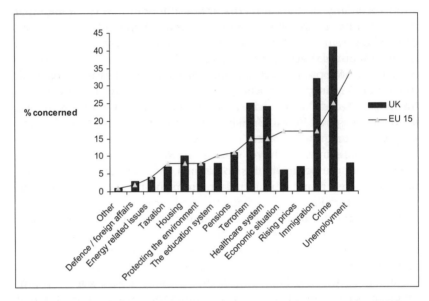

Figure 2.2 *Top public concerns in the UK and EU (Eurobarometer data, 2007).*

around' and about 'our own children getting hurt or abducted' topping polls of local or community concerns.

The UK was not unique in this pattern of concern. The public in Spain showed an almost identical pattern of concern by 2007, and the pattern in Denmark was also very similar. All three countries have suffered from terror attacks, but this has blended with more ubiquitous concerns about crime and immigration to create a potent blend of fear and vulnerability.

Of course, such opinion surveys are designed to elicit some concern. There are almost no surveys that ask 'what do you think is going well these days?' But are countries like Britain and Spain right to be worried? Similarly, economists and most politicians emphasize that the benefits of free labour and trade greatly outweigh the costs of foreign workers 'taking' a few jobs at home, but struggle to persuade the public of this.

Most importantly, if we want to address our fears, we need to look hard at their roots before launching into policy solutions that may be pointing the wrong way.

Crime – High and Rising?

The UK has a relatively high crime rate – second only to Ireland in the most recent European crime victimization survey. Given our relatively strong economy, and vocal media, it doesn't seem that surprising that it comes out as a top public concern. In contrast, in the US, public concerns about crime fell from 76% in 2001 to 46% in 2009, though with quite a lot of volatility in between.[1]

What is more puzzling is why more than two-thirds of Britons think that crime is rising, a proportion that has remained largely unchanged for over a decade. Over that same period crime fell by more than a third, as measured by the British Crime survey, our most reliable and robust measure.[2]

Similar falls in crime have occurred in many other countries. After rising for decades, crime in the USA began to fall in the early 1990s and has fallen even more substantially than in the UK, where it fell from around 1995. Falls in crime since the mid 1990s have been shown in victim surveys in France, Italy, Germany, Spain, Netherlands, Sweden, Finland and Estonia. In fact there are few OECD countries where crime has not fallen over the last decade, two notable exceptions being Ireland and Belgium.

Falls in crime have been particularly marked in relation to car and other property crime. This is thought to have been as a result of 'target hardening' – manufacturers and owners making things more difficult to steal. Crime is also thought to have been driven down by a fall in the proportion of young people in the population and, more controversially, by the proportion of 'unwanted' young people as a result of abortion and birth control.[3] Since crime is both disproportionately committed by young people and targeted at them, demographic shifts to smaller family sizes and higher life expectancy have helped to reduce crime too.[4]

So why do people *think* crime has got worse? One clue comes from the finding that while people think that crime has got worse at the national level, they tend to think it has got better where they live. Similar effects are found for education and health – people are relatively positive about their personal and local experiences, but think it is atypical. The standard interpretation of these findings – local good, national bad – is the preponderance of negative stories in the media. Systematic analyses confirm the everyday suspicion that newspapers massively over-report violent crimes over other crime types, helping to inflate people's estimates of their occurrence. Beliefs about crime are also affected by the particular newspaper that you regularly read, confirming a negative effect of the tabloids in particular.

There's little doubt that the media does have an effect. It particularly drives up the belief that crime is rising at the national level, but its role is mainly to reinforce a pattern of thought in our own heads. Essentially, we're not very good at estimating probability. We estimate by using various mental shortcuts or 'heuristics', which sometimes lead us to make serious errors. One of the best documented of these shortcuts is that we 'guesstimate' the probability of something occurring from the ease with which we can conjure up an example of it occurring. The classic example is of people's fear of crashing on an airplane, versus their relative comfort about travelling by car. The high profile given to otherwise rare airplane crashes makes us overestimate how often they occur.

A tighter example of the same thing is to ask yourself whether you think there are more English words that begin with the letter 'r' or that have the letter 'r' as the third letter. Most people reach the conclusion that there are more words that begin with the letter 'r', because they can rapidly think of examples, whereas it's more difficult to generate words (like word!) that have the 'r' third. In fact, there are roughly three times more words with the 'r' third than first.

Additionally, we have a tendency to both remember and pass on to others scary and negative incidents. It's not just the newspapers, it's us. Studies have suggested that people are up to seven times more likely to tell a friend about a negative than a positive experience. Negative events also loom larger in our own memory, often for good reason. For example, if you have ever had food poisoning, the chances are that you can remember what you ate and where it was, even if it was ten

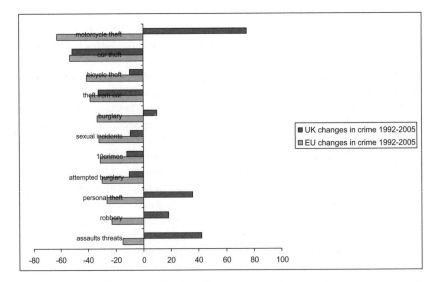

Figure 2.3 *Change in crime victimization rates from 1992 to 2005 across EU countries. Impersonal thefts, such as from cars, have fallen faster than crimes against the person, such as robbery, and especially in the UK.*[5]

or twenty years ago.[6] And how many times have you recounted the story in the years since?

The fact that violent crime has fallen less fast than other forms of crime – though has still fallen in a majority of European countries – may help to explain why we tend to overestimate both the absolute rate of crime and its trend. Fears linked with knife and gun crime, however objectively rare and almost regardless of the trend, loom especially large in our personal estimates of what is going on.

Crime has a particularly powerful impact on our psyche, way in excess of its 'objective' or economic cost. Victims of burglary, let alone assault, often report strong feelings of being violated, and their anxiety and distress greatly outstrips the economic cost of what they had taken, or damage done. Indeed, when the UK Home Office quotes the massive costs of crime – normally when it is trying to get money out of the Treasury – the big numbers come from trying to put an economic cost on the distress and anxiety caused rather than more conventional loss or damage. There's something about the intentionality – another person hurting or harming us – that we seem programmed to be particularly sensitive to, compared with the impacts of misfortunes that we interpret as impersonal 'accidents', like illness or slipping over on ice, even though these may be far more frequent and devastating.

Returning to the travel example makes the point. Thousands of people die on the roads every year in the UK alone, with per capita road-deaths in other counties generally even higher. Yet we would regard it as extremely bizarre for somebody to say that they were afraid to go out in a car or to cross the road as a pedestrian because of the fear of a road accident (see Figure 2.10 on probabilities later in the chapter). At the same time, we take it as quite unremarkable that more than a quarter of Europeans report feeling unsafe or very unsafe on the streets after dark – a proportion that rises to a third or more among Britons, Poles, Spanish, Portuguese and Italians.

Perhaps it should be no surprise then, given how we estimate risk and feel about crime, that 30% of Europeans estimated that they were 'likely' or 'very likely' to be burgled in the most recent international crime victimization survey, while the actual number who were burgled in the previous year was 1.6%.[7] In other words, we overestimate the probability that we will be burgled by nearly *20-fold*.

It's a tricky claim to say that we worry too much about crime, because this rests on a judgement that we are 'irrational' to feel so strongly about it. But what we can say is that people are prone to systematically and massively overestimating their risk of victimization, and that in this sense at least their fear is inflated.

Why are Some Countries More Afraid than Others?

As we have seen, people greatly overestimate the chances that they will be the victim of a crime such as burglary in the next year, but there are also significant variations in how much people overestimate the risk across countries. For example, the Greeks overestimate the probability of being burgled by nearly 30-fold, with close to 50% of Greeks feeling that it is likely that they will be burgled next year (whereas the actual victimization rate was 1.8%). In contrast, 'only' 14% of Danes thought that they were likely to be burgled the next year, despite the fact that their victimization rate, at 2.8%, was substantially higher than that of the Greeks.

This curious cross-national pattern is shown in Figure 2.4. At a glance one can see that countries with higher rates of burglary – such as the UK – do tend to have higher proportions of people who fear they will be burgled, though statistically this relationship is weak (the correlation is 0.34 and statistically non-significant). However, if we compare fear of burglary to another variable – levels of 'social trust', or the extent to which you think people in general can be trusted – we find a strong and statistically significant relationship (correlation = –0.70; prob. < 0.001). In essence, low-trust, generally southern European countries such as Greece, Italy, Portugal, Spain and France report particularly high estimates of whether they will be burgled, while high trust, generally Scandinavian, countries such as Denmark, Netherlands and Finland report lower estimates, regardless of their actual burglary rates.

We can explain even more of the variability in people's estimates of being burgled if we add into the mix levels of 'self-interested values' – how acceptable people think it is to do things like: keep money that you have found; cheat on your tax return or benefits; and avoid fares on public transport. Countries where people think it is more acceptable to do these kinds of self-interested activities are also the ones where estimates of the risk of burglary are highest (correlation = 0.62; prob < 0.01), as well as also reporting lower levels of social trust (correlation = –0.51; prob < 0.05). A statistical model that contains all three of these variables – actual rate of burglary, social trust, and self-interested values – explains nearly 70% of the cross-national variation in people's estimates of the likelihood of being burgled.[8]

A very similar pattern helps to explain the large cross-national differences in people feeling that it is unsafe or very unsafe on the streets after dark in the local area. There is only a very weak relationship between objective crime rates and such fear (correlation = 0.2; statisti-

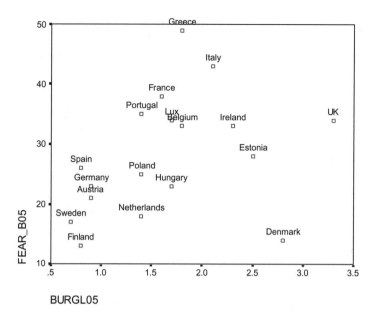

Figure 2.4   *Perceived likelihood of burglary by burglary victimization, by country, 2005.*

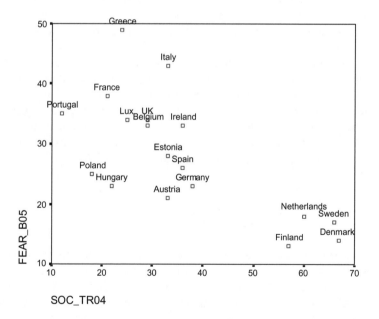

Figure 2.5   *Perceived likelihood of burglary by social trust, by country, 2005.*

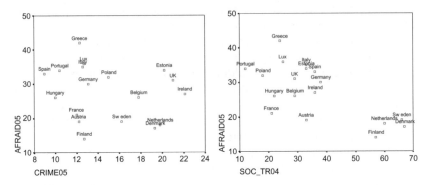

Figure 2.6 *Feeling unsafe on the streets at night has almost no relationship to objective levels of victimization, but does relate to prevalent levels of social trust – note the distinctive cluster of high-trust and low-fear Scandinavians.*

cally non-significant). But there is a very strong relationship between prevalent levels of social trust – thinking that other people are generally trustworthy – and levels of fear (correlation = –0.68; prob. < 0.01). Countries where people feel very unsafe – such as Greece (42%); Italy (35%); Estonia (34%); Spain (33%) – are all relatively low trust countries, whereas in high trust countries roughly half as many people report feeling unsafe, such as Sweden (19%); Netherlands (18%); Denmark (17%) and Finland (14%).

The conclusion is that people's fears of crime have a great deal to do with how they feel about people in society in general, and relatively little to do with cross-national differences in objective risk. Fear of crime is, to a large extent, showing a mirror to ourselves – a glimpse into the hidden social wealth or poverty of a nation. If we think it is acceptable to cheat other people and think that those around us can't be trusted – 'you can't be too careful', in the words of the question – then we start to see danger in every shadow.[9]

Reducing Actual Crime

Just because fear is driven by other factors, in addition to actual crime rates, doesn't mean that it is not important or should not be a focus of policy attention. The UK, for example, does have a relatively high crime rate, and we can and should seek to reduce crime through policy intervention.

Thoughtful senior figures in the Home Office and Ministry of Justice would describe government policy as not just to reduce crime, but also to reduce fear and ensure that the public, and victims in particular, feel that justice is done. But the danger is that fear reaches the point that it distorts policy away from effective strategies to reduce crime and deliver justice. For example, public appetite in the UK for locking up offenders is head and shoulders above that of any other European country. More than half of Britons (52%) favour a prison sentence for a recidivist burglar, with the next nearest country being Ireland at 38%. This is a very expensive and not very effective way of dealing with crime. Typical estimates are that, at best, about 5 percentage points in the 30% fall in crime rates in the UK since the late 1980s comes from the near doubling in the UK prison population over the same period.

A number of the drivers of crime are reasonably well understood. Economic growth tends to drive up drug crime (as people have more money to buy drugs), whereas inequality tends to drive up violent crime (as people at the bottom of the pile fight for respect). The number of young people, as a proportion of the total population, also affects crime as mentioned above, as both offenders and victims tend to be young adults. But it is clear that perhaps the biggest single factor affecting crime is culture. Japan is the best known illustration. While crime rates were rising relentlessly across most of the OECD through the 1950s, 1960s, 1970s and 1980s, various sources suggest that Japan, almost uniquely, appeared able to resist the trend.[10] This is widely attributed to the very strong social norms that made anti-social behaviour unacceptable together with a very distinctive form of what Braithwaite called 'reintegrative shaming'.[11] In most countries, and especially within the Anglo Saxon world, we think of offenders as bad people (as do offenders), whereas in Japan there is a much stronger sense that offenders are ordinary people tempted into doing something bad. As countless TV shows remind us, the script for an Anglo Saxon offender when caught is to angrily fight back at the police and those around, with mutual contempt in large doses all around. In Japan, so Braithwaite argued, the script was different. The offender would ask for forgiveness and feel genuine shame, but in return would be forgiven and reaccepted by the wider community. Not exactly a Hollywood blockbuster, but it turns out to be a cultural formula for low crime.

Evidence-based ways of reducing crime

The hard fact is that many of our everyday instincts are wrong about what will reduce crime. A recurrent example is the repeated popularity of programmes that take young people who are starting to get into trouble to visit a prison, to show them the reality of prison life and 'shake them out of it'. But it doesn't work. If anything, the evidence shows that it makes the young person *more* likely to commit crime and end up in prison. Similarly, longitudinal data shows clearly that a young person who is diverted away from the criminal justice system – such as through out of court warnings or settlements – is much less likely to offend again than a young person with a similar profile but who gets sentenced and enters the formal criminal justice system.

Some of the more evidence-based, though sometimes controversial, ways of reducing crime are listed below.

Target-hardening. It is generally agreed that one of the key factors that has driven down crime rates, especially of property crime such as car theft, has been product and security changes that simply make things more difficult to take. Working with manufacturers, businesses, homeowners and insurance companies to make crime harder, such as security codes or fingerprint recognition at restart is an unsexy but effective way of driving down crime. Situational crime reduction is also highly effective, such as ensuring there is a good supply of taxis in town centres late at night so that people who have had a little too much to drink aren't standing around arguing over the only taxi in town.

Drug treatment and partial legalization. Up to 80% of certain crime types, such as shoplifting and burglary, are thought to be drug related. Visibility of drug related activity is also known to be an additional driver of fear. A key point to understand is that the best drug strategy depends on the maturity of the drug market in question. When a new drug enters the 'market', it can be very effective to criminalize it and police it aggressively. However, once a drug has been around and in use for decades, criminal justice sanctions become much less effective, such as with addicts who have been on heroin for 20 years (or alcohol, in the case of the US prohibition). At this point, a better strategy is to focus efforts on managing the harms. This may involve 'legalizing', or medicalizing, the supply of long-established drugs to chronic users to undermine the criminal suppliers and to stop the person needing to steal or prostitute themselves to pay for the habit. International evidence suggests that such approaches can reduce associated crime by up to 60%. There may also be positive benefits in terms of changing the situation on the ground in the source-producing countries, such as Afghanistan in the case of heroin.[12] Of course, alcohol consumption is also strongly implicated in crime and helps to explain some cross-national variations in offending, though its treatment receives far less policy attention.

Diversion. A low-tech and effective way of reducing crime is simply making sure that potential offenders, notably young men, have got something to keep them busy. Structured youth activities are far superior to traditional 'youth clubs', providing both short and long-term crime reduction benefits. Even having controlled for all other known factors, young people who are involved in structured activities (e.g. the scouts, sports teams or military corps) have much better long-term outcomes both in terms of reduced crime and increased pro-social behaviour later in life.

Early years interventions. Some of the most successful, well-evidenced crime reduction programmes don't look like they have anything to do with crime at all. The Nurse Family Partnership, developed in the USA by David Olds and currently being piloted in both the UK and Germany, provides regular support to young, at-risk mothers-to-be by a health visitor before the birth of their first child. This support, with fortnightly visits, continues until the child reaches the age of two. The support starts with medical advice, but soon naturally expands into supporting the young mother with decisions around parenting, relationships and work. Follow-up evidence from the USA shows dramatically lower offending and arrest rates at age 15, compared with control groups, for the children of mothers who went through the programme.

Parenting programmes. These have been found to significantly reduce conduct disorders, and seem to work just as well whether the parents took part on a voluntary or obligatory basis. Current estimates are that a pound spent on a well-designed parenting programme will reduce around twenty-eight times more crime than the same money spent on high profile policing. Skilled parents prove much better placed to 'police' their children than the occasional police officer passing by. For older children and teenagers who are already getting into serious trouble, more intense programmes such as Multi-systemic therapy (MST) can be effective.

Increase certainty and immediacy of punishment, not severity. An important general principle of crime reduction seems to be that it is generally more important that criminal or anti-social behaviour is detected and rapidly sanctioned than that the sanction be severe (especially if this delays it or reduces its certainty). For example, a good way of reducing violence in town centres is for the police to be out early issuing Fixed Penalty Notices (FPNs) around unruly behaviour to establish the appropriate behavioural norm, rather than wait till later in the evening and intervene with stronger punishments associated with more serious behaviour. Similarly, community policing can be highly effective where it gives a range of adults the confidence to intervene in the precursors of crime, rather than walking-on-by until serious offences have been committed. Linked ideas are community punishments and restorative justice – helping the offender come face to face with victims and giving them a clear and immediate understanding of the consequences of their actions for others – and these are best done early in an offender's 'career'. (See also Box 2.1 for a further extension of this principle.)

Rehabilitation. It's often debated how well prison does, or doesn't work. The answer is that it works a bit (through incapacitation), but at immense expense. But if we are going to have prison, the real no-brainer in terms of cost effectiveness is treatment programmes while the offender is inside. High on my list would be the RSVP programme developed by Jim Gilligan in California, but not yet – to my knowledge – being used in the UK; but others include residential drug treatment and vocational training while in prison.[13]

Good fences make good neighbours. Communities with high 'collective efficacy' – where people know each other and intervene in the precursors of crime – have much lower crime rates. Physical layouts that make it easy for neighbours to meet and recognize each other; make the area less permeable to strangers; but that don't force neighbours to interact strongly, support the growth of good neighbouring relations and collective efficacy. Closing off alleyways that cut across housing projects is a well-known example. It is also possible to support collective efficacy by creating e-neighbour lists or by communities creating local directories of neighbours, including their interests and details.

Change the norm. A lot of crime reflects 'what goes' – the prevalent social norm. An intense intervention in a given place and time can flip the social norm. For example, intense place-focused zero tolerance programmes around drugs, alcohol-fuelled violence or gang crime may be more effective than spreading prevention programmes more widely if they change the behaviour of a whole peer group at once. But they still need to be more sustained than a short-term blitz.

In sum, a scan of the list above shows something rather striking – most of what governments are under pressure to spend more money on, such as more police, don't really feature. As Mary Tuck, the head of the Home Office's Research and Statistics department, used to say privately in the early 1990s – crime is the policy area where the discrepancy between the evidence and policy was largest. It has got better since then, such as the significant resources put into drug treatment programmes or the growing focus on target hardening, but politicians across countries – but perhaps especially in the UK – remain under enormous pressure to spend money on popular programmes rather than those that will do most to reduce crime.

We shouldn't despair. We do have lots of evidence about what works. We just have to use it. What we really need is a tabloid campaign demanding that politicians follow the evidence to reduce crime – now that would be something to see.

Box 2.1   *Should punishments be graduated by certainty of conviction?*[14]

A basic principle of law is that people should only be convicted if guilt is proven 'beyond reasonable doubt'. So if a judge or jury is not sure, they should let the person go free, or prosecutors should find a lesser charge with which to convict the person. However, everyday natural justice operates on a slightly different principle, which is that sanctions are conditioned not only by the severity of the offence, but by the certainty of guilt. If you come home and find a broken vase on the floor, and your kids pointing at each other, the chances are that you'll tell them both off but to a lesser extent than if you were sure who did it. The advantage of giving a lesser punishment when you're not sure is that it fits with the idea that certainty (and immediacy) of consequence is more important than severity.

In practice, the legal systems of most countries find ways of enabling lesser punishments for less certain judgements. In the UK and USA, for example, civil judgements – that normally involve fines rather than imprisonment – can be made on the balance of certainty rather than the higher threshold of 'beyond reasonable doubt'. An interesting question is whether we should make this trade-off more explicit. For example, should juries be asked to give a sense of their certainty of guilt, not just guilty or not guilty. A judge would then be expected to take this certainty into account when issuing a sentence. In crude terms, juries would be allowed to find people 'probably guilty', which would be associated with lesser sentences. In this way, more people might be convicted, but with no increase in the total quantum of punishment issued. This might be particularly important in relation to crimes such as rape, where convictions are notoriously low.

Immigration

In December 2007, concern about race and immigration reached a thirty year high in UK polls, with 46% of the public listing it among their top four concerns.[15] Perhaps this should be no surprise – the UK has, over recent years, experienced what is probably an unprecedented level of immigration. Roughly a million people came to join the UK's relatively vibrant labour market, mainly from Eastern Europe but also from across the globe.

Though concern about immigration moves up and down each month depending on media coverage and concern about other issues, the peak level of concern has been edging up year by year: 35% in 2003; 36% in 2004; 40% in 2005; 45% in 2006; and 46% in 2007. Previous historic highs in the UK were in May 2002 (39%); September 2001 (27%) and August 1978 (27%). During much of 2007 and early 2008, race and immigration was the top issue of concern to Britons. Even with the advent of the economic crisis of 2008 and into 2009, it remained consistently as one of Britons' top three concerns.

The simple explanation is that these concerns just reflect levels of immigration. Of course, the UK is not alone in experiencing high levels of immigration, so one way to test this hypothesis is to see whether countries which have had higher levels of immigration have higher levels of concern about immigration. As can be seen in Figure 2.7, this does not seem to be the case.[16] For example, countries such as Sweden, Germany and Ireland have relatively low levels of concern despite having relatively high levels of foreign born residents, whereas Spain and Denmark have far higher levels of public concern yet have roughly half the level of foreign born residents.

An optimistic interpretation is that the increase in concern about race and immigration in countries such as the UK, Spain and Denmark simply reflects falls in other concerns, such as about the economy and

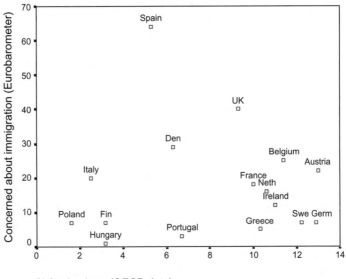

Figure 2.7 *Public concerns about immigration by percentage of foreign born, by country: there is a relatively weak relationship between overall immigration levels and public concern.*

public services. There is, after all, plenty of evidence for public concerns about immigration in the 1970s and 1980s, at least in Britain, with race riots, struggles around discrimination, and regular reference to the issue of immigration in political speeches. Could it just be that as other concerns have dropped away, concerns about immigration stand out in comparison? However, as in the discussion on crime above, a fall in other concerns doesn't explain why it is race and immigration that has come to the fore rather than, say, the environment.

Policy wonks tend to separate immigration into several distinct policy issues. First, there is the issue of legal, generally economic, immigration. Second, there is the issue of illegal immigration and of asylum seekers. Third there is the issue of 'race', or more particularly, as the Canadians call it, of 'visible minorities' which can include people who aren't immigrants at all. Finally, there is the issue of how terrorism may relate to immigration, such as around the control of borders, which we will pick up in more detail in the next section. Of course, in the media, and sometimes in political speeches, these issues are often blended together, though arguably they are really quite different.

Economic migration and its effects

Let us start by looking at the facts around these issues, then return to the matter of public concern. What are the impacts of mass immigration, and are the public right to be concerned? The economics of this have now been poured over in some detail and, viewed through an economic lens, immigration looks generally very positive. Immigration is both a symptom of, and boost to, economic growth. It is estimated that immigration into the UK over the last decade has probably been boosting economic growth rates by at least a quarter of a per cent per annum, with evidence of similar effects in other countries such as the USA, Canada, Germany, Switzerland and so on.

One of the surprises has been that immigration has made possible the maintenance of industries that would have otherwise have faded away through the lack of a cheap and motivated workforce. For example, UK agriculture, which had been contracting, has expanded on the backs of hard-working immigrants from Eastern European countries. Higher skill sectors have also relied heavily for their growth on workers from other countries, by directly supplying workers to City firms through to the health service, and indirectly by making it easier for high skill women who have children to return to work because of the availability of domestic and childcare help.

Contrary to the fears (or hopes) of many, wages don't seem to have been driven down by the influx of workers from overseas, but

rather the number of jobs has increased – a pattern noticed in previous decades in relation to immigration in the USA. The existence of
the minimum wage may help here by preventing a wage race to the
bottom for legal workers, and by providing an anchor for the wages
of illegal workers.[17] Hence, employment rates have increased in almost
every socio-demographic segment in the UK over the last decade,
including older workers, single mothers and those with disabilities.
The big exception is those with no qualifications among whom employment rates have fallen (and those with mental health problems). Of
course, those without qualifications have also been hit by competition
from workers in low-wage countries resulting from the re-location of
manufacturing jobs (such as to China) and from the mechanization and
shrinking of unskilled tasks, so that even without immigration they
may have found their positions in the labour market squeezed, though
by how much is difficult to be sure.[18] There are also benefits that flow
back to the countries from which immigrants left, in the form of the
money that migrants send home. It is estimated that these financial
flows exceed formal aid programmes by several-fold.

So the economic case for immigration mostly looks like a no-brainer
to the receiving country. The point is easily made by thinking about the
problems facing countries that are suffering net *migration*, like much of
Eastern Europe after joining the EU. In those countries, many of their
most able and entrepreneurial workers leave to come to places like
the UK, potentially leaching the giving country of skills and revenue.
Or think of the complaints of previous generations about 'brain drain'
to the USA, or the concerns of Scottish or Irish communities worrying
about their viability as most of their young people moved elsewhere.
If you could choose, the chances are you'd rather be an economically
successful nation dealing with the 'problem' of immigration than an
economically faltering nation dealing with net migration.

Finally, having large numbers of economic migrants tends to actually help a country when it enters recession. As the work dries up,
economic migrants tend to return home, containing levels of unemployment and reducing spending on benefits.

Social effects

Net economic benefits don't necessarily mean that there are net social
benefits. Here the picture is more complicated, but still tends to be
more positive than is often made out.

Some commentators have hinted that immigration brings in its wake
waves of crime and disorder. In the USA, where this has been most
closely studied, the results are striking – and strongly contradict the

doom-mongers. It is found that immigrants, on average, commit crime at a much lower rate than the domestic population. One of the reasons seems to be that migrants are much more focused on getting work and taking advantage of a strong, conventional economy. In some cases their legal status may be 'grey', and they are afraid of losing, or not gaining, full citizenship. The children of immigrants are also found to commit crime at a lower rate than the domestic population, so fears over citizenship cannot be the only reason for the low crime rate. It is only by the time you reach the third generation, the grandchildren of the original immigrants, that their crime rate begins to converge on that of the American average.[19]

Of course, this is not to say that the crime rate of all immigrant groups will be lower than the average. Organized crime in particular tends to show a degree of ethnic specialization, just as do many sectors of the real economy, such as taxi driving or restaurant working as people find employment through family and peer networks. But in general, the evidence is that immigrants commit crime at a lower rate and therefore, if anything, may have helped reduce crime.

However, it is more difficult and controversial to judge the impact of immigration on culture and everyday habits (which could in turn indirectly affect crime if immigration lowers levels of 'collective efficacy' or the preparedness of communities to trust each other and intervene in the precursors of crime). There is no doubt that societies are changed by mass immigration, and this can be very unsettling and sometimes unwanted. The influx of Poles into the UK has boosted attendance at Catholic churches across the UK, reversing decades of seemingly terminal decline. Polish delis are springing up across the UK just as Chinese and Indian supermarkets sprang up a generation before. Due to geographical clustering, these influxes change the character of high streets and residential areas, with different colours, sounds and scents.

Most subtly, at least in the short term, immigration tends to create 'breaches' of everyday habits and norms. Societies are characterized by large numbers of everyday habits and norms that most of us are not aware of. For example, Northern Europeans tend to maintain a larger personal space (physical distance) from others compared with most of the rest of the world. But there is no written code telling Northern Europeans that 18 inches is the right distance to stand away from another person. So when Brits, Germans and Swedes find themselves mixing with people from cultures where the normal interpersonal space is 12 inches or less, the Northern Europeans will continually feel invaded while, as they try and back away, the other person will feel that they are being cold and stand-offish (literally).

These habits may seem prosaic, but we know from social science experiments – as well as from *Candid Camera* and its successors – that people often react very strongly to such breaches of social norms. Famously (within sociology) Garfinkel used to send out his students to deliberately break some everyday social norm and document the consequences, such as telling his students to answer questions such as 'how are you?' *literally*. The typical reaction was bafflement, irritation and anger.

Just like *Candid Camera*, Garfinkel's breaching experiments are often viewed as an amusing illustration of the arbitrary nature of the rules that guide our everyday behaviour – amusing but not very important. I don't think that's right, not least because it's these everyday norms that enable us to get along with each other, reducing conflict and oiling the works of a myriad of everyday social and economic transactions. If it's only a transient adjustment, it's no big deal, but if it leads to a more permanent set of tensions, then it is. This, of course, is no longer just about the effects of immigration, but of racial and group differences in society, which we shall turn to shortly.

Asylum seekers and illegal immigrants

Intellectually, it's not really quite right to put asylum seekers and illegal immigrants together. An asylum seeker is someone who is fleeing danger and persecution. An illegal immigrant is someone who wants to come into a country, normally for economic reasons, but isn't entitled to residence because they are neither in danger in their home country nor entitled to stay to work. The lack of entitlement typically reflects the lack of an agreement between the countries in question and/or that the person's skills are unwanted. But administratively, the two categories are strongly linked, with immigration officials having to decide on a case-by-case basis which category an individual falls into.

Many politicians, certainly in the UK, identify this mixed group as the main source of public discontent. Ministers and Members of Parliament privately describe the deeply divisive nature of immigration issues at the local level. They talk of surgeries taken up by asylum seekers, and failed asylum seekers, and of local resentments to the 'unfair' or advantageous treatment that residents feel asylum seekers are getting. A frequently cited example is the claim that councils give housing and new furniture to asylum seekers, seemingly skipping over existing residents and those on the local housing list. Many of these stories may be overstated and, of course, local residents tend not to see the counter-stories of the tough conditions that asylum seekers and illegal immigrants generally live in. But it is also clear that many progressively minded MPs have been shocked by the sense of entitlement of some asylum seekers who have come into their surgeries, particularly around access to public services.

The public concern hinges around fairness. Data from the British Social Attitudes surveys suggests that the public have very strong and hostile views towards those they see as unfairly free-riding on public services. Interestingly, they are relatively at ease about those who have paid their taxes and made a contribution getting access to public services after two years of residence (see below). This fits with other analysis by Tony Health that the British have a strong conception of 'earned citizenship' – in common with other Anglo-Saxon countries – rather than the more ethnically based citizenship of many nations.

The political response has been to seek to increase the rate of deportations, both in the UK and elsewhere. In some places, notably the USA and Spain, there have also been periodic amnesties allowing existing illegal immigrants to convert to full or partial citizenship. But policymakers have found themselves between a 'rock and a hard place' on this issue. In the short term it makes perfect sense to offer amnesties, including allowing failed asylum seekers to work and earn money instead of claiming benefits. But in the long term the fear is that amnesties put out a signal to further illegal immigrants that you will get to work, and thus encouraging further influxes.

This issue was one of the reasons why Tony Blair became so keen on the development of ID cards (or more accurately, an ID database and electronic border controls) as he came to see it as the only way in which we would be able to track those who were coming and going from the country, including those who overstayed. He felt that it was the only way that public confidence would be restored in the immigration system and head off damaging social tensions.

Race and 'visible minorities'

One of the great uncertainties, and grounds for deep unease among many thinkers, is whether the public concern voiced around economic migration, illegal immigration and asylum seekers, is just the tip of a much bigger iceberg of racial tension and mutual dislike. Putting it bluntly, the policy worry is that public concern about immigration is the 'acceptable' expression of a dislike of all the minorities in society, and especially those that are growing.

The social psychological literature, together with the history of conflict between groups, is not encouraging. Psychological experiments going back to the 1940s have shown repeatedly how subjects show strong in-group favouritism and out-group prejudice, even when the groups are defined in an overtly arbitrary manner. For example, in the famous 'Robber's Cave' experiment, boys randomly assigned into two competing groups rapidly engaged in hostilities between the groups, regardless of whether those involved were previously strangers or friends. Similarly, bloody conflicts in many countries, especially over limited resources, have split nations along ethnic and racial lines even when these group categories rested on the slimmest basis. Human judgements and social habits appear hardwired to foster prejudice, at least under conditions of conflict over scarce resources.

Further concerns have been raised by the finding, particularly in US data, that increasing ethnic heterogeneity is associated with reduced levels of trust. In US data, increased heterogeneity leads to falling 'social trust' not only between groups, but within groups too.[20]

A final cause for concern, or at least reflection, is one of the great unexpected results of the cross-national values surveys that started in earnest in the late 1970s – the lack of value convergence across countries. Across the world, many aspects of life have been converging, and particularly around modes of economic production and consumption. New forms of technology, regardless of where they were developed, rapidly become ubiquitous across the world, be these cars, phones, televisions or sneakers. Often known as 'McDonaldization', the presumption is that the same would happen with people's values. After a quarter of a century of detailed research, the conclusion has to be – at least for now – that this value convergence is not happening. Covering issues such as religiosity; trust; attitudes to marriage and family; social and moral tolerance; political engagement; and feelings of nationalism, a recent review concluded:

> . . . we have found evidence of limited cultural change and almost no evidence of convergence between 1981 and 2001. We may further speculate that, if convergence is infrequent – almost non-existent – in our sample of mostly advanced, industrialized countries, it is much less likely to be observed in less developed societies.
>
> Y. Esmer (2007), p. 97[21]

In other words, while in some countries fewer and fewer people are agreeing with the statement 'a woman's place is in the home', believing in God or thinking that it is acceptable to cheat on benefits, in other countries the beliefs are going in the opposite direction. If values are not converging, is the great multicultural experiment doomed to failure and conflict?

If this is the pessimists' charter, let us also consider the more encouraging view. While the psychological evidence shows the powerful effects of group identification and prejudice, it also shows the conditions under which it is overcome. Essentially, when individuals from different groups interact on equal terms, and especially where they have a shared interest, inter-group cooperation and friendship follows, though it takes time. Sometimes prejudice and friendship sit paradoxically side by side, such as in classic studies of mining communities within the USA where inter-racial comradeship underground stood side-by-side with strong social and racial cleavages above ground. A contemporary policy equivalent is how disadvantaged communities with strong ethnic tensions often unite around a common concern such as anti-social behaviour or drugs.

Equally important is a subtle finding, within the same values literature that has failed to find convergence across countries, that within-country group differences are generally small compared with between country differences. For example, if we compare the values and attitudes of a Christian and Muslim in the USA or UK with that of a Christian and Muslim in India, we find that nearly all the difference is explained by the nation, and very little is explained by the religion. In other words, a Muslim living in America has much less in common, in terms of values and expectancies, with a Muslim in India than with a Christian also living in the USA.

This, it seems to me, is a very important finding. It tells us that there must be very powerful forces within a country that drive value convergence, at least across generations. It doesn't mean that there won't be tensions, or that there won't be some groups that resist convergence, but it tells us that a more serious tension will often be between generations within a group rather than between groups. And, for the most part, this is exactly what we see. We return to these intriguing questions in the next chapter.

Immigration and prejudice – what's the nature of the problem?

Revisiting the data on race, immigration and public concerns, I have to confess that I was very worried about what we'd find. In essence, I thought the story might turn out to be brutally simple – that the high levels of immigration over recent generations driven by powerful economic forces and the liberalization of movement was triggering a major rise in intergroup tension and prejudice. But that genuinely does not seem to be the story.

The World Values Survey has a series of questions about who you would *not* like to have as a neighbour – not a very politically correct question, but nonetheless a very interesting one. Across countries and waves of the survey, around 15% of respondents said they would

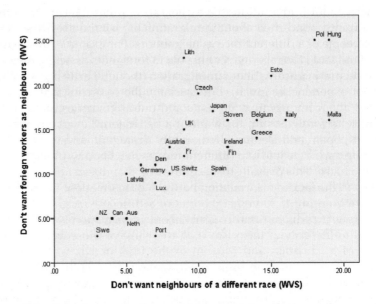

Figure 2.8 *Percentage saying they would not want to have foreign workers as neigh-bours against percentage saying they would not want neighbours of a different race (WVS; correlation = 0.80; prob. < 0.001).*

rather not have people of a different race as neighbours. Perhaps unsur-prisingly, it turns out that those countries where people didn't want neighbours of a different race were generally the same countries that didn't want foreign workers as neighbours either.

Around 1 in 5 of people in Eastern European countries such as Poland, Hungary and Estonia say they do not want to have foreign workers or those of a different race as neighbours. In contrast, in coun-tries such as Sweden, Netherlands, New Zealand and Canada, less than 1 in 20 express this view.

It turns out that those countries with highest levels of historic immi-gration, and therefore the highest levels of actual foreign born and ethnically diverse neighbours, are the countries where people are *most* at ease with such people as neighbours (the correlation is –0.61; prob < 0.005). Similarly, those countries where people are most relaxed about having neighbours of a different race, such as Sweden, are also those where people are most likely to agree with the statement that 'immigra-tion is good for the country'.[22]

But here's the interesting twist. A comparison of Figure 2.8 (levels of dislike for neighbours of a different race) and Figure 2.7 (levels of concern about immigration, see earlier) shows that the countries that are currently concerned about immigration are *not* the ones who don't want people of a different race as neighbours. For example, the publics of Poland and Hungary are very hostile to foreigners as neighbours yet have very few concerns about immigration (though partly because they are not experiencing much). But crucially, the countries that are concerned about immigration do not stand out as countries that express hostility to foreigners or, for want of a better term, everyday racism. The UK, Spain and Denmark look pretty average in terms of hostility to foreigners or people of a different race as neighbours (though Malta is quite high). This overall story – of the dog that doesn't bark – is confirmed in the lack of a correlation between concern about immigration and not wanting to have neighbours of a different race. As we shall see below, it turns out that concern about immigration is much more related to fears about terrorism than to dislike of those from a different race.

But before we get too complacent, the data also holds two significant warnings. While this dislike of having neighbours of a different race has been falling in many Eastern European countries – often from shockingly high levels – it has been, if anything, edging up in a number of traditionally more tolerant European countries. For example, from the late 1980s to early 2000s, the proportion saying that they would not want someone from a different race as a neighbour fell from 40 to 12% in Slovenia; from 30 to 17% in Slovakia; and from 20 to 9% in Latvia. In contrast, during the same period the proportion saying they would not want neighbours of a different race rose from: 3 to 7% in Denmark; 5 to 9% in France; 10 to 19% in Spain; and 6 to 16% in Italy.

Second, the headline figures conceal deep differences of views about immigration within the publics of Western European nations. In Britain, only 1 in 10 of the 'liberal elite', who constitute about a quarter of the population, agree with the statement that 'there are too many immigrants in Britain'.[23] In contrast, 9 in 10 of Britain's 'traditional poor', and 8 in 10 of the working and lower social classes agree with the same statement that there are too many immigrants. The middle classes lie somewhere in between but closer to the working class view, with around 6 in 10 tending to agree that there are too many immigrants. There are very few issues on which the public is so profoundly split. It is also a cleavage that is being aggravated by the rising unemployment of recession.

The standard account of this deep cleavage is that it is those with lower skills whose salaries tend to be squeezed by the new-comers, whereas for the liberal elite they supply a steady stream of low cost services from staffing Starbucks to providing domestic help at home.

Economic analysis suggests that this 'rich-win, poor-lose' may be over-stated, especially once the newcomers sharpen their language skills and rapidly move up the job market. However, for those at the bottom of the pile, any threat – either cultural or economic – tends to be felt far more profoundly. A clear illustration of this phenomenon was what happened to public support for the UK Government during the petrol strikes of the late 1990s. As petrol began to run out, support for the Government was largely unaffected in the liberal elite, but it collapsed spectacularly among 'D's and 'E's (lower socio-economic groups) even though they were the people in the population least likely to even have a car. For those with little to buffer them, any extra disruption or threat is felt much more sharply. Concerns about immigration are having a similar effect – whether rationally or otherwise, prompting deep anxi-eties in the bottom third of the socioeconomic pile.

These deep cleavages in attitudes to immigration are reflected in the papers we read. Nearly half of UK tabloid readers in the mid 2000s said that race and immigration was one of the most important issues facing the country – 48% of *Express* readers and 46% of *Daily Mail* readers – compared with only 19 and 20% of *Guardian* and *Independent* readers respectively. It is difficult to know to what extent these attitudes are fostered by the newspapers, versus whether the papers merely reflect the views of their audiences. But outside the liberal elite, among the more established middle and upper classes, concerns also run high – 44% of *Financial Times* readers also saw immigration as a major concern.[24]

So what's going on? There is a liberal elite – around a quarter of the population – that is relaxed and even welcoming of immigration. At the other extreme, the bottom quarter of the population is very anxious about immigration, a fear rooted in both cultural and economic anxiety – though the latter probably objectively overstated in relation to immigration. In between, a swath of the middle classes is anxious but persuadable. In this group, attitudes are shifting away from an ethnic conception of citizenship, based on where you are born and your racial heritage, towards one based on earned citizenship: people who make a contribution are welcome to stay. In this sense, the major-ity is holding its judgement, for now at least. A final concern, especially at the time of writing, is how much a downturn in the economy and rise in unemployment will harden attitudes against immigrants and minority groups – even if these groups themselves are ones that are hardest hit.

Whether we like it or not, the policies around immigration, asylum and race are messily entangled – as is the issue of terrorism (see below). Nonetheless, a few specific policy options are worth a mention:

- Border controls and an ID or entitlement database. These can be used to reduce abuses of welfare and public services, and creates a framework for other more sophisticated policies. But they are expensive.
- Setting up immigration and asylum seeking centres inside source countries (though source and other countries have tended not to be so keen on the idea). The cost of dealing with asylum claims is much lower, both for the nations and individuals concerned, if it can be done closer to home.
- A bond system within which asylum seekers are allowed to work but a chunk of the money is kept in a bond and only returned after they leave the country. This is easier to imagine working alongside a tighter system of ID and border controls.

A rounded response really requires us to consider a broader set of debates, including our notion of common citizenship. This will be taken up further in the next chapter.

Terror

As noted above, while there is little relationship between public concerns about immigration and crime across EU countries, there is a strong relationship between concerns about immigration and concerns about terrorism (see Figure 2.9; correlation = 0.67, prob. < 0.001). Essentially, terrorist attacks serve to heighten concerns about immigration.

By its very nature, terrorism consists of violent attacks deliberately designed to cause maximum fear and anxiety. Attacks involve multiple casualties, are random, dramatic and highly intentional. This ensures that they get lots of media and mental attention – we can all imagine ourselves and those close to us as the victims.

In objective terms, the probability of someone dying in a terrorist attack is much less than that of dying in a traffic accident or from illness, but these risks don't have the same imaginability or malice of intent. Even the terrible death toll of 9/11 in the USA – of 2,974 people – is dwarfed by the number of people in the USA who are victims in a year of homicide (around 17,000); of suicide (32,000) or who are killed in motor vehicle accidents (42,000). If we aggregate these data over a 10-year period so that we mix 2001 with more typical years, the relative risks become even starker. In the decade containing the 9/11 tragedy, the average American, compared with the probability of dying from terrorism, was:

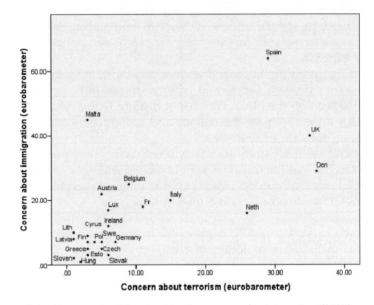

Figure 2.9 *Concern about immigration by concern about terrorism (2007).*

- more likely to be shot by a law enforcement officer or to be electrocuted;
- around 5 times more likely to die from a hernia or common flu;
- around 50 times more likely to die from each of accidental poisoning; falling; or homicide; and
- more than 100 times more likely to die from suicide or in a motor vehicle accident.

Terrorism attacks also generally pose little threat to the integrity of a modern democratic state though, as in the case of the Madrid bombings, they can affect the course of elected governments within them. The Madrid train bombings led to a change of government, and consequent policy in Iraq, though more because of the handling by the Government of the day than through some simple direct effect.

Of course, the real imponderable that weighs heavily on the mind of any democratic leader is of the risk an attack using a weapon of mass destruction. In the face of this possibility, however remote, it is not surprising that countries such as the UK doubled their expenditure on the security services in the years following 9/11.

The UK, Spain and Denmark have also been shocked by the emergence of domestic based terrorism. Though often linked to the war in Iraq, empirically there is no overall relationship across countries

Cause of death (1996-2005)	Relative risk compared with terrorism
Terrorism	1
Shot by law enforcement	1.3
Electrocution	1.6
Accidental gunshot	2.7
Hernia	5.3
Flu	6.2
Accidental poisoning	44.6
Falling	46.6
Homicide	55.1
Suicide	103.0
Motor vehicle deaths	134.5

Figure 2.10 *Relative death rates in the USA (selected causes) compared with terrorism from 1996–2005.*[25]

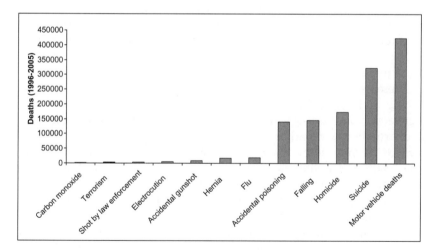

Figure 2.11 *Number of Americans dying from selected causes, 1996–2005.*

between the occurrence of Islamic-inspired terrorist attacks and the
country having had troops in Iraq – though this is not to say that it did
not feature in the minds of particular attackers. It is also striking that
the individual profiles of the attackers have not fitted the easy stereotype of a deprived or uneducated individual or recent immigrants. But
there are some patterns.

It is clear that, at least within the UK, attackers have been drawn
from a relatively narrow range of communities. It is certainly wrong
to lump all the different Muslim communities together in terms of
risk profiles over the last decade. For example, key suspects picked
up by the security services in the early to mid 2000s – either following or before an attack – were more than fifteen times more likely pro
rata to come from the Pakistani UK community than the Bangladeshi
community (despite the fact that the latter are if anything more disadvantage). Afro-Caribbean Muslim converts, though small in number,
have proven to be a particularly high risk group. Even within a given
'community' the probability of being involved in violent extremism
is not evenly distributed. For example, second and third generation
Pakistanis have been far more likely to be involved in extremism than
their first generation parents and grandparents. Similarly, it was found
in the wake of the domestic terror incidents in the UK of the mid
2000s that although there were many Muslim local councillors in the
areas from which the bombers were drawn – indicating a 'community'
that was well integrated – these tended all to come from one or two
mosques or sub-communities. There were other Muslim communities,
seemingly living side-by-side, that were almost entirely disconnected
from mainstream local politics and institutions.[26]

It seems that the most fertile ground for current extremism is where
strong and conflicting currents of identity mix – an individual torn
between generations and worldviews. There is normally a charismatic
individual who then draws together a small cell in a way that is very
similar to that of the emergence of a cult, not unlike those seen in
the 1960s, 1970s and 1980s. Those involved gradually cut themselves
off from contact with those outside the cell, and with this separation
the normal comparisons and challenge that this contact would have
brought are lost.

Individuals who don't feel a part of any community are the most
vulnerable to recruitment into terror cells, or indeed other cults. Poverty
or disadvantage does not seem to be a prerequisite. Widespread depri-
vation or disadvantage may be more likely to lead to mass protest
or unrest rather than cell-based terror, as seen in the mass unrest
among the high unemployment minority communities around Paris at
a similar time to when a tiny minority of the UK's minorities – otherwise generally doing economically better – engaged in terrorist attacks.

We once conducted an exercise in the Prime Minster's Strategy Unit after 9/11 to try and identify possible targets for terror attacks. After a couple of hours we concluded that there were so many potential targets that a determined and imaginative would-be-terrorist had almost no-end of options. Instead, our best bet was to understand and affect the conditions that led to an individual or community to consider and be sympathetic to terror. So what might 'prevention' policy look like? It might include:

- engaging more deeply with our domestic minority populations over issues in foreign policy – this would also help to better inform policy. Though disagreements and tensions will still arise, at least all sides will have a better mutual understanding.
- Encouraging more open debates which allow extremists to voice their views but in a context where peers can challenge and judge these views. The psychological literature shows that one of the most effective ways of 'inoculating' a younger generation against extreme views is to expose them to its own bad advocates.
- Supporting self-confident and better connected communities. The evidence is that cohesive and internally vibrant communities are more, not less, likely to integrate and connect into mainstream institutions, political structures and communities.
- Creating more opportunities for young people from 'at-risk' communities to be able to put into action their desire to help others they identified with such as through volunteering on aid programmes (see next chapter).
- More open and self-confident 'branding' of the country's own extensive aid programme. It always seemed striking that while US aid would be delivered to distant needy populations, and to television screens, with prominent stars and stripes, aid from the UK would be delivered with 'DFID' logos that nobody outside of Whitehall would recognize as having anything to do with the UK.[27] It is certainly the case that many minority communities seem unaware of the large scale of UK aid, relative to other countries, going to help Muslim and other countries across the world.

Conclusion

A number of nations, including the UK, Denmark and Spain, developed a striking pattern of concerns through the early years of the twenty-first century. In crude terms, fear of other people has come to the fore – not a fear of invading armies or superpowers, but of those around us. We might think of it as a crack in our hidden wealth. There was – and is – a sense of dangerous strangers in our midst. And there is evidence that these fears are also affecting how we see the economic crisis of 2008–9.

Concerns about crime, across nations, do bear some relationship to differences in risk. But concerns about crime are viewed through a distorting lens of generalized distrust of other people which greatly magnifies its impact. This strongly shapes political debates, distorting policy away from evidence-based interventions to punitive and harder measures. As Tony Blair once demanded in the context of a conversation on punishments for anti-social behaviour 'I don't just want eye-catching initiatives, I want eye-watering ones' (i.e. painful). In this context, evidence-based initiatives have to be smuggled in under the radar, or at least presented through the media in tough, 'eye-watering' ways. At least the good news is that there are plenty of evidence-based interventions to reduce crime, and that across countries, crime is generally falling.

Concerns about immigration and race have also risen over the last decade, though are clearly not new. History teaches us to take these concerns very seriously, even when they feel uncomfortable to the liberal elite from which most policymakers are drawn. Though the economic effects are generally benign, the social and political effects of immigration are more problematic. Border and immigration controls remain central to policy, and when in place can enable more sophisticated responses such as the use of repayable bonds by economic migrants. If countries would coordinate, asylum reception centres close to source countries would also make sense.

Concerns about immigration, at least within Europe, prove to be closely linked to concerns about terrorism. It is very difficult to judge what is the 'rational' level of concern to have about terrorism, given that some of the extreme possibilities are so awful, such as the use of a dirty nuclear bomb in the heart of one of our major cities. It is not just politics. We look to government to think through and protect us from unlikely but high impact risks that we as individuals can do little about. But it does seem that our level of concern is disproportionate. It may be that the psychological profile of terrorism – as its perpetrators intend – inflates our concern. It is visible, memorable, intentional and plays to our strong sense of loss aversion. That said, there are things we can do. In particular, there has been a relative neglect of prevention, such as drawing in some of the more disaffected youth that are vulnerable to the cults of terrorists – especially since such interventions can pay dividends in other ways as well.

During my period of working for the British Prime Minister from 2001–7, these three issues – crime (and anti-social behaviour), immigration and terrorism – took up a lot of time and focus, and indeed were ones that I personally spent a lot of time on. But ultimately they need a response that goes deeper and broader than some snappily designed polices, even ones that are evidence-based. They also need a matching 'positive' agenda – a way of rebuilding our social wealth. In short, they need a common understanding of citizenship, acceptable behaviour and a sense of shared community. It is to this flip side of 'not getting along' that we now turn – to a positive agenda of actively 'getting along'.

Appendix

Pearson correlations at national level between: not wanting neighbours of a different race (N_RACE, World Values Survey data); not wanting neighbours who are foreign workers (N_FWORK World Values Survey data); agreeing that immigration is a good thing for your country (IMMIGOOD Eurobaromenter); the percentage of the foreign-born in the country (FORIEGNB OECD); and percentage unemployed in 2007 (UNEMPL07 OECD).

Correlations

		N_ RACE	N_ FWORK	IMMIGOOD	FORIEGNB	UNEMPL07
N_RACE	Pearson Correlation	1	0.797**	−0.448*	−0.609**	0.388
	Sig. (2-tailed)	0.0	0.000	0.032	0.004	0.056
	N	29	29	23	20	25
N_FWORK	Pearson Correlation	0.797**	1	−0.730**	−0.545*	0.107
	Sig. (2-tailed)	0.000	0.0	0.000	0.013	0.611
	N	29	29	23	20	25
IMMIGOOD	Pearson Correlation	−0.448*	−0.730**	1	0.270	−0.122
	Sig. (2-tailed)	0.032	0.000	0.0	0.311	0.560
	N	23	23	25	16	25
FORIEGNB	Pearson Correlation	−0.609**	−0.545*	0.270	1	−0.282
	Sig. (2-tailed)	0.004	0.013	0.311	0.0	0.273
	N	20	20	16	20	17
UNEMPL07	Pearson Correlation	0.388	0.107	−0.122	−0.282	1
	Sig. (2-tailed)	0.056	0.611	0.560	0.273	0.0
	N	25	25	25	17	27

** Correlation is significant at the 0.01 level (2-tailed).

* Correlation is significant at the 0.05 level (2-tailed).

3

The Politics of Virtue

We have let money devalue the very characteristics that define our
humanity and that enabled our species to survive: our universal capacity to care for each other, to learn from mistakes, to come together to act
in concert . . . There is other work to be done. There is another economy
that needs tending, the core economy of home and family and village.

Edgar Cahn, 2002[1]

In March 2007, we held a 'citizens' summit' at No. 10 at which sixty
members of the public were brought together for a day to discuss
what they wanted public services to be like, and what they thought
the respective roles of the citizen and state should be. A number of
the ideas for discussion involved how citizens might be rewarded, or
sanctioned for particular behaviour. For example, should people who
regularly recycle get a discount off their council (local) tax, or should
there be a charge according to how much unrecycled rubbish people
put out?

Economic theory suggests that these kind of sanctions make sense –
taxing bads and rewarding goods. In fact, we found that the public at
the summit generally were not very keen on these types of sanctions
and rewards. It wasn't because of the practical issues (what happens
if someone else puts rubbish in your bin). It was because many people
felt that most of these behaviours were ones that a decent, normal
citizen should do anyway, and they shouldn't need to be rewarded for
doing them (though they did generally favour sanctions for those who
consistently failed to do the 'right thing').

In general, participants had a clear sense of what being a good citizen meant, and what a good society felt like. The phrase that was used repeatedly to capture this was 'respect and caring'. They were talking about the hidden wealth of society.

Now, after six years of working for Tony Blair, I knew that we'd spent a lot of time on the 'Respect' side of that equation. Indeed, I'd personally led the work within the PMSU on the Respect campaign in the run-up to the 2005 election. The work was strongly rooted in the public's desire for us to act against anti-social behaviour, adding to the armoury of legal instruments such as Anti-Social Behaviour Orders (ASBOs) – with parenting orders and support and various other 'tough love' measures. It was a policy response to some of the strong and growing public concern in the UK about crime and 'yob culture' (see previous chapter).

The Respect agenda was certainly popular. It provided the only consistently positive story for the Home Office throughout that period.[2] My political colleagues in No. 10 felt that the Respect Campaign may have won them an extra 30 to 40 seats at the 2005 election. The policies it contained also had a respectable evidence base, especially the parenting programmes and other supportive measures that backed up the use of injunctions and the wider signalling of what constituted acceptable behaviour.

But 'caring' tended to take a back seat. Of course, it was caring in that we were trying to help people who were at the receiving end of anti-social behaviour. It was caring in the sense that the 'tough love' of intensive family intervention support projects or parenting programmes could create some basic structure and habits of family life within which a child and adult had a chance to thrive – or at least survive – in. And other policy measures, such as the Every Child Matters programme were there to provide support. But the overriding aim of the Respect campaign was to contain anti-social behaviour, not to care *per se*.

Beyond 'Respect'

Tony Blair's agenda was that of a liberal lawyer, and it was perfectly tuned into the public concerns of the early to mid 2000s expressed within the Respect and related drives. The example Tony often gave to illustrate the issue, including I recall at the launch of the campaign, was that of an old lady being spat on, or shouted at, by a rowdy drunk. It was an example that immediately drew a sense of revulsion. Tony would go on to show, with devastating effectiveness, how our civil and criminal justice systems struggled with this type of everyday problem. If a policeman had to intervene, by bringing the drunk down to a police station, booking them, and then going through a whole lengthy legal process to end up with a small fine – he or she just wouldn't bother. The example set up the case for why we needed low-level sanctions, such as on-the-spot fines (fixed penalty notices) that didn't require a high level of proof or legal process, or even ASBOs – civil injunctions that were relatively easy for authorities to establish but if violated led to severe sanctions.

Within Tony's examples, you could see his conception of the good citizen. A good citizen was essentially a person who refrained from bad behaviour. In this sense it was deeply liberal and Anglo-Saxon – the good society comes from restraint and mutual respect. Ironically, Tony himself was always – and still is – dedicated to the public good; extraordinarily generous in the time and effort he gives to helping charities and others. But that didn't mean that he expected the same of others.

The raft of new sanctions and measures were sometimes criticized for chipping away at freedoms and due legal process – normally by lawyers – though the measures had a strong moral logic of proportionality which built on already existing distinctions between criminal, civil and minor sanctions such as cautions (see also Box 2.1 in previous chapter). Less noted, and perhaps more important for the current discussion, was the asymmetry between the vigour with which punitive sanctions were applied relative to 'positive sanctions'. Thousands of ASBOs were sought and obtained telling offenders what *not* to do, but at the same time you could count on the fingers of your hands the total number of support orders that were issued to instruct offenders what they *should* do.

The phrase 'respect and caring' that the public used at the Downing Street summit suggested an appetite for something more than good citizenship built around restraint. Obama, Brown, but also Cameron (Opposition leader in UK) and a number of leading politicians in other countries share this intuition – an instinct that our notion of good citizenship needs to be about more than just restraint or respect. It is about something more active – about giving something back, or positive mutuality. But they also know that this is hazardous political territory.

Religion, Ethics and Secular Society

Politicians have an uneasy relationship with religion. In the UK, Blair kept his religious beliefs tightly under wrap while in office, knowing the public would react against it. In contrast in the USA, a President would struggle to be elected without a basic level of public Christian display. Across nations, politicians talk about values, but it's a dangerous game, especially with a free media ready to compare what they say with what they do. Prime Minister John Major's famous 'back to basics' speech, with its strong values content haunted his administration, as Minister after Minister were found to fall short of its implied moral prescriptions and the public ridiculed the right of politicians to lecture them on morals. Yet an everyday sense of moral values and a shared sense of what is acceptable behaviour, is key to making a society work – it is part of the 'hidden wealth' of a successful nation.

Freud argued that religions, and other Weltanschauung or worldviews, had three functions. First, they offered an explanation of how the world came to be. Second, they offered the comforting promise that, whatever the hardships or injustice of the present, a better future awaited the virtuous in this world or the next. Third, religions justified and supported ethical systems. In essence, such ethics made it possible for people to get along, at least within the same religious group.

In most secular societies, science has the first function covered, and the legal system has had a good go at covering the latter two. But despite the apparent redundancy of religion in a modern society, religious beliefs have proven very robust. This robustness has been one of the great surprises to sociologists studying value change over the last quarter of a century.

Formal religious activities, such as church attendance or baptisms, have fallen in the majority of Western European countries, including in a number of traditionally very religious countries such as Ireland, Poland and Spain. But in central Europe and the former Soviet Union, Africa and parts of South and central America, religious attendance has been increasing in many countries. In predominantly Muslim countries where we generally lack time-series data, the percentage of people attending a mosque or other religious temple once a week or more is on average higher still and typically in the range 30 to 75%.[3]

Digging a little deeper, we find that formal religious attendance is relatively low compared with religious beliefs. Across a basket of countries, we find that around two in three people say that they 'get comfort and strength from religion', though less than a half of them say that they attend religious services once a week or more. In terms of specific beliefs, it seems the 'attractive' elements of belief, such as believing in heaven or life after death, have fared rather better than 'negative' elements, such as belief in hell or the devil (see Figure 3.2). Belief in God stands out as especially widespread.

Belief in God remains extremely widespread – and much higher than levels of formal religious attendance. While it has drifted down

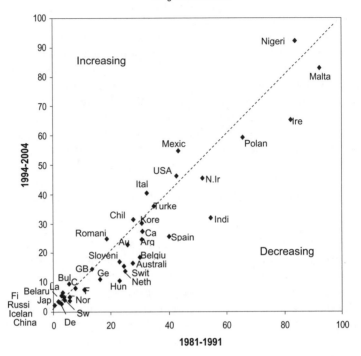

Figure 3.1   *Religious attendance of once a week or more, 1981–2004.*

in most Western European countries, there has been a resurgence in expressed belief in other countries, particularly in Eastern Europe and the former Soviet Union. Belief in God remains at over 90% in the majority of countries, and there are only two countries out of 81 in the 1999–2004 World Values Survey in which less than half the population say they believe in God (Vietnam and the Czech Republic). There is a moderate, but far from perfect, correlation between changes in levels of belief in God and church attendance at the national level (r = 0.33).

Researchers in the 1970s and 1980s generally expected religiosity to fall. They got the headline trend wrong for a couple of reasons. First, the countries on which early conclusions were based – essentially Western Europe – turn out to be relatively atypical. Second, they were misled by the strong age profile of religious beliefs. Younger people tend to have far less religious beliefs giving the impression that there is a big shift underway towards less religious beliefs. But it turns out that as people age they tend to get more religious, even if they don't

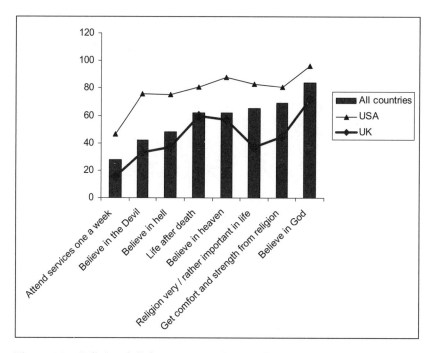

Figure 3.2   *Religious beliefs across countries (WVS data, 1999–2004).*

necessarily become as religious as their parents. Third, even within Western Europe, many countries have taken in many immigrants who are more religious than the original citizens. Finally, many researchers are secular, and presumed that a rational world would follow their lead.

But what of Freud's central claim that religions justify and support a society's moral or ethical code? Even among those who lack religious beliefs, the argument that religion props up ethical beliefs is often used to accept their role in society. On this, an obvious place to start – at least for Western European countries within the Christian–Judaic tradition – is with self-reported adherence to the Ten Commandments.[4]

We might note that far more people say that these commandments apply to themselves than they feel that they are followed by 'most people' in their society. This could indicate a major problem with the survey sample, or more likely, the strong psychological tendency to think of ourselves as more moral than others. It is also striking that the commandments that are about how you should treat God – not taking his name in vain; not worshipping idols; and having no other Gods – command much less support than those regulating how people should treat each other.[5]

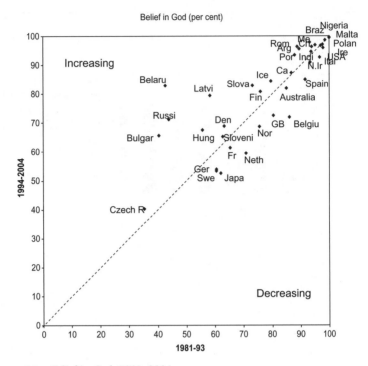

Figure 3.3   *Belief in God, 1981–2004.*

People who believe in God are significantly more likely to report that they followed the commandments – and they were much more likely to follow those that relate specifically to God. This might be seen as a test of Freud's hypothesis that religion props up ethical beliefs. But although the other correlations are statistically significant – in the range 0.15 to 0.3 – they are not very strong.

Believing in God – or going to religious services more often or getting comfort from religion – was also correlated with attitudes to various morally debatable acts. Those who were more religious were strongly and significantly less tolerant – or permissive, depending on your point of view – of morally debatable personal and sexual acts, such as sex outside of marriage, abortion, divorce, homosexuality, suicide and so on. The more religious were also slightly less tolerant of acts of self-interest, such as keeping something you found, or of overtly illegal acts, such as stealing cars or accepting bribes, though the effect was weak.

However, if we track these correlations over time, a very interesting pattern is seen. Across European countries over the last 25 years, there has been a clear and consistent drop in the association between peo-

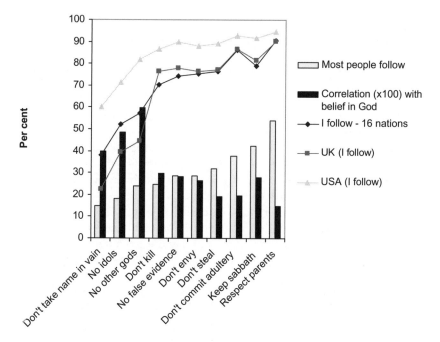

Figure 3.4 *Belief in the 10 commandments (1981–3), across countries and correlation with belief in God, ranked by percentage who feel that 'most people' follow them.*

ple's religious beliefs and their moral values.[6] In other words, it used to be that if you knew someone's religious values within a country, you would have a pretty good sense of what their other moral and ethical values would be. This is much less true today. Even though there is no simple downward trend within these countries in religious beliefs, these beliefs have become less morally consequential.

In contrast, within North America – particularly the USA, but also Canada – the correlation between people's religious beliefs and their other values has become stronger. In essence, North America is coming apart along religious and secular lines – with a parallel rise of the very religious and the very secular – whereas within Europe these lines are disappearing.

Moral decline?

We should be wary of the doom-merchants who tell us that society is in moral free-fall. It seems to be a characteristic of every generation that at least some people will feel that society's moral fibre is under threat:

> The world is passing through troubled times. The young people have no reverence for their parents: they are impatient of all restraint; they talk as if they alone knew everything, and what passes for wisdom with us is foolishness for them.
>
> Attributed to Peter the Hermit, eleventh century; quoted in Raven (1952).

We have at least one advantage over eleventh-century hermits: several decades of population surveys. There are large national differences in moral tolerance. For example, Southern Europeans are much less tolerant than other regions of personal–sexual acts, whereas Northern Europeans and especially Scandinavians are much less tolerant of acts of self-interest than Southern Europeans.

However, despite differences in national views, and the shifting relationship between religion and moral values in Europe and North America, the pattern of *change* in moral values over recent decades is broadly similar across Western countries. People have generally become considerably more tolerant of a clutch of personal–sexual behaviours, notably: homosexuality, prostitution, euthanasia, divorce and taking soft drugs (see Figure 3.5). A number of these changes are

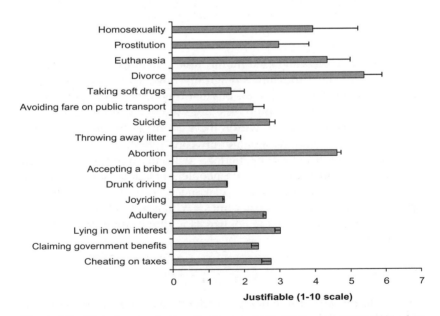

Figure 3.5 *Changing moral values for Europe and North America (1990–2001 where bars show 1990 values and lines show change to 2001); ranked by level of change.*

very substantial – notably towards homosexuality – and characterize a key shift in society towards greater personal–sexual permissiveness (or tolerance depending on your point of view).[7]

Yet there has not been a rise in tolerance for all types of morally debatable behaviour. A glance at the lower half of Figure 3.5 shows that there are a cluster of values on which people have generally become, if anything, rather less tolerant, including cheating on taxes, claiming benefits that you are not entitled to or lying in your own interest.

The weakening influence of religion does not seem to have led to an undifferentiated rise in acceptance of morally debatable acts, and certainly not a general 'moral collapse'. In fact, there seems to be an underlying logic to the general pattern of changing moral values in Western nations: acts between consenting adults that don't seem to harm others have become more acceptable, regardless of traditional views, while acts that harm others have tended to become less acceptable. In this context, it is worth noting that attitudes to adultery have hardened, despite being strongly correlated with other personal–sexual attitudes that have in general been characterized by increasing tolerance. Unlike most of the other personal–sexual behaviours (such as homosexuality), adultery doesn't just affect consenting adults, but implies that someone is being cheated and probably hurt.

So it turns out that sociologists only got it half wrong about the demise of God and religion. The God of contemporary Western Europe is a pretty anaemic version of his former self. We have selectively clipped out the bits we don't like, such as Hell and the Devil, and religion has become increasingly inconsequential to our other beliefs, including our morality. But there has not been a great moral collapse. Indeed, one could argue that patterns of value change are following their own, generally secular, moral logic of development.

Religious beliefs remain very consequential in much of the world, and the secular–religious divides between, and within, many nations could prove to be more important than the traditional and more visible conflicts between religions that have characterized previous generations. The tensions look especially great in North America where the liberal views of seculars have leapfrogged over those of their previously more secular European cousins of a generation before.

It is clear from this pattern of change that secular societies have mechanisms that refine and promote distinctive ethical beliefs and behaviours – somehow ticking off the last of Freud's functions of religion through secular means. But big questions about ethics and identity in secular societies remain, including whether there is something else that people still look for that secular societies have yet to give them. We noted in Chapter 1 that being religious seems to boost happiness, and our models suggest that around two thirds of this effect comes from the satisfactions and support received from being part of a community. For some reason, this function doesn't seem to make it onto Freud's list. Religious beliefs and practices perhaps offer something that secular societies still struggle to capture – such as around identity, a feeling of connection, and the marking of key transitions in life.

The Economy of Regard

Imagine you have just spent a pleasant evening at a friend's house. They cooked dinner for you and a couple of other friends. At the end of the evening, you say how wonderful it was, take out your wallet and put £50 ($100) on the table, kiss the hostess and take your leave. It just wouldn't be right.

The idea of using money to 'pay' for dinner in such a situation feels *so* wrong, in most Western countries, it makes most people cringe to think of it. Why does it feel so wrong? The answer seems to be that friends cooking us dinner isn't part of our normal economic exchange – instead it is a part of what has been variously called the 'gift economy' or 'the economy of regard'.[8] Regard seems to be the currency of the hidden wealth of nations.

In simple terms, the economy of regard concerns the myriad of ways in which people help, show affection, care for and support each other in everyday life. Familiar examples include looking after our own children or those of a close relative; looking after an elderly parent; or simply keeping an eye on a neighbour's property when they are away.

Unlike in the 'real' economy, the relationship between the giver and receiver is absolutely key. It matters who is giving and supporting, and why they are doing it. In contrast, when we buy a new dishwasher or dvd, all that really matters is the objective quality of the good and the price at which we get it.

Evidence from time-budget studies gives a powerful sense of the scale of the economy of regard. Time-budget studies involve asking people to keep a diary of how they spend their time. If you average this across a large sample of adults from all walks of life, across ages and across weekdays, holidays and weekends, you get a picture of what, on average, we spend our time doing – or what's sometimes called 'the great day'. Figure 3.6 shows this for the UK, using data from 1961, 1983 and 2001.[9]

Figure 3.6 shows how much less time is spent doing manual paid work since the early 1960s, and how much more time is now spent on leisure. The data show how only a minority of our time – about

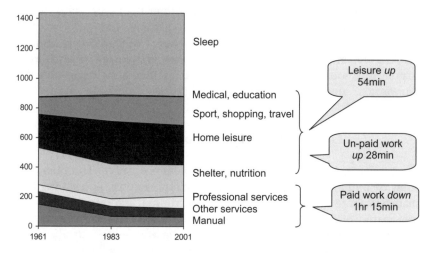

Figure 3.6 *Use of time, from 1961–2001. Only a small portion of our time is spent in paid work, and the long-term trend is less paid work, and more leisure and un-paid work. (Data from the Geshunny's work on the UK time-budget surveys; data for adults over-18).*

23% of our waking time – is now spent in paid work. In contrast, we spend more than three-quarters of our adult lives engaged in 'unpaid work' – cleaning, washing, looking after our kids, building flat-pack Ikea furniture etc – and in leisure – playing sport, shopping, reading, watching TV etc. Of course, this use of time is not evenly distributed across our lives or across the population: some people are more heavily employed than others, and most of us wind down our paid employment later in life.

A lot of this time and activity is spent engaged in the economy of regard. Obvious examples are time spent looking after kids or elderly relatives – or caring for other people. When researchers have tried to cost the value of all unpaid work that we do, by calculating how much it would cost if we had to pay someone to do all that work (such as looking after the kids or cleaning our houses), the figure comes up at around that of the country's GDP. And that's if you put the substitute labour cost in at a minimum wage type level – it is an even bigger figure if you value this labour at a higher rate.

But that's not the end of the matter. It turns out that much of the 'real economy' is driven by the economy of regard too. The obvious examples are buying presents for our friends and relatives, but less obvious is our loyalty to work-mates, or how we choose to buy services or goods from people we know and like rather than who gives us the best price (see also Chapter 1).

Far from being a fringe activity, the economy of regard turns out to be the rock on which much of our economy and society is anchored. Arguably, it's the real economy that is the fringe activity around the economy of regard.

Good Fences Make Good Neighbours

Not all our interactions with other people are positive. The phenomenon of crime, as discussed in the previous chapter, is testament to that. But there are plenty of other, non-criminal interactions that are less than a pleasure. There's the work-place bore; the neighbour who you dread bumping into; and even at home and among family, there are inevitable tensions and disagreements.

As we have grown richer, one of the main things we've used this wealth for – and particularly in Anglo-Saxon countries – is to try to minimize these types of negative interactions. At great financial cost, each household now has its own washing facilities (so that we don't have to go to the communal wash-house or laundrette); its own TV and entertainment systems (so we can shape our own entertainment rather than listen to communal programmes of music or shows that we don't like); and we're prepared to go to great length and cost to have our own car or transport (rather than rely on public transport).

Hirsch coined the term 'the economics of bad neighbouring'[10] to describe the underlying logic in relation to neighbourhoods. There will always be a risk of an annoying or unpleasant interaction with a neighbour or someone else in a public space. The more people in that space the more likely that negative interaction is to take place. So we withdraw behind our own front door, so we don't have to risk bumping into the neighbour we hate. Indeed, we will often pay a premium to allow us to withdraw from these public spaces so that we can avoid the possibility of a bad interaction. This can lead to a vicious spiral where the only people left in the public space are the ones that no one else likes, as everyone else has withdrawn.

What if we just design spaces so that everyone has to pass through them and interact? It turns out that one of the worst things for positive relationships is to force people into unwanted interactions. An elegant example of this is provided by the natural experiment of students in different types of accommodation.[11] From a design point of view, one of the most efficient forms of student accommodation is a simple double-loaded corridor, with a row of bedrooms on each side and a block of toilets and showers all grouped together. The good thing about this design is that the chance of not being able to brush your teeth or get a shower in the morning is very low, as it would be very unlikely that every cubicle would be used at the same moment. In contrast, if you distribute the bathrooms so that each is shared by just say three rooms or room-mates, it becomes much more likely that when you need to use the bathroom it will already be in use.

Yet it turns out that students generally dislike the 'efficient' corridor design, and are much happier in the 'suite' type arrangement. Students living in the corridor design dislike it because they feel they can't control who they may bump into when they go into the relatively public space of the corridor. To put it another way, there's bound to be at least one or two people among the 40 or so other students on the corridor that they don't much like, and at least a few who they feel they don't know either way. So the students adopt a strategy of withdrawal, avoiding going out into the corridor and avoiding eye contact or interaction with others when they do.

This strategy of withdrawal, and the feeling that interactions with other people are unpleasant, generalized into other settings. Researchers found that, even when taking part in activities in other parts of the campus, students from the corridor design were more likely to avoid interaction with other people such as making eye contact and engaging in conversation. In experiments, they were less likely to engage in cooperation and more likely to engage in conflictual strategies (and were more comfortable when doing so). It also affected their relationship with room-mates, as corridor-design students were much less likely to choose the same room-mates in the next year.[12] In short, the inability to control who and when they would bump into other people led the corridor-design students to find contact with other people aversive and to adopt a strategy of generalized withdrawal.

Much the same pattern is found in residential neighbourhoods. A massive study of the 1970s British 'good neighbours' schemes ended with a simple conclusion, borrowed from the poem by Frost, that 'good fences make good neighbours'.[13] An even more literal and dramatic illustration of this effect was provided in an early study of the notorious Pruitt-Igoe in St. Louis in the USA – a massive project of 43 11-storey blocks built in 1954 to house 12,000 people. Despite winning various architectural awards, the project became plagued with crime and high vacancy rates. Researchers found that the design appeared to foster problems, noting that 'Pruitt-Igoe provides no semi-private space and facilities around which neighbouring relationships might develop.'[14]

In a perfect natural experiment, a mesh fence was put up around one of the Pruitt-Igoe blocks while contractors were working on it. During the six months of construction vandalism and crime fell, and residents began to sweep their hallways and pick up litter. Because of the changed character of the building, residents petitioned to have the fence left after construction work was completed, and this was agreed. Two years later, the crime rate for the building was 80% below the Pruitt-Igoe norm, and the vacancy rate was 2–5% compared with the project norm of 70%.[15]

This structuring of social space helps to explain a range of impacts of the built environment on wellbeing. For example, Willmott found in a study of Dagenham in the 1960s, that residents living on 'banjos' (cul-de-sacs) seemed to be happier than those living on through roads, a result that was subsequently replicated on large data-sets.[16] People living on smaller roads and cul-de-sacs can be far more confident that those they see outside their front doors are neighbours, and the lower level of traffic also makes it a more pleasant space to interact in. In contrast, various studies have found that residents in houses at the ends of small streets but that face directly onto a larger through-route, are much more likely to become social isolates.[17]

My own research on the effects of the environment on mental health in the early 1990s reached the same conclusion. Designs and schemes that force people together, unless the numbers involved are very small, tend to lead to withdrawal and aversion, not to cohesion and positive relationships. Of course, schemes that preclude interaction aren't great either, as they inevitably lead to isolation and loneliness. The ideal is where the design creates easy opportunities for neighbours to interact with each other – confident that those they are interacting with are actually neighbours and not total strangers – but enabling them to choose when and where they will interact. Hence the point about 'good fences' – or maybe more accurately 'good fences and good porches': they give people the ability to choose who they will interact with and when.

These design issues are as salient as ever. I recently participated in a television programme about crime and anti-social behaviour which included revisiting a number of high profile incidents where a resident had been attacked, or even killed, by youths living close by. In every case, the location was characterized by a physical design that made it difficult for residents to gain a sense of control over interactions outside their house.[18]

The good news is that physical interventions – especially if twinned with resident efforts to build social capital – can have dramatic positive effects. For example, in one of the estates I worked on in the 1990s, alleyways were closed to the public in a part of a 'Radburn layout' housing estate that had become characterized by withdrawal, fear and high rates of depression.[19] This simple intervention meant that when someone opened their front door, if there was a person there, they were almost certain to be a near neighbour, rather than a relative stranger cutting through the estate as would have been the case before the intervention. Levels of social support – the perceived helpfulness and willingness of neighbours to help each other – rose dramatically over the year following. Levels of anxiety more than halved, and levels of depression – as measured by a clinically validated scale – fell by 80%.

Similarly, in a follow-up to the original Baum and Valins study of student accommodation, it was found that simply installing a series of doors to break up the long corridor into much smaller sections eliminated many of the negative effects.

In short, the character of social relationships are powerfully affected by the extent to which the physical spaces around homes give residents the opportunity to interact with others, but also the ability to choose when and with whom to interact. This finding is important not just for designers of physical environments – and increasingly for virtual environments – but because of the clues it gives about the factors that are key for positive social interaction in general.

Crowding Out Regard

There is a fascinating – and important – question: do the broad dynamics of modern societies and economies foster positive interaction, virtue and mutual regard – or do they 'crowd it out'? The answer to this question is not a simple one, not least because successful societies are economies that are themselves generally built on a foundation of trust and virtue (see Chapter 1 on economy).

Studies of court records going back over the last 500 years, twinned with our best estimates of population numbers for the relevant European countries, suggest that we have generally been getting better behaved to each other.[20] It is estimated that the murder rate in a typical Northern European country in the late middle ages was around fifty times higher than today, fuelled by a mixture of alcohol and the acceptability of violence to resolve disputes (plus some contribution from the lack of medical expertise). In Britain, such violence began to fall in the sixteenth and seventeenth century cities of Oxford and London. This fall continued for hundreds of years, gradually fanning out from the cities – a pattern that continued until roughly the 1950s.

What happened? In simple terms, it seems that we got a lot more polite. Elsewhere I've argued that people gradually developed common codes of understanding so that relative strangers could get along with each other with less friction. Others have argued that the process was linked to the emergence of the 'modern self' – a more reflexive pattern of thought within which we are more self-aware, and aware of the consequences of our behaviour for others. But whatever the detail, there is clear evidence that we figured out better ways of getting along with our fellow citizens so that we could work with others, buy and sell goods, including with people we'd never met before.

One of the key ways we learned to get along with others was to build institutions, practices and codes that created a framework within which relative strangers could trust each other. Common ethical codes offered by religions – backed with the threat of an omnipresent God who would punish misbehaviour in this life or the next – helped to clip behaviour that harmed others such as violence and cheating, and encouraged helpful and cooperative behaviour. In addition we created legal institutions that reinforced property rights, contracts and fairness meaning that relative strangers could transact with others and invest their labour without having to rely solely on soft trust and morality.

We also got the hang of abstract currencies. This fantastic innovation greatly facilitated our ability to transact goods and services, because as long as we trust the money, we don't have to trust the person who is giving it to us. This trust is in turn underwritten by a set of institutions that back the currency, that 'promise to pay the bearer' and that work to ensure its continuing value by controlling its supply and by paying a return on it (interest). These features are very important to the success of a currency, and their importance is illustrated by the collapses that happen when they are absent. For example, if a central bank prints, or issues too much currency, then its value falls and hyper-inflation can result. Similarly, but more subtly, if interest is not paid on cash held in that currency – or even negative interest – then people will avoid holding onto the currency resulting in is value falling or even people ceasing to use it altogether.[21]

Now here's the interesting twist. If we buy the argument that there is a sort of parallel 'economy of regard' (see Chapter 1), then we need to consider how the dynamics and incentives of the real, currency based economy interact with it. In essence, the question is whether the real economy might 'crowd out' activity in the economy of regard.

Edgar Cahn argued that it does. He pointed towards how efficient economies reward rare skills, such as understanding company accounts, or inventing and marketing new products, or being really good at football. In contrast, skills and abilities that are virtually ubiquitous will attract little premium in the conventional economy. Unfortunately, Cahn argued, the list of ubiquitous skills includes much of our humanity, including taking the time to care for, or respect, another person.

Bernard Lietaer, an expert on currency systems, has taken this argument further. He argues that when conventional currencies are introduced to societies that previously lacked them, they dramatically change their social character. In short, they drive a dynamic of competition around maximizing returns on investment – excellent for efficiency, but not great in terms of some of the more cooperative social fabric that they squeeze out. Attention is also sometimes drawn to the unfortunate dynamic that in poorer areas – where cash is short – the lack of currency actually inhibits activity that would otherwise have occurred. For example, imagine unemployed and hungry Mr White who knows how to fix roofs, while around the corner Mrs Brown is a good cook but can't do much because of a leak in the roof. Since neither of them have money, they sit hungry and wet. We restrict the supply of currency for good reasons, but it does have at least some perverse effects.

There are also some related effects at the micro-level, where the introduction of an extrinsic reward or currency seems to crowd out pre-existing intrinsic motivations to act. This was demonstrated in the 1960s with studies on young children who were given paper and crayons, some of whom were then rewarded for doing colouring while others received nothing. When later given the opportunity to do more colouring, it was found that the children who had previously been rewarded were much less likely to engage in the activity – the extrinsic reward seemed to have displaced the intrinsic motivation to colour.[22] Similar changes to motivation, and consequent behaviour, have been reported for a wide range of activities, famously including payment for blood donation or, more recently, the introduction of fines for parents picking up their children from kindergarten. There is also evidence that once 'marketized', the behaviour stays that way in our thinking even if the extrinsic reward is later withdrawn. It has even been found that the mere presence of a symbol of money changes how people behave. For example, experiments by Kathleen Vohs found that simply having a screensaver in the background with a dollar sign led to subjects being significantly less helpful to a hapless assistant than when a neutral screensaver (of a fish) was on.[23] Symbols of money also made subjects less likely to ask for help too – in essence, it made them act more individualistically and independently of others.

Oiling the Economy of Regard: The Case for a Complementary Currency

These arguments above set up the case for an 'alternative' – or more accurately, 'complementary' – currency that can oil the works of the economy of regard in a similar way to how conventional economies oil real economy transactions.

The most familiar examples of such a currency or system are 'Local Exchange Trading Systems' or LETS. These have evolved to deal with the problem mentioned above, of hungry Mr White and rained-on Mrs Brown failing to transact. Instead of having to go to the bank, users effectively create their own cash or credits when they need it. Mrs Brown gets Mr White to fix the roof, and he ends up with a credit which he can use to 'buy' cakes from Mrs Brown and vegetables from Mr Black. It is more flexible than bartering, because the transaction can form a much longer loop than a simple trade between Mr Brown and Mrs White.

Such schemes can become very large. St. Louis has a LETS scheme with around 12,000 people in it. A more common pattern has been the emergence of lots of small local LETS banks within a country or region. For example, by the early 1990s there were estimated to be more than 200 LETS banks across Australia, and 400 in the UK.[24] Such schemes are also attracting renewed interest because they tend to promote trade and activity within the local area and are therefore relatively 'green'. But in as far as LETS can facilitate the trading of all kinds of goods and services, they also have a weakness which is that as they grow they become more and more like a conventional currency.

An interesting example is the Swiss WIR, founded in 1934 by business-men Werner Zimmermann and Paul Enz as a result of currency short-ages after the stock market crash of 1929. WIR is short for *Wirtschaftsring* and the word for 'we' in German, reminding participants that the 'economic circle' is also a community. According to the cooperative's statutes, 'Its purpose is to encourage participating members to put their buying power at each other's disposal and keep it circulating within their ranks, thereby providing members with additional sales volume.' It has around 65,000 members, mainly small businesses and the self-employed, trading around 2 billion Swiss Francs (or $1.8 billion) worth of services between them per year. But in a tell-tale and controversial decision in the 1950s, interest started to be paid on credit held in the system – in short it has become more and more like a normal currency.[25]

It is no coincidence that LETS and other complementary schemes have often arisen in places, and times, when conventional cash is short, and particularly in areas of high unemployment. But one reason for their success is problematic – it's a great way to avoid tax. If I spend most of my time fixing roofs in exchange for cakes, vegetables and other local services, I could claim that my conventional income is very low and I shouldn't have to pay much tax. Similarly, if local businesses start paying workers partly in the alternative currency, such as in Ithica dollars or the WIR, what is the impact on the local and national tax base?

In the USA, where many local alternative currencies exist, the Treasury has had to think hard about the tax treatment. The line they have is that these transactions are taxable. So if you pay your plumber or roofer in LETS, you're supposed to work out the value in real dollars and pay tax on this as you would normally – and in good old-fashioned greenbacks (dollars). But the Treasury do make an interesting exception – they don't treat 'timedollars', Edgar Cahn's invention,[26] as taxable, and I think they are right to make this distinction.

Timedollars are credits that participants get in exchange for time that they give almost always to help or support other people. Within Cahn's system, everyone's time is valued the same (which is of course very different to the real economy). Though Cahn doesn't use the phrase, his system operates primarily in the economy of regard. In contrast, LETS tend to become micro-economies that blend both regard-based and conventional economic transactions – often shifting from the former to the latter as they grow. Timedollars may also blur the boundary between the two, but they tend to end up staying mainly in the economy of regard.

A purer example can arguably be seen in the Japanese complementary currency of 'Fueai kippu' – or 'caring relationship tickets'. Japan currently has the most aged population of any nation, with roughly a fifth of the population already over 65. It also has a strong tradition of family based care, not least in relation to its tradition of ritual bathing. These demographics present a big problem, but one that the system of Fueai kippu greatly helps to address. Imagine I am living in Tokyo, but my elderly parents live 200 miles away so it is difficult for me to care for them. Instead, I care for an elderly person who lives close by, and I transfer my credits back to my parents. They can then use these to 'buy' care where they live. But because Fueai kippu are earned through care, not money, the whole transaction feels different and far more acceptable. And the evidence shows that this system leads to more caring activity, not just displacement – just as theory predicts.

Another example, this time from the USA, is Elderplan – a social HMO – within which more able members provide care to others in exchange for credits. Hence someone having fully recovered from a medical procedure might help someone else who has just gone through it, with shopping or getting around. As members age, the type of help that they might offer may change from more physical work towards offering company or advice.

Finally, and perhaps most impressively, Lietaer points to the way in which Bali has maintained a dual currency for centuries. Alongside conventional cash, Bali has a system of 'Narayan banjar' (work for the common good of the community). Typically this currency is used within the 'banjar' – a community of 50 to 500 families. It is used for projects that the community democratically agrees on, such as putting on a festival or putting up a new building for the local school. In such projects, conventional currency is used to buy in materials and specialist labour that cannot be sourced within the community, but the rest is bought using the complementary currency.[27]

A recurrent theme of these complementary currency systems is that the interactions they stimulate are experienced as qualitatively different from those within the real economy. They seem to be powered by, and reinforce, a different motivation. Apart from the regard that undertaking such acts brings in the eye of the receiver or community, acts are undertaken with an unknown and uncertain distant reward – they are primarily motivated by care for others and a sense of connection to the community.

Why not just volunteer? It is estimated that, on average, around a third of people who engage in such schemes in Western countries have never volunteered before. There seem to be several reasons why such currencies stimulate extra activity above volunteering, not least being that people seem to value the reciprocity or gift exchange built into complementary currencies. We seem to be hard-wired not just to be good Samaritans, but to be reciprocators. Researchers have found that volunteering seems to boost well-being, but these positive feelings soon evaporate if volunteers just feel they are being 'used'. There seems to be a hormonal system that lies behind this effect linked to oxytocin – sometimes known as the 'trust and lust' hormone because of the role it plays in reinforcing our positive feelings in relationships. Studies have shown that this 'feel-good' hormone is released in our brains when we do a good deed for another person, but it is actually triggered when that other person acknowledges or reciprocates the good deed.

This seems to be evolution's neat way of achieving the great advantages of cooperation, but without turning us into dupes. Complementary currencies resonate and amplify this mechanism, and can also help solve the informational problems about keeping track of who has been a 'good citizen' over long periods of time.

Implications: The Space between Formal Welfare and Family

One of the strongest trends in modern societies is towards 'beanpole' families – smaller within generations but more stretched across generations. This pattern is driven by wealth – the resources to live more independently – and longevity. Other linked trends are the well-known demographic shift towards older societies and the dramatic reduction in the dependency ratio (the ratio between able adults and dependents). A more subtle consequence is that risks have become much more concentrated and potentially more devastating.

Essentially, this is the law of small numbers. In a large extended family, if someone becomes sick or loses their job, the burden can be spread across thirty or forty family members. However, in a household or family of three or four – let alone in the fastest growing household size of one – such an event places a massive and potentially catastrophic burden on the household.

To caricature, the left has traditionally turned to expansions of the welfare state to address these types of risks, whereas the right has tended to favour personal or family-based responsibility. Either way, this century has witnessed a massive growth in professional care services in both the public and private sectors. In the USA, for example, the proportion of the workforce in professional care services rose by five-fold over the twentieth century, from 4% in 1900, to 19.2% in 2000.[28] Much of this growth reflected the move of women into the labour market, bringing with it new freedoms and autonomy.[29] A similar story applies to income support, with a massive growth of both State welfare benefits and private insurance, these developments themselves helping to make possible the riskiness of small household living (see also Chapter 4 and 5).

But there is an important space in between the individualizing and nationalizing of risk and care-giving. In most countries, the extended family continues to play a big role. Financial transfers from older family members to adult children within Europe range from around 1,500 euros per annum in Sweden to 10,000 euros in Switzerland. Despite complaints about the demographic burden, on average older generations give roughly twice as much to their adult children than the other way round – with an average of 2,914 euro given to 1,470 received – and though the gap closes with age, a net transfer remains even among the very elderly.[30] A similar pattern exists for the giving of time: the amount of support given to children and grandchildren substantially exceeds the amount received

– an average of more than 900 hours a year given and just over 600 received.[31]

This space is also partly occupied by volunteering and third sector organizations. Such volunteering only weakly embeds any notion of reciprocity, as noted above. People are expected to do it without an expectation of return: it is altruistically based, not reciprocity based.

A key challenge for governments and communities is how to foster the informal welfare or mutuality that exists between states and individuals. Recent research shows how our extended social networks have massive impacts on our health and well-being, but unlike individuals, households or geographical communities, 'networks' are very hard for conventional administrative systems to get a grip on. And the challenge is further complicated by the idea that there are obligations and affiliations that we have to others that cannot be discharged through the conventional economy.

Yet if the economy of regard is as substantial and important as suggested here, then even small increases in its 'efficiency' should have massive payoffs. So what might governments, or perhaps large third sector organizations do, to stimulate the economy of regard? In my view, there is a strong case for the creation of a state, or series of local government sponsored, complementary currencies to stimulate and oil the workings of the economy of regard. This would be primarily rooted in exchanges based around health and social care, and in the education system around mentoring and peer support. The primary focus should be supporting help and support between non-kin, since families can already do this for themselves. Further detail is suggested in the conclusion of the chapter.

Some people worry that such a currency would itself crowd out the virtue in current voluntary exchange. I think this is wrong on several counts, and not least on the evidence to date. It would force many public providers to think about what could be asked of the talents of citizens. But it is absolutely key that the currency is reserved for this special class of care-based exchange, and not used to pay for labour. On this point, the economist Bruno Frey makes a useful distinction between payment that is perceived as controlling, and that which is perceived as 'acknowledging'.[32] While the former rapidly crowds out intrinsic motivation, the latter does not. That is what a complementary currency has to achieve – acknowledgement, not control.

National Identity

If we Europeans, together with an increasingly secular minority of North Americans – don't get our ethics and identity from religion, then where do we get it from? Where does secular identity and ethics come from? Do we get them from our fellow national citizens, our local community, or our nation state? Is identity part of our hidden wealth?

The classic way of establishing national commitment and identity is to ask if people would be prepared to fight for their country. It turns out that, across countries, there are great variations in the proportion of the public that say they are willing to fight for their country. Willingness to fight is particularly low in the former Axis and fascist powers of the Second World War, with less than half saying they are willing to fight in Japan, Germany, and – until recently – Italy. Willingness to fight is also particularly low in Iraq, Belgium and Spain – all countries with strong and sometimes violent regional and ethnic fault lines. In contrast, willingness to fight is reported by more than 90% in nations such as Vietnam, China, Turkey, Bangladesh and Morocco. Within Europe, it is relatively high in the Scandinavian nations, and hovers around the 70% line elsewhere.

Another measure is to ask people if they are proud of their country. Again this varies highly, but is only modestly associated with the classic measure of willingness to fight. Nations such as Japan, Germany

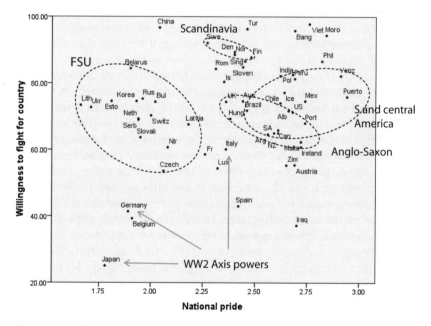

Figure 3.7 *National pride and willingness to fight for country (WVS, 2001–3).*

and Belgium score low on both measures; Vietnam, Morocco, Bangladesh and the Philippines score highly on both; while Anglo-Saxon countries score reasonably on both. But the nations of Eastern Europe and the former Soviet Union are surprisingly willing to fight for their countries given their low levels of pride in their nations. Iraq is at the other extreme, with high levels of national pride, but low levels of willingness to fight.

There is also an interesting discrepancy between the trends in these two measures of national identity over time. Willingness to fight has fallen in 4 out of 5 countries over the last two decades. In contrast, national pride has, if anything, risen in a small majority of countries – with a fall in the minority of people who say that they are not proud of their country.

Using a variety of data, researchers have concluded that – at least in leading OECD countries – national identity is gradually changing from one based on ethnicity or blood, to one based on 'earned citizenship' (see also Chapter 2).[33] This change is manifest in British data that shows that, while worried about excessive immigration, the public are relatively accepting of immigrants who have worked and paid taxes for two years or more, including their having access to public services.

At the same time we have seen the spectacular emergence of new nations across the world, and particularly in Europe. It seems like long buried 'minor' national identities in the Balkans, the former Soviet Union, the UK, Spain, Belgium and elsewhere have emerged to recreate the tapestry of small nations of centuries ago. This seems to be driven by a number of factors including the ending of the cold war, the emergence of supranational governance and, arguably, the growth in individual prosperity and associated value change. In short, the underlying economic and military logic that drove the dominance of the twentieth century nation state has waned, just as the dynamic that drove the competing empires of the nineteenth century waned before it.

Nonetheless, despite the loosening of the legal and military dominance of the nation state, there is strong evidence that nations generally remain surprisingly distinctive in terms of their values and habits – though not in quite the way that politicians are apt to describe it. There is a temptation for polemicists in every nation to claim a clutch of desirable attributes as distinctively characteristic of their nation. Within the UK, political leaders are especially fond of the distinctive British commitment to 'tolerance, fairness and the rule of law'. But, of course, many other nations also claim a strong attachment and identification with such values and habits. Across nations – and certainly within Europe – there is a high degree of consensus that the key objectives and values of their nation should be the promotion of peace and respect for

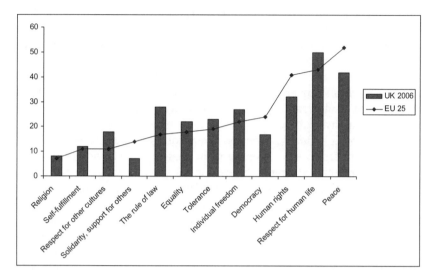

Figure 3.8 *Value priorities of European national publics (Eurobarometer, 2006).*

human life, with similar general agreement that religion and personal self-fulfilment are less central.

The belief – often quite sincere – that our own nation is more attached to a key set of virtues than other nations is very reminiscent of the individual level finding that we think that our own behaviour is more moral and virtuous than that of others around us (see above how respondents rated themselves as twice as likely as 'most people' to follow the Ten Commandments). It is a phenomenon long studied by social psychologists who have noted how we attribute positive attributes to ourselves and our group, and disproportionately project negative attributes onto others and to out groups. Indeed, scores of such 'self-serving attributional biases' have been documented, and it is found that they swing into action very rapidly – and even where the groups have been transparently and arbitrarily assigned just for the purpose of a short experiment.[34]

Soft National Identity: Within Nation Convergence of Norms

Nations are characterized by distinctive values and habits, even if they aren't necessarily as universally positive as we tend to paint them in our minds and our political narratives. The UK, for example, does have a distinctive combination of value priorities, relative to other European nations, around respect for human life, the rule of law and other cultures – and correspondingly less emphasis on human rights, democracy and solidarity and support of others. We also take an unusual level of pride in our army and our history. Basically, we Britons tend to be relatively liberal, especially economically, mixed with a slightly authoritarian streak.

A fascinating finding, mentioned earlier, is that there is little evidence of convergence across nations in these value clusters (Inglehart, 2007; Esmer, 2007). It seems that economic growth and prosperity are pulling most nations away from a cluster of 'survival' values towards a more 'hedonic' set of concerns – and only weakly away from traditional religious beliefs. But this is not leading to value convergence, even across a relatively narrow range of Western European nations (see Figure 3.9). Indeed, one of the very few values around which nations are converging is the importance of teaching children 'respect and tolerance' – including of different values![35]

Yet while there is a modest divergence occurring in values between countries, there is, if anything, a tendency towards *convergence* of values *within* countries. We can show this by taking a similar basket of values and countries to those explored in Esmer's analysis of differences between countries, and looking at whether the spread of values within countries is broadening or narrowing (i.e. seeing how the standard deviations of particular values have changed between 1981 and 2001).

It is such a favourite refrain of commentators to talk about how much more complicated and diverse our societies have become. This implies that we should find strong increases in variability (or standard deviations) of a range of values over time within nations – just as we do between them. Using a basket of 15 variables – including political protest, religious beliefs, sexual tolerance, attitudes to neighbours of a different race, national pride and life satisfaction – there are indeed countries where a majority of these variables are becoming more variable (i.e. where more of the standard deviations are rising). Such countries – where citizens are tending to become more different from each other in their attitudes – include Britain, Belgium, Ireland and, even more strongly, Poland, Estonia and China. But in a majority of countries the differences between fellow citizens seem to be getting *smaller*. This convergence of values has been particularly pronounced in the Netherlands, Sweden, Denmark, Portugal, France and Italy, but was also strong in nations such as South Africa, Mexico, Latvia, Romania and Iceland.

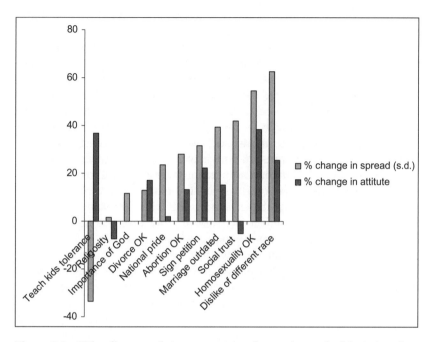

Figure 3.9 *Value divergence between countries: changes in standard deviations from 1981 to 2001 in 19 nations suggest that on a variety of values countries are getting more different (based on WVS data from Esmer, 2007). Ranked by increasing spread within nations.*

In short, these results are in dramatic contrast to the standard accounts of globalization which normally suggest that across countries we are getting more similar – what is sometimes known as 'McDon-aldization' – while within countries we are getting more diverse. The data on values for the last 25 years strongly suggests more or less the reverse. In general terms, the values of nations are tending to *diverge*, while the values of citizens within those nations are tending to get *more* similar. In this sense, distinctive national values and habits seem to be alive and well, and this 'soft' form of national identity remains a powerful force.

There can be no doubt that common habits, assumptions and history greatly facilitate the ability of people to get along, even if they do not constitute a fully fledged Weltanschauung or classical system of ethics. To borrow a prosaic example from the previous chapter, the British tend to maintain a lot of personal space compared with Southern Europeans. Arguably it doesn't really matter how big this personal space is, but it does matter that there is consensus about what it is, so that a stable equilibrium emerges.

These soft habits and values are reinforced by a nation's institutions, including predominantly national media, and by the public's attachment to and respect for these institutions. These include state institutions – such as, in the UK, Parliament, the Monarchy, the police, the National Health Service – and civil institutions such as the BBC and other media, charities such as the NSPCC or the National Trust, and even private sector 'institutions' such as Marks and Spencer or Boots.

Yet most of all, there must be a logic of common interests that underpins common identity, habits and ethics. In the UK, the constitutional expert Robert Hazell has emphasized the extent to which the Union – of the different nations that make up the UK – is essentially voluntary. This is especially clear in the case of Northern Ireland, where the Good Friday agreement makes explicit that it is up to the people of Northern Ireland whether they wish to remain in the Union or not, but in principle also applies elsewhere. This is a remarkable historical turnaround – the creation of a world where nations and empires are built on voluntary membership rather than force.

War

It is an interesting question whether the modest value divergence between nations (along with value convergence within most of them) is setting the scene for future conflicts. Optimists might say that this pattern – twinned with the strong and growing emphasis in most countries on the expression of tolerance in children and between people – is a sign that modern nations are finally figuring out how to live together.

An analysis of contemporary wars reminds us that this happy state of affairs – the nation as a cluster of voluntary clubs living happily together – is far from universal or complete. Most wars in the world today are civil wars. They also tend to be in nations in which people are too busy or afraid to conduct value surveys.

In a typical year, around two such civil wars start. Where these wars will happen can be quite accurately predicted using statistical models.[36] The most powerful predictor is simple – the majority of civil wars occur in countries that have already had a civil war in the previous decade. An unsurprising additional risk factor is strong ethnic or religious cleavages within the nation. Hence, for example, Iraq topped the CIA rankings of countries most at risk of civil war even before the US-led invasion to topple Saddam, because of its deep underlying ethnic and religious cleavages.

Less immediately obvious is the finding that nations with rich natural resources with high value but that can be relatively easily extracted – such as diamonds – are also at high additional risk of civil war. Where such resources exist, groups compete with each other to get control of these resources, often with spiralling violence. If you can get some guns, you can take over the mines and then get the cash to get even more guns to secure your dominant position. Mix in an existing ethnic cleavage, and you've got yourself the ingredients for a lengthy civil war.

As nations and economies mature, the economic logic seems to tip away from civil war. The division of labour involved in the manufacture of industrial goods and services locks people together in extended chains and webs of connection. Modern welfare states reinforce this interconnection by solving collective action problems around public goods from roads and infrastructure to the enforcement of justice and property rights.

By the turn of the nineteenth century, the strongest of nation states were vying with each other rather than fighting internally, swallowing up weaker nations and eventually slogging it out with each other in the world wars. It is no wonder that game theorists such as Von Neuman were so interested in the logic of conflict between nations. A fascinating and important question is whether the economic and social logic of our emerging world is one in which violent group conflict is being crowded out by more profitable endeavours. Perhaps Von Neuman and other architects of the cold war and the logic of Mutually Assured Destruction (MAD) did after all get it right, or perhaps the relentless integration of the world economy will bind us all together so that the gains of peace increasingly outweigh the costs of war.

In the context of the data in the previous section, the question becomes whether the cold logic of MAD and economic integration will overpower the hot logic of a drift to value divergence between nations. As we have seen, 'McDonaldization' of values outside small clusters of countries is very much a myth. Be this around religious beliefs, moral values or attitudes to women, the regions of the world are diverging. Are these the ingredients for a new World War, or is it the last hurrah of a millennium of national conflict, just as evolutionary pathways sometimes fan out before extinction?

Conclusion

This chapter has tried to explore the broader dynamics that affect whether we can get along with our fellow citizens. In contrast to the hard, generally negative and relatively familiar policy contours of the previous chapter – around crime, immigration and terror – this chapter has focused on areas that many policy specialists would view as distinctively soft, if not downright flaky. Reciprocity, religion and shared values aren't the normal stuff of policy debate – at least not in the UK. But they do seem to be an integral part of the hidden wealth identified in earlier chapters. Where does this take you in policy terms?

Rights and responsibilities. For many politicians in the Anglo-Saxon world, the dynamics described in this and the previous chapter help make the case for a tougher approach to rights and responsibilities – the explicit expression in the welfare state and elsewhere of a 'something for something' deal between citizens and the state. Familiar policy examples are active employment policies – the cutting off of benefits if you don't actively look for work or get into training; criminal justice sanctions; and co-payment mechanisms, such as charging for excess rubbish collections or contributing to the cost of medical appointments (especially if patients fail to turn up).

There are economic and efficiency arguments for such 'deals' between citizen and state, or community. There are also moral arguments linked to people's sense of fairness that others are not taking unfair advantage or free-riding on the goodwill of the community. These types of mechanism, contract or 'compact', are important for both reasons, and their absence can significantly undermine public support for the welfare state (at least within the Anglo-Saxon countries – other European nations don't seem to feel this issue so keenly). But there are limits to how far this approach can be pushed. There are practical issues around how elaborate the assessments should be of whether an individual citizen or community should be responsible for a given cost, and difficult ethical questions often arise about the consequences of negative sanctions for third parties, such as the impact of benefit withdrawal on claimants' children. There are also more subtle problems around the dynamic of distrust that can be created around welfare entitlements that are subject to strong tests of rights and responsibilities – if you treat everyone like a rogue, that's what they'll feel like and may just become.[37]

Harnessing positive reciprocity and the economy of regard. Much of our lives, and certainly much of what we care about, is rooted in an 'economy' of reciprocal and caring relationships. But despite this, the economy of regard tends to get viewed as the poor relative of the 'real economy', if not neglected and even crowded out by the dynamics of the real economy.

We should consider whether all able adults should be expected to contribute a minimum number of hours of community or local service, such as six hours a year, or 350 hours over a lifetime. Contributing hours might include, for example, the care of non-kin; mentoring or coaching in school; or the supervision or maintenance of local communal spaces or parks.

The economy of regard could be strengthened through the use of 'complementary currencies' or formal 'thank yous'. These currencies would enable citizens and communities to keep some track of the contribution that they make to others. They would be used to get and acknowledge help when citizens need it, or could be given to others to get extra help. This currency should not be simply exchangeable with 'real money', and if this does happen the 'exchange rate' should be high to signify the value of the complementary currency. These currencies should not therefore be another LETS scheme, though these may have merit of their own.

An obvious place to start is to build such currencies around the social care system for the elderly or infirm, rather like the Japanese system of Fueai kippu, or the US Elderplan system. With this as a backbone, it should be possible to extend into care of the young, mentoring, and some of the more human aspects of public services (on which more in Chapter 4).

The practical issues are considerable when viewed through the lens of a bureaucratic state, but much less so when envisaged in terms of local self-regulating networks. The classic policy-wonk argument against will be that this isn't worth the bureaucratic hassle – just think of the checks involved in allowing adults to mentor young people – and the big third sector organizations aren't too keen on the idea of floods of 'unskilled' volunteers, let alone ambivalent adults who aren't sure they want to be doing it anyway. But the evidence is that most people would happily give a small slice of their time, empathy and skills to help those around them if the barriers were low enough – and especially if it seemed to be the social norm. There are plenty of needs and plenty of goodwill; just not the push or scale of framework to connect the two. Such a scheme would collectively force us to make the connection.

If we could boost activity in the economy of regard by even a few per cent, the fiscal and well-being impact would be immense. The logic is not that of the altruism of volunteering, but of true reciprocity. Unlike traditional rights and responsibility approaches, the dynamic would be a virtuous one of greater trust and mutual respect.

Box 3.1   Creating a state-sponsored complementary currency

How might a government go about creating a currency of 'thank yous' to support and oil the workings of the economy of regard?

- Create a framework for care-based complementary currency, together with the institutions to support it – including the design of secure notes or e-credits. These could be grown at local community level but with a common currency.
- The currency would be used to support care of the elderly and infirm; peer-to-peer support; and community projects.
- An obligation or strong expectation could be created for citizens to contribute a certain number of hours or credits over a lifetime, or over given phases of life.
- The giving of credits to those most in need, possibly including a basic level to all citizens.
- Underwrite the currency, such as enabling care-credits to be exchanged for certain 'goods' within public services – such as extra TV channels in hospital or extracurricular specialist training in schools.[38]

For example, school children might routinely acquire credits from the mentoring of peers or younger children (see also Chapter 4), which they could use as young adults to get tuition or apprenticeship training. Parents – or all adults – might be obliged to give a certain minimum number of hours to schools – say six hours a year – in a local area which could be used by a host of educational and youth institutions for mentoring or perhaps for parenting support for others. Later in life, the credits could be used to 'buy' supplementary care and support – or could be earned and either given to grandchildren and other family members for education, or could be banked for when the person themself needs them for care.

Secular props for ethical habits. Religion is losing its power to shape and support ethical habits in Western Europe, though not elsewhere. Despite this, there is no evidence for a general 'moral decline' or undifferentiated rise in permissiveness. People are tending to become more relaxed about what consenting adults do in the privacy of their own homes, but they generally show no increases in tolerance for overt acts of selfishness or behaviours that will harm others.

But an understanding of the impact of our behaviours on others, and the internalizing of this understanding into our actions, requires spaces and places for reflection and conversation. The modern media; conversations with friends and family; the odd chat down the pub and (increasingly) online forums offer many such spaces. But it's not clear whether we have quite pulled off the trick of connecting these interactions with the key moments of people's lives. This is also important given our very strong tendency, and very human habit, of seeing only virtue in our own acts and selfishness in the acts of others. We need times when we can see ourselves through the eyes of others, and structured moments when we can test our own personal sense of morality against that of the community around us.

Citizenship ceremonies, school graduation ceremonies and civil marriages begin to bridge the gap between the realm of collective ethics and personal experience. My guess is that we will see the emergence of more such points around which key transitions are marked in secular echoes of traditional religious ceremonies – such as around the transition from child to teenager, the right to vote, or the birth of a child – times not only of personal celebration and reflection, but of reflection on the moral and ethical habits that enable us to get along with each other in secular societies.

Conflict prevention. We are confronted with very conflicting evidence about terrorism, diversity and the nation state. The cross-national evidence suggests that there are very powerful forces that generally drive value convergence across ethnic and religious groups within advanced industrialized nations. Yet at the same time, new nations are appearing – or reappearing – at a remarkable rate, and globalization and ICT seems to be allowing people to choose to maintain identifications with nations that they no longer live in to an unprecedented extent. The future balance between these forces seems very unclear.

One policy conclusion for the developing world – for which you don't need a complicated account of value change to reach – is that it is well worth expanding the peacekeeping operations of UN and other international bodies in the wake of civil wars. Given that the average cost of a civil war is estimated to be around US$75b, spending US$0.5b a year to keep a peace-keeping force in place for 10 years after any civil war looks like a no-brainer. Building up trade and the ties of international economic integration may also be a no-brainer – not just because of how it appears to catalyse economic growth but because of how it changes the logic of conflict.

But what about the wild-card of value divergence between nations? David Held, the scholar and proponent of the rise of 'cosmopolitan democracy' has a persuasive line that it's going to work out OK, provided that we strengthen our international institutions adequately. But it may be that we need to do more on the soft, cultural side too. It is difficult to nail down the effects of educational exchanges, holidaying overseas, the Eurovision song contest, loans of art between national galleries, or international sporting events. Perhaps we should try harder to estimate the impacts of these 'soft activities', for it could be that the mutual understanding they bring are the best investment we can make to save our grandchildren from Armageddon.

A different kind of state? Viewing the world through the lens of the economy of regard has deep implications, and I cannot claim to know them all. Does it mean a bigger role for local and neighbourhood governance? What does it mean for regulators, and what they do? What does it mean for the nature of our economy itself, how we measure what it is we produce and the implicit incentives built into our 'real' currencies and market institutions?[39]

At the very least I think it means shifting policies in the direction promoting virtue rather than squeezing vice. We are now moving into the realm of speculation, but to cut back to the topic of well-being in Chapter 1, it feels like happier nations are better at this balancing act. Their instinct is to see the best in a troubled youth, not just the problem. Their natural public campaigns are about opportunities for betterment and mutual service, not stamping out knife crime or anti-social behaviour (and the inadvertent reinforcement of the problematic 'declarative norm' that this brings).[40]

Let's end this chapter with a final example that spans my personal and policy life. In the UK we have massively increased our spending on the health service, from a little over 5% of GDP to nearly 10% in the space of about 10 years. Clearly, part of what we want to achieve is a health service with better health outcomes, and preferably with a reasonable degree of efficiency so that it doesn't swallow our entire economy. But the health service we want for our children and our grandchildren is surely more than an efficient machine. It's about treating each other with respect, dignity and compassion – a way of building the hidden wealth of our society. In that sense, it is not something that we can just leave to some doctors in white coats – it is something that we all need to be a part of.

I have a younger son, now ten, who needed a tracheotomy for the first four years of his life. This involved a lot of contact with the health professionals – most of it fantastic, some of it terrible – and lots of carrying around pumps and equipment, sleepless nights of care, and periodic crises just like a scene from ER. As he grew older, and fortunately no longer needed his artificial airway, my wife and I offered via the health professional we had dealt with, to help any other family or parents who had a child with a tracheotomy – such as if they wanted to talk about it or just wanted someone else to look after their child so they could take an evening off. Of course, we were never asked. Maybe no one had the need, though I doubt it. More likely, our health service with its professionalism and worry about litigation doesn't really know what to do with such offers, and perhaps other parents would hesitate to ask. But it is not so difficult to imagine a future in which our institutions, our markets and our habits have more room for a different kind of exchange. It must be possible to combine our drive, as policymakers and citizens, for efficient and effective public and private institutions with our human desire for affiliation and care.

4

Fairness and Inclusion

It is about our sovereign value: fairness. It is about potential never explored; talent torn-off unused, the inability to live a life free from the charity of others. The objective is timeless: we want to expand opportunities so that nobody whatever their background or circumstance should be left behind.

Tony Blair, 5 September 2006[1]

Every politician, and pretty much any citizen, is in favour of fairness and social inclusion. They just don't agree on what constitutes it; how important a priority it is; or how you can achieve it.

Fairness has lots of aspects, and is something that humans seem very concerned about. Most people would consider it unfair to be punished for something they did not do; to be forced to work for another without pay; or to suffer injury from another without compensation. Most, if not all, of the activity of the legal and criminal justice system is concerned with such issues of fairness.

Laboratory experiments suggest that most of us have a deep sense of fairness, and are prepared to pay quite a high price to see fairness done – at least for ourselves. A classic example is where two people are given a sum of money to divide between themselves and keep – the ultimatum game. One participant is given absolute control over how the money is divided, and the other is simply given the option of accepting the deal or rejecting it, in which case neither gets anything. Classic economics tells us the person dividing up the money should rationally take nearly all of it, and the other person should accept it whatever, since something is better than nothing. But it is found that if the divider takes more than about three-quarters of the money, the other person will generally reject the deal, even though it means they both get nothing. We just can't bear the idea of the other person taking so much – it feels too unfair.

Evolutionary accounts suggest that this desire for fairness may be hardwired, as it strengthens the incentives in a social group to coop-erate with others. Sociological, and even economic accounts, suggest that such habits make sense in settings where people interact with each other frequently over time – people who don't 'play fair' get excluded from the group. Such a sense of fairness almost certainly constitutes a part of the hidden wealth of successful societies.

But what about fairness when it comes to societies of millions, espe-cially in respect to the division of resources? In much of Europe, the polit-ical language and emphasis tends to be on 'social inclusion'. Attempts are made to give all citizens enough resources to participate in society through relatively generous income support and publicly funded uni-versal healthcare and education systems. In Anglo-Saxon countries, the emphasis has tended to be more laissez faire with a sharper sense of the 'deserving' and 'undeserving' poor. Anglo-Saxon political lan-guage has tended to be more around reducing barriers to opportunity and reducing 'exclusion', rather than 'inclusion'. Hence in Anglo-Saxon nations income support for the unemployed and other benefits has tended to be less generous, and state funded health and education less comprehensive (such as in relation to who pays for Higher Education).

Income Inequality

Income inequality is the simplest, and perhaps most widely used measure of how resources are distributed across a modern society.[2] Within country income inequality tends to fall with development, as wealth and income spreads and an affluent middle-class emerges. But inequality tends to grow again as the economy matures – or at least it has in recent decades. One comprehensive analysis showed that in the twenty years from 1980–2000, inequality rose in 70 out of 73 developed and developing nations.[3]

This pattern of change overlays an extraordinary range of income inequality across countries, especially among countries with lower incomes. As we shall see, an argument can be made that high income inequality is not necessarily unfair – though it is difficult to see this 'fairness' in the extreme contrast between the inequality of Brazil or

Colombia versus the relatively low inequality of countries with similar average incomes such as Egypt or Bulgaria (see Figure 4.1).

Levels of income inequality are higher in Anglo-Saxon countries than in mainland European countries with otherwise similar overall levels of wealth. Levels of income inequality are especially low in Scandinavian countries, where the ratio of the incomes of the top 20% to bottom 20% are around four-fold or less compared with roughly double this differential in the USA or UK. However, even US levels of income inequality look modest compared with those of South America where the ratio of incomes between the top and bottom 20% range from around 18 to around 28-fold (and the top to bottom 10% ratios range from 40 to 70-fold).

There is some evidence that the extremes of inequality get clipped as nations develop economically. You can see an indication of this in Figure 4.1 – the most unequal countries all have incomes of less than \$US15,000p.a.[4] Similarly, there is evidence that the relatively equal incomes of the former Soviet Union nations are moving to the OECD 'norm' as their economies develop and integrate into the world economy.

That said, the very long-run trend of income inequality *between* countries – that is from the 1820s to the current period – has been of divergence. Over that same nearly two centuries, levels of inequality within countries have not changed very much. To put this in human terms, the main reason why Bill Gates and Warren Buffett are so much richer than everybody else in the world is because they live in a rich nation such as America.

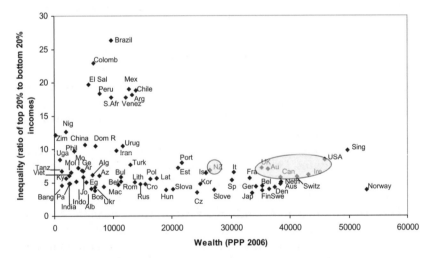

Figure 4.1 *Income inequality vs. wealth: inequality shown as ratio of incomes of top 20% to bottom 20% (World Bank data, 2006); wealth shown as income expressed as purchasing power parity (IMF, 2006). Anglo-Saxon nations highlighted.*

But Gates created the software that allows most of the world's computers to run (even if we don't always love it), while Buffett has spent a lifetime ensuring that the most innovative and efficient companies got the resources they needed to grow and prosper. Isn't that both fair and efficient?

So What? The Impact of Poverty and Inequality

Why should we care about the fact that some people are poor? A primary reason is clearly because of fairness or justice. We may feel that every child or adult should have a chance in life to succeed based on their individual effort and ability, and should not be condemned to hardship or poverty by accident of birth. We might also employ an efficiency argument too – that it makes economic sense to utilize the talents of all in a society, not just of the lucky few.

The moral argument rests heavily on the claim that being poor or 'disadvantaged' really is unpleasant and consequential. This claim is also politically important for the obvious reason that if most people think being poor isn't that bad, then there will be little support for doing anything about it.

As one might expect, the poorest fifth of the population are much less likely to own material goods that the majority take for granted, such as washing machines or having a second pair of shoes, and are very much less likely to be able to afford luxuries, such as being able to have a holiday away from home. But there are big non-material differences too. Those from lower socio-economic groups are typically two to three times more likely to suffer from premature death from a variety of causes, and their children are much more likely to die or be hurt as a result of an accident at home or from being hit by a car on the street. They suffer more crime, see their neighbours more but trust them less, and suffer more from obesity and alcohol abuse. Here we start to see a darker side to the hidden wealth of nations – and the consequence of its uneven spread.

Yet even these kinds of statistics are sometimes discounted on the basis that these figures largely reflect lifestyle and habits, and even that it is patronizing and middle-class centric to use these statistics at all. Just because someone chooses to smoke or drink, or lives without all the luxuries that the middle class take for granted doesn't make a case for injustice or misery.

One way to look at this issue is to ask people directly about how happy or satisfied they are with their lives (see also Chapter 1). When we do this we find that people on lower incomes and in lower socio-economic groups report significantly lower levels of life satisfaction

	Richest 1/5	Poorest 1/5	Ratio
Income			
Pre-tax (2006/7)	£72,900	£4,900	14.9
Post tax income	£56,100	£10,110	5.5
Post tax inc. benefits in kind	£52,400	£14,400	3.6
(as % of total income, 2006)	45%	6%	7.5
Wealth distribution	(top 25%)	(bottom 25%)	
Total wealth	72%	Close to zero	-
Less housing	85%	or negative	
Household *lacking* (2006):			
Bank account (or post office account)	2%	6%	3.0
Central heating (2003)		10%	
Freezer		12%	
Two pairs of shoes per adult	(close to 0)	15%	-
Washing machine		15%	
Household contents insurance		32%	
Money for 1 week holiday per year		52%	
A personal computer		70%	
Health			
Smoking (male, 2004)	15%	62%	4.1
Life lost to alcohol (months, male, 2004)	6 months	18 months	3.0
Obesity Men (2006)	21%	25%	1.2
Obesity Women (2006)	18%	32%	1.8
Health risk factors (2 or 3 of: smoking,	Class I	Class V	
high alcohol consumption, and poor diet)			
Men	9%	28%	3.1
Women	4%	19%	4.8
Age standardised mortality rates, men	Mang / prof	Manual	
aged 25-64			
Circulatory diseases	741	1,522	2.1
Cancer	918	1,491	1.6
Respiratory diseases	98	292	3.0
Digestive diseases	164	368	2.2
Accidents	94	206	2.1
Suicides	94	200	2.1
	(bottom 1/3)	(top 1/3)	
Not very/not at all happy (WVS)	12.5%	4.8%	2.6

Figure 4.2 *Inequality in the UK: a selection of recent statistics.*

and happiness than those in higher socioeconomic groups. Broadly speaking, the relationship is curvilinear – small increases in incomes at the lower level are associated with much bigger increases in subjective well-being than similar size increases in income at the top end.

Some have made the argument that well-being measures fail to capture the true hardships of poverty and disadvantage because people report their well-being relative to their own previous life experience – so the very poor might say they are happy just because they are doing just about as well as they could expect given their position in life. As we have seen, the poor do report much lower well-being, but there is an odd empirical finding which supports these 'false consciousness' concerns. If you ask people to rate their happiness on a 10-point scale, you find that the lower end – i.e. 1 to 5 – is dominated by those from lower socioeconomic groups. Similarly, as you move up the scale, you find the 7 to 9 range dominated by the higher socioeconomic groups. But, for some reason that is not well understood, there tends to be more low socio-economic respondents who say '10' – but what might be interpreted as the 'naively happy'.

A more detailed take on well-being is to ask people about their satisfaction with specific domains of their life. This is shown in Figure 4.3 for a recent sample of the UK population. The lightest bars show the level of satisfaction for those from lower socioeconomic groups ('E's) whereas the black bars show the levels of satisfaction of the higher socioeconomic groups ('AB's). As can be seen the 'AB's report higher levels of satisfaction with virtually every aspect of their lives. The gap is particularly large, as you might expect, for satisfaction with 'future financial security' and for 'standard of living'. But it is also very substantial for satisfaction with 'achievement of goals'; 'day to day activities'; 'relationships' and 'health'. Indeed, the only domain of life where the 'AB's report less satisfaction is with 'community'.

Inequality or poverty?

There are important empirical and political arguments about whether such negative impacts are associated with inequality *per se* or just poverty.

In the UK, when Seeborn Rowntree conducted his groundbreaking survey of York in 1899, he concluded that just over one in four people were living below the 'poverty line' – that is they lacked the most basic resources, such as being able to afford enough food to maintain a healthy weight or resist illness. His radical conclusion was not that these people were lazy, but that work did not pay them enough to afford the most basic necessities.

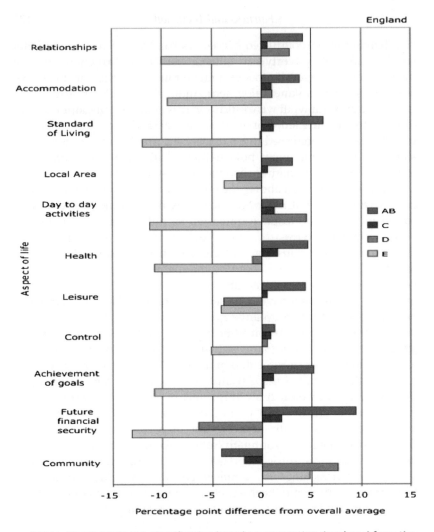

Notes: Social grade is a classification based on occupation developed from the National Readership Survey. Examples of occupation in each grade include:
AB: Doctor, solicitor, accountant, teacher, nurse, police officer;
C: Junior manager, student, clerical worker, foreman, plumber, bricklayer;
D: Manual workers, shop workers, apprentices;
E: Casual labourers, state pensioners, unemployed.
Separate grades A and B, and C1 and C2, have been joined (to AB and C) due to very similar distributions.
The results presented here show the difference between each group and the overall average.
Source: Defra

Figure 4.3 *Satisfaction with different domains of life by social class (UK, 2007; data from DEFRA).*

When Rowntree conducted his second survey in 1936, he found that levels of absolute poverty had fallen considerably, largely because of more generous wages. By this period, he found that the major cause of absolute poverty was unemployment. Again, this didn't seem to be about laziness, but about what we would now call structural unemployment.

Rowntree conducted a final survey in 1951. By this time, absolute poverty had been reduced to small pockets. The advent of the welfare state and full employment policies looked like they would go on to finish the job of eliminating absolute poverty for ever.

Yet, as we have seen above, the effects of class differences and 'relative poverty' did not disappear. It seems that people at the bottom of the pile continue to have much worse outcomes, even though in absolute material terms they are often much better off than many of the affluent of previous generations. This has led to heated political and academic arguments about whether the object of policy should be the reduction of poverty, or a reduction in inequality. Blair, for example, was always careful to say that the objective of policy was not the reduction of inequality *per se* – which could have implied we should drag down the incomes of the rich – but was the lifting up of the poor to join the rest.

The evidence, in short, is that both absolute poverty and inequality have impacts on outcomes. Absolute effects include the health effects of inadequate diets, such as those documented by Rowntree at the end of the nineteenth century, or the excess winter deaths that are still seen in the poorly heated homes of the poor elderly today. However, there is strong evidence for relative effects too. Humans are very social creatures, and to be stuck at the bottom of a social hierarchy takes its toll. The evidence suggests that this toll is paid not only by those at the bottom, but that even those at the top of a more unequal society pay a price in terms of their physical and mental health.[5] The greyer causal areas are where behavioural and cultural habits mediate the social class differences, such as smoking or diet.

I don't want to dwell on this well-rehearsed argument.[6] The political compromise is to focus on a measure of relative poverty, such as the proportion of the population on less than 60% of median incomes (a UK target). In principle, this can be reduced by pushing up the incomes of the poorest and leaving the top earners alone – but it is obviously harder to do if the earnings of the rich keep rising at above the average rate.

Meritocracy

In the run-up to the 1997 election in the UK, a story broke about the pay of Cedric Brown, the boss of the newly privatized public utility company British Gas. Brown's pay had soared in the wake of the privatization of the company, which had a national monopoly on the supply of natural gas to the British public. The company argued that now it was private, it had to pay the going rate for keeping its top people. But the public weren't convinced. People felt genuinely outraged that the bosses seemed able to award themselves a huge pay rise overnight for doing essentially the same job – and that the public had to foot the bill.

In contrast, at around the same time, there were plenty of stories in the UK about figures such as Richard Branson, who was paying himself far more than Brown. But while Brown became a hate figure – the personification of a self-serving 'fat cat' – Branson remained popular. Why? The public distinguished between someone who took personal risks, invested their own capital and built up a business (Branson) and someone who they felt got a huge hike in pay for no good reason and for no personal risk (Brown). In 2009 we have a similar example around the bonuses for shamed bankers, versus the struggles of small businesses and workers. It's about fairness and appropriate reward.

It is clear that these judgements of fairness can't be reduced to differentials in income. People care deeply about 'procedural fairness' – often more so than about differentials in outcomes. For example, studies of criminal justice systems have found that feeling that the process was fair often matters more than the objective outcome for how people feel afterwards. Even for those at the sharp end of the law and who get punished, if the process seemed to be 'just' – the judge and jury heard all the evidence and circumstances, and carefully weighed these in reaching their conclusions – they can and will genuinely feel 'it was a fair cop'. Similarly, when media stories run about the levels of pay of top bosses, politicians, film stars or sports stars, people discuss whether these levels of pay are 'fair' – and their conclusion rests on more than how much the pay is.

Interestingly, the public tend to apply the same logic at the other end of the pay spectrum too, at least in Anglo-Saxon countries. One of the most popular and emblematic policies of Labour in 1997 was the proposed reform of the benefits system, itself borrowed from Scandinavia and the USA. Labour proposed that able-bodied but unemployed individuals who were not actively looking for work or in training would face having their unemployment benefits cut. The policy tapped into the same moral logic of the Brown-Branson difference – that there was a distinction between deserving and undeserving poor, just as there was between deserving and undeserving rich (plus evidence of better outcomes from elsewhere).

The logic of fair and unfair inequalities powers the idea of 'meritocracy' – the idea that some people deserve to be paid or promoted more. Meritocracy is attractive to progressives on both left and right who contrast it with more rigid and traditional notions of society where your place in life depends on who you know or who your parents were. Meritocracy can be promoted on both economic and social justice grounds. A more meritocratic society should be more economically productive because the most skilled and able people will be allocated to their optimum roles. It is also more just because resources and responsibilities are allocated 'fairly' – on the basis of effort and skills, rather than on the basis of arbitrary assignment or the abuse of power.

The American dream is often cited as the practical embodiment of meritocracy. No matter how low your origins, with hard work, determination and a little natural ability, you can make a good life for yourself – to be rich and influential, if not necessarily happy (see also Chapter 1 on prosperity). In such a model, pay and success should follow the contribution you make. And Americans really do think this. In an innovative question tucked away in the first World Values Survey in 1981, respondents were asked whether they thought that it was fair that where two secretaries were doing the same job, but one worked faster and more efficiently, that the faster worker should get paid more.

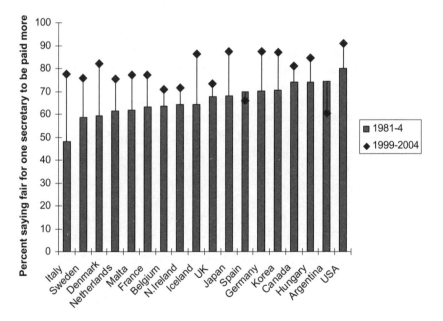

Figure 4.4 *Is it fair for one secretary to be paid more than another in the same job if she works harder? Percentage agreeing that it is fair, by country, 1981–2004. Most countries have become more North American on this measure of fairness.*

Around 80% of Americans thought this differential in pay was fair. In contrast, and in the same year, less than half of Italians agreed.

Interestingly, in the twenty years since, the world has generally moved towards the American viewpoint of meritocracy. Sixteen of the eighteen nations asked this question in both the early 1980s and early 2000s have moved substantially towards the view that it is fair for the secretary who is more productive to be paid more (the exceptions were Spain and ultra-high income inequality Argentina). The Italians are now close to 80% in agreement, while the Americans themselves have moved past 90% agreement.[7]

Even Cuba, after half a century of wage parity, decided in 2008 that more productive workers should be paid more after all. The official notice stated that 'the socialist principle of distribution will be achieved wherein everyone earns in accordance with his contribution, in other words, pay in accordance with quality and quantity'.[8] In future, Cuban workers who fulfil production quotas will get 5% bonuses, and managers could get up to 30% – not quite a USA-style market and certainly not South American style inequality, but interesting nonetheless to see the same moral and economic logic at play.

So the world has become more meritocratic in its attitudes – and why not? Who could disagree with the idea that the hardworking should be rewarded more than the feckless – that the prodigal son does *not*, after all, deserve to get half the fruits of his brother's labour (see box)? Younger readers will probably feel baffled that more than half of Italians once thought that the productive secretary *shouldn't* get paid more.

The prodigal son

The parable of the prodigal son illustrates the issue of meritocracy – with most citizens now taking a very different line to that of the traditional biblical conclusion.

There are two brothers. One stays at home and works hard while the other goes off on a long jaunt of fun-filled adventure – the prodigal son. After a year or so, the prodigal son has used up his money and inheritance and comes back home. What is his entitlement? The generous spirited lesson is supposed to be that the prodigal son gets forgiven and shares equally in the fruits of the family farm. But citizens today, especially in countries such as the US and China, have a very different view – they think it's morally wrong that the prodigal son gets such a good deal. They feel that the hard-working son should get to keep most of the efforts of his hard labour.

There are, of course, both tricky practical and ethical issues buried in the notion of meritocracy. Most importantly, you have to decide what constitutes merit. If a person is blessed with high intelligence, and therefore high productivity – do they then 'merit' higher pay? If merit relates to their productivity, then the answer is clearly 'yes'. But if merit relates to their effort and agency, then the answer may not be so clear.

A linked issue is how advantage is transmitted across generations. If a person comes from an advantaged background – noting that even in a meritocracy some people will end up with more resources – then they probably get access to better schools, better networks, and perhaps 'better' parenting. How are we to handle the *unfair* advantages bestowed on the children of *fairly* rewarded parents?

An important empirical point is that while meritocracy may be more fair – and certainly more efficient – than an aristocratic, rigid class or caste-based society, it is not necessarily less unequal. In essence, most conceptions of meritocracy shift the basis of inequality to one that has a stronger economic and moral logic, but still leave open many questions about fairness.

Social Mobility

Even in my time in government, I saw several cohorts of Ministers become very interested and excited about the idea of social mobility, only to drop it quietly a little while later. Of all of them, the interest in social mobility has run especially deep for Gordon Brown, the UK Prime Minister from 2007. So what makes social mobility such an interesting concept, and how come it keeps getting dropped?

The basic idea is simple. Social mobility is a measure of the extent to which people's life chances are determined by, or free of, their origins of birth. It is a simple idea, but quite tricky to measure because you need information not only about the individual, but also about the circumstances of their parents. In essence, to know about social mobility today we have to wait for fifteen or twenty years to see what becomes of today's children as they enter adulthood and the labour market.

Researchers distinguish between two different basic measures of mobility. *Absolute* social mobility measures tell you about what proportion of people are moving up in the world in terms of social class, income or some other key outcome. This measure tells as much about how a society and economy is changing as about fairness *per se*. If there is strong economic growth and an expansion of more professional and high-skilled occupations, the majority of young people should be 'winners' in an absolute sense – or in Kennedy's famous phrase, a rising tide of growth should lift all boats. In contrast, *relative* social mobility filters out the overall background of change, or the rising tide, to estimate what the relative chances are of someone born from a given background succeeding in life compared with the chances of someone from another background born at the same time.

The story on absolute social mobility is generally a good one, and quite easy to understand. In most countries there has been considerable absolute growth in higher occupations and real wages over the past century, though the rate of growth has changed from generation to generation. For example, Americans born in the 1930s – growing up in the post-war 1940s and 1950s – were almost twice as likely to be upwardly socially mobile than downwardly mobile. But for those born in the 1960s and 1970s, the net difference between upward and downward mobility had narrowed to just 3% – more people were still going up than down, but the rate of change was much more modest (see Figure 4.5).

A similar story can be seen in the UK. The 1950s and 1960s saw a period of rapid expansion of the middle classes as service sector, professional and managerial jobs grew and manufacturing and unskilled manual work shrank as a proportion of the economy. There was, to

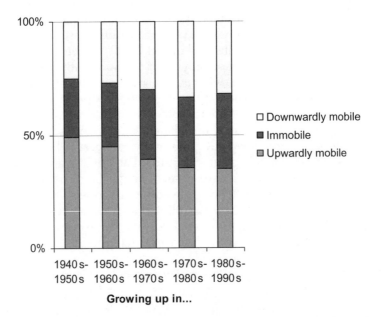

Figure 4.5 *Absolute social mobility in the USA by generation (General Social Survey Data, 1988–2004). Cohorts born in 1930–9 through to 1970–9.*

use John Goldthorpe's encapsulation, 'more room on top'. To give a sense of the scale of this change, in around 1900 about three in four men in the UK worked in manual occupations, but by 2000 this had collapsed to about one in four. Researchers argue about how much the rate of this absolute upward mobility has fluctuated over time, but generally speaking there's not much argument about the direction of travel or that this has generally been a good thing. Far fewer people experience the combination of hard physical work, long hours and often dangerous conditions that many of our grandparents endured. Absolute mobility, and the transformation of working life that it relates to, is not to be sniffed at.

The story around relative social mobility is more complex. Relative measures seek to compare our success in life not only with our parents, but to others in our own generation. For example, we might ask what are the chances that a child will end up *rich* if born to poor versus rich parents? Similarly, what are the chances that a child will end up *poor* if born to poor versus rich parents?

Figure 4.6 shows the answer to this question by putting two graphs side by side. The graph on the left shows how much people from the bottom quarter of the population, in terms of their parents' incomes, went on to earn relative to others (using US and UK data). The graph on the right, in contrast, shows what happened to those from the highest income quarter of the population. As one can see at a glance, the children of the poor tend to stay poor, and the children of the rich tend to stay rich. This relative mobility – or lack of it – can be expressed in

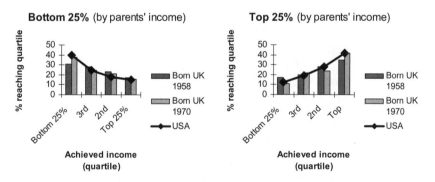

Figure 4.6 *The rich tend to stay rich, the poor stay poor. The relative social mobility of the children of the top and bottom quarter of the income distribution for those born in the UK in 1956 and 1970, and the USA at around the same period. Note how the stickiness of our origins became stronger between these two UK cohorts. (UK data from Blanden, Gregg and Machin, 2005; and US from Peters, 1992; quoted in Beller and Hout, 2006).*

various ways. For example, while 42% of the children of high income parents end up in the top quarter of the income range (in both the USA and UK), only around 15% of those from lower income parents will make it into that bracket – a difference of about 2.8-fold. The higher the ratio, the lower the level of relative social mobility in the society.

The graphs also show how relative social mobility appears to have fallen in the UK between the 1958 and 1970 cohort – a matter of great controversy within the UK. In essence, relative income mobility in the UK seems to have drifted down towards that of the USA (which does not seem to have changed much over the period).[9] In other words, children growing up in the Britain of the late 1970s and 1980s had less of a chance of escaping from poor backgrounds than did those who grew up in the 1960s and early 1970s.

The observant reader will note one other important point about these mobility graphs – the chances of slipping down from the top of the income ladder are noticeably lower than the chance of climbing up from the bottom. Those born into low income families in 1970 were 2.4 times more likely to end up stuck at the bottom than climb to the top, whereas those born into high income families were 3.8 times more likely to stay at the top than slide to the bottom. In other words, upper middle class families are better at stopping downward mobility than poorer families are at achieving upward mobility. To put it another way, more of the mobility at the bottom end of the distribution is movement in and out of the lower three-quarters of society, whereas for the top quarter there is a 'glass floor' that stops the children of the affluent falling down (or the rest of society from climbing up). Again we glimpse a downside – at least for those at the bottom – of the hidden wealth of nations.

This observation gives an important clue both as to what happened in Britain to make relative social mobility fall between the 1958 and 1970 cohorts, and as to why politicians tend to fall out of love with the concept once they get a closer look at it.

Explaining changes in relative social mobility

A number of detailed analyses have been conducted to explain why relative social mobility fell in Britain in the 1970s and 1980s. The explanation is a surprising one – particularly to progressive politicians – the expansion in higher education.

In common with many countries, there has been a dramatic expansion in the proportion of people going into Higher Education in the UK. The number going to university doubled in the 1960s, though was still low by today's standards. Even by 1980, only around 13% of young people went on to university. However, a particularly dramatic expansion in the proportion of young people going to university occurred in the late 1980s and early 1990s with the conversion of a host of institutions into new universities. The proportion of under-21s going to university rose from 15% to 28% between 1988 and 1992. This happens to have coincided almost exactly with when the 1970 cohort were coming of age.

The question is: who took up these new opportunities? Figure 4.7 shows the answer – the most affluent. Between the 1956 and 1970 cohorts, the proportion of the most affluent 20% (by background) going on to university rose from 20 to 37%. In contrast, there was almost no change in the proportion of the poorest 20% going to university, which edged from 6 to 7%.

At the same time, the financial returns from getting a degree remained particularly high in the UK as the demand for graduates matched, if not exceeded, supply. So whether intentionally or otherwise, the rapid expansion of HE actually led to a drop in social mobility as the more affluent and educated children (in terms of school grades) of the better off were more able to take advantage of the new opportunities.

One good bit of news for the UK is that the evidence for the subsequent cohorts suggests that relative social mobility has remained roughly stable despite further expansion of HE. This is thought to

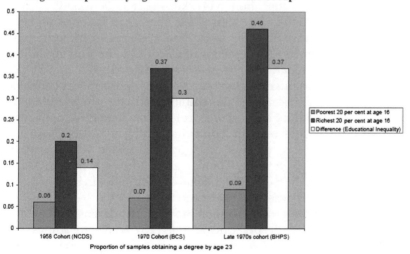

Degree Completion by Age 23 by Parental Income Group

Source: Blanden, Gregg and Machin (2005) Table 5.4.

Figure 4.7 *Degree completion by parental income (from Blanden et al., 2005).*

be a result of the steadier pace of expansion matched with underlying improvements in school grade performances across social groups at age 16 and 19. On the other hand, the published evidence to date suggests that relative social mobility hasn't risen either, despite the massive increases in education spending at all levels from 1997 – though there is tentative evidence from the very latest unpublished data that this mobility may be rising.[10] If this data is confirmed, it will be truly remarkable – the first time in more than a generation that relative social mobility has risen. But even if it is true, the chances are it won't be confirmed until after the next general election – perhaps 15 years after the Labour Administration came to power, and probably after they have left.

Now one can begin to see why politicians are initially so drawn to the idea of increasing social mobility and then quietly move on. It's very tough, and it takes a very long time. More relative social mobility also implies more *downward* mobility, and no one is very keen on that, especially the affluent families and individuals concerned, and even more so in the context of low absolute mobility. Your best bet as an elected government is to hope to expand educational and top-end labour market opportunities to make 'more room on top'. But, as the rapid expansion of HE in the late 1980s in the UK showed, it's the most advantaged that tend to win in the scrabble for new places. If you want these new opportunities to be disproportionately taken by the less advantaged, you have to work very hard indeed.

A final warning comes from a breakdown of social mobility figures across the UK nations. In general, those born in 1970 did much better than their parents, with a big expansion in professional occupations and a contraction in routine or manual work by the mid 2000s. This absolute occupational mobility was especially marked in Scotland, where the occupational structure caught up with the more professionalized profile of England. But this did not translate into relative social mobility. In England, 63% of those with parents who were professionals ended up as professionals, compared with just 11% of those with parents in routine occupations – a six-fold advantage. In Scotland, the figures were 69 and under 6% – more than a 12-fold advantage. Despite the much larger increase in professional opportunities in Scotland, relative social mobility was actually lower.[11]

This is something that Gordon Brown, the current Prime Minister, genuinely and deeply cares about, and wants to address. As we have seen, history is against him – but can it be done? Should we dare to hope from the glimmer of promise in the unpublished academic studies that policy can drive up levels of relative social mobility?

Box 4.1   Genetics and class

There is a long-standing and notorious argument that higher social classes (even races) have an inherent or genetic basis to their superiority. This argument was revisited in the 1990s with the publication of the book *The Bell Curve* which highlighted how IQ is a more powerful predictor of earnings in the USA than social class origins. Since there is very strong evidence for the heritability of IQ – current estimates are typically in the range 50 to 75% – *The Bell Curve* created consternation by pointing out that social class must itself have a strong genetic basis.

Critics have tended to focus, with only partial success, on whether *The Bell Curve* fails to account for how social class origins shape the child's IQ. In my view, there are much more fundamental, and in many ways more troubling, questions to think about in relation to this subject. Progressives overly focus on trying to knock down the argument that there is some genetic basis to social class destinations, partly because they (wrongly) think this argument undermines the case for environmental interventions. They would do better to reflect on what are the implications for the justness of the distribution of earnings that result from this uneven distribution of abilities. The distribution of earnings is substantially socially determined, even if the abilities underneath it are not. A higher natural ability means that a person is likely to be more productive, but doesn't tell you whether that person should earn 5, 10 or 100 times more than someone else. Indeed, you might even make the case that – if you could independently measure it – a person with higher natural ability should be 'taxed' at a higher marginal rate to account for the fact that for the same marginal effort they can produce far more than someone of lower ability.

A linked result is that, in a more meritocratic society where environmental factors are more evened out, heritability estimates should be *higher*. In this sense, higher heritability estimates are to be celebrated.[12] An illustration of this effect can be found in *The Bell Curve* itself, in the massive jump in the gap between the IQ's of Ivy league students and the average – from around one standard deviation in the 1930s to more than three standard deviations by 1990, i.e. the Ivy League has become more meritocratic. Shouldn't we celebrate that earnings are now based more on genes than social class origins (though not make the Bell-curve mistake of attributing ethnic differences in IQ to genes)?

One troubling question is whether the rise in 'assortive mating' – people having children with partners of similar ability, could inadvertently change the shape of the distribution itself. Increasingly meritocratic sorting in education and the labour market matches us to partners who are more and more like is in terms of cognitive ability. To caricature, does this mean that the super-brainy will eventually spawn a hyper-able super-class, while at the other end, a new genetically-based underclass will emerge? The evidence to date is that 'regression to the mean' – the fact that the abilities of our kids tend to drift to the average regardless of our own abilities – seems to overpower the effects of past assortive mating.[13] But it would certainly be a deep irony if the creation of a more meritocratic society created the genetically-based class society and underclass that the Victorians suspected, but did not really have.

International differences in social mobility

Things that governments can't do anything about are best thought of as facts of life, not policy problems or challenges. The question is what category is relative social mobility in – a fact of life or a tractable policy problem?

As a young research fellow at Nuffield, Oxford, I recall a seminar by Gordon Marshall comparing the social mobility rates of the recently re-unified East and West Germany. The core finding was analytically dull, but politically very striking. Marshall found that the levels of social mobility in pre-unification East and West were basically the same. However, Marshall noted that the claims made about social mobility by the governments of the East and West had been very different. In the West, nobody claimed or expected society to be especially fair in terms of social mobility – it was obvious that having educated and affluent parents gave you advantages in life. But in the East, the ideology made much stronger claims about fairness and mobility: it was claimed that the communist system ensured that all had equal chances in life. Marshall's argument was that low social mobility *per se* was not a political problem, but the discrepancy between the Eastern claims of high mobility and the reality was a big problem. He speculatively proposed that this discrepancy helped to de-stabilize East Germany and bring the wall crashing down. Marshall may have overstated the case, but it's a pretty powerful political warning nonetheless.

Are there countries that have significantly higher levels of relative social mobility? The answer is clear – yes. But despite the claims of the American Dream, it's not the USA. Using measures of occupational

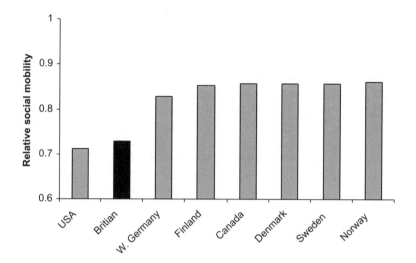

Figure 4.8 *Relative social mobility in income compared between countries. (Data from Blanden et al. 2005. The number is 1 minus the intergenerational partial correlation between parents, or father, and adult child using cohorts born from 1958 to 1970. On this measure, perfect social mobility, where parental income had no effect on their child's income, would be 1, and perfect immobility would be 0.)*

mobility – whether labourers' children get to be bankers, or vice versa – US mobility is average at best. If we use the tougher measure of relative income mobility, the USA ranks very poorly – if anything lower than the UK, and certainly lower than countries such as Germany (East or West). It turns out that it is Scandinavian countries that consistently top measures of relative social mobility by income (see Figure 4.8). Interestingly, the normal Anglo-Saxon uniformity breaks down in this case, with Canada performing much better than the USA and UK.

The generally accepted explanation of this pattern is that low inequality goes with high social mobility. One way of thinking about this is that in more equal societies, the steps on the ladder of life are much closer together so that it is easier for people to make the inter-generational jump from one step to another. In countries such as the UK and USA, it is not just that the more advantaged do better in the education system – though this is true, and especially in the UK.[14] It's also that the more educated do better in the economy, with particularly high returns to education in the USA and UK.

Several conclusions can be drawn. First, it is possible to achieve higher levels of relative social mobility than currently seen in the UK and USA. Second, it is not an easy political way out. Some politicians

are attracted to the idea that high levels of inequality may be acceptable if this inequality co-exists with high levels of social mobility: a
meritocratic society. But the stubborn fact seems to be that equality and
social mobility generally go hand-in-hand. Sooner or later, a concern
with meritocracy and mobility brings you back to inequality, the details
of how advantage and disadvantage is transmitted, and to grey shades
of judgement about what is fair.

Inequality – One or Many?

As a number of thinkers have noted, inequalities would be OK as long
as they didn't sit together. If wealth, income, intelligence, beauty and
so on, were uncorrelated there could be plenty of inequality but still
no simple ranking of advantage and disadvantage.

Focusing on the UK, John Hills – a long-time leading researcher on
inequality – argues that something seemed to 'snap' in the connection
between the rich and poor in the late 1970s. The 1980s saw substantial
increases in all forms of inequality, such that it was not very interesting
to break it down into different measures. During this period, Britain
became a far more unequal society on most dimensions, with only
New Zealand notching higher rates of growth in inequality among
comparator OECD nations.[15]

From 1997, the picture changed. The Labour government made bold
commitments to reduce relative and absolute poverty, and introduced
a number of measures to help achieve this including tax credits (extra
income paid to those in low income work); raised child benefits; and
more generously funded state services in general. These policies led
to a much more even growth in incomes in the period post-1997 in
contrast to the previous two decades. But even all this effort simply
halted the growth in income inequality – and made little in-roads into
reversing it (see Figure 4.9).

If we look beyond income inequality, into some of the more hidden
forms of wealth, the post-'97 story gets more complicated. Hills argues
that while everyone was focusing on incomes, other forms of inequality
worsened. With a big growth in the value of housing, capital inequalities have risen too. It is now estimated that only around a third of
young people in the UK will acrue sufficient incomes and savings to
buy a house on their own. A further third will buy a house with help
from their parents or grandparents – help needed to overcome the
massive growth in the size of the cash deposit necessary to buy a house
over the last decade. At least a third of young people – those who lack
either a very high income or wealthy parents – have little or no prospects of ever buying a home. Sadly, despite falling house prices, the

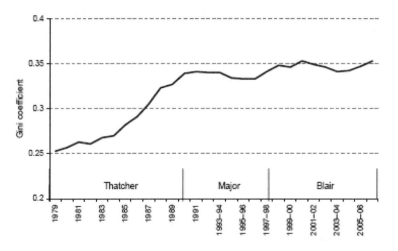

The Gini coefficient, 1979 to 2006–07 (GB)

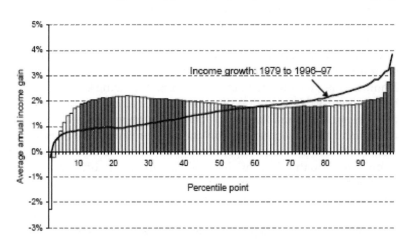

Real income growth by percentile point, 1996–97 to 2006–07 (GB)

Figure 4.9 *Changes in income inequality in the UK (IFS analysis, 2008).*

credit crunch has made the situation even worse. Though prices have fallen, access to credit has fallen even faster, leading to a net worsening in affordability for the capital-poor.[16]

In terms of financial capital, a new cycle and driver of inequality has emerged. Those families where the previous generation bought a house are now in a position to lever that asset to help their children, helping maintain the buoyancy of the housing market as they do so. In contrast, those who did not buy in the previous generation can do little to help their children and can only watch as housing prices and borrowing requirements continue to outstrip their ability to buy.

There is evidence for a similar dynamic playing out in terms of educational attainment. As a former Chief Economist at the Department for Education and Skills explained, 'trying to reduce educational inequality in the UK is like squeezing a long balloon – if you squeeze down in one place, it simply bulges out at the next'.[17] Sure enough, even as the government managed to reduce educational inequalities in say, the proportion of children getting basic qualifications at 16, the gap generally grew in terms of the numbers getting the next level of qualification. Similarly in Higher Education, new and expanding markets have emerged in post-degree qualifications as the more affluent seek additional ways to differentiate themselves from the increasing numbers of young people getting 'ordinary' degrees.

The differentiation in education and skills is not limited to formal educational qualifications. Social and emotional skills – or 'soft' skills – are a key differentiator in the labour market, and one that the best schools work hard to cultivate. Yet it is not a factor that has, to date, been measured by exams or the performance frameworks of local and national government. Empathy; an ability to read the intentions of others; and the ability to get on with other people, are 'people skills' that are valued by many employers and society as a whole. There is some evidence that one of the reasons why middle class kids were better able to take advantage of the expansions of Higher Education of the late 1980s was the effects of inequalities in such soft skills.

Surprisingly, given the growing understanding of their importance, there are very few systematic studies of social class differentials in soft skills, though psychologists have long since developed measures designed to capture them. This means that we have little idea whether inequalities in soft skills are growing, though we do have evidence that the financial returns to such skills are growing.

Finally, there is evidence of growing inequalities in what are known as 'social' and 'cultural' capitals. These terms are sometimes used interchangeably, but strictly speaking 'social capital' refers to social networks and to norms that facilitate trust and cooperation, while 'cultural capital' refers to having knowledge about the prevalent cultural activities of your society. In other words, social capital refers to how many people you know and if you can trust them, and cultural capital refers to how many books you've read and if you can hold a conversation about opera, football or ripsticks. Both can have powerful social and economic consequences.[18] For example, it has been estimated that around 80% of jobs are got through personal networks, so if all your friends are unemployed you are at a big disadvantage. In many countries, and especially in the UK, the poor have lower levels of social and cultural capital, and less valuable forms of them, and this helps to explain the propagation of disadvantage. There is also evidence that these gaps have become larger over time – at least in the UK. Through the 1980s and early 1990s, the poor became less connected, engaged and trusting, while the affluent have become more connected, engaged and trusting.

There are relatively few models that look at the impact of several of these capitals at once, or the interactions between them. There are none, to my knowledge, that look at the effects of all these capitals at once.

If we want to do something about deep-seated social and economic inequality, and to create a fairer and more meritocratic society, we will need to broaden our lines of attack – or more constructively, our lines of support. Government polices, in the UK and elsewhere, have tended to focus on a relatively limited range of the 'capitals' that affect life chances. A lot has happened around income support and financial incentives to get people into work, and quite a lot around seeking to address differentials in educational attainment, with at least some impact. But if truth be told, the downstream consequences have been smaller than many hoped. Earnings inequalities have remained stubbornly unchanged, and though the numbers in poverty have been reduced, it has been mainly by pulling those closest to the margin across it. Absolute attainment has been driven up, but educational inequalities and their strong links to parental background remain barely dented. And wider inequalities, such as in life expectancy or accident rates by social class remain similarly largely untouched.

If we sought to address the longer list of fundamental inequalities, would we have a bigger impact? There have been some interventions on this longer list, but these have been very modest in comparison to the billions spent on income support and classic education. For example, the UK government introduced the 'baby bond' to ensure that every child would have at least a small amount of capital when they reached 18. This policy was supported by evidence from longitudinal data that such capital inequalities had big impacts on life chances even having controlled for other known factors.[19] It seems that having a few

Capital or resource	Returns and trend
Employment (income)	Growing wage inequality and polarization into 'work rich' and work poor households through 1970s and 1980s. Effects partly capped by in-work benefits and other interventions, though the last decade has also seen a rise of the in-work poor.
Financial capital	Growth in property values, and polarization in cross-generational ability to support first purchase of home. Longitudinal data show marked impacts on later life chances of even relatively small capital endowments. There has been a large increase in the proportions of first-time buyers who have bought with the help of cash from their parents, up from less than 1 in 10 a decade ago to around 1 in 2 today.
Human capital (classic)	Reduction in some educational attainment gaps. But there is a particularly strong link between social class and attainment in UK and evidence of the emergence of new attainment gaps. Returns to Higher Education are strong and have, if anything, grown despite the rise in the number of graduates. While unemployment has generally fallen, it has risen among those with no formal skills or qualifications.
Human capital (soft skills)	Evidence of growing returns to soft skills in labour market, but scale and trend in social class gap uncertain.
Social capital	Strong returns to social capital. Evidence of widening gap in levels of social capital by class. Trend in returns unknown.
Cultural capital	Good evidence of returns, partly mediated by educational attainment. Large social class gaps. Trends unknown.

Figure 4.10 *Different capitals and indications of trends (UK).*

hundred pounds, or dollars, in the bank changes the major life choices that young people make. Analysis also shows that capital inequalities have a bigger impact than income on differentials in life satisfaction.

Critics argue that the size of such baby bonds will be too small to have the hoped for effect. An early proponent of the idea, Bruce Ackerman, suggested an endowment of US$80,000 per child. In the UK, Julian Le Grand (later the No. 10 health advisor) suggested an endowment of around £10,000 (US$20,000). Massive asset price inflation, notably in housing, has also raised the bar of capital costs and put a question mark over whether baby bonds, or child trust funds, of a few hundred pounds will be enough to really make a difference – either economically or psychologically.

There has been the beginning of a focus on soft skills – such as through the UK SEAL programme in UK primary schools or Roots of Empathy in Canada – but it remains very much the poor relative in the educational system. This is despite the evidence that pro-social behaviour in young children is often a better predictor of their subsequent educational attainment than their early cognitive ability.

Social capital has been talked about quite a bit, but we haven't done much about it. Supporting parenting skills has at last become a serious topic of policy concern, at least for the parents of children who are getting into trouble. But it is still the case that, while new parents get endless guidance on the process of birth, they can expect little or no guidance or support around what might make them more effective parents once the child is out of the womb. Similarly, while there is an endless stream of chatter about community, there is very little of rigour or robustness about what we actually might do about it, or how we might systematically build social trust (see Chapter 3). Few policymakers want to get into the minefield of how we might build more socially mixed communities and networks – or bridging social capital, as the literature calls it – and understandably so. At the same time, capital inequalities are providing a powerful new driver for social segregation, expressed through where we live, where our children go to school, or where we go to shop or play.

Finally, there has been some policy activity on cultural capital, but it has mainly been at the margins. A programme of ensuring that all children have at least some books at home has been developed – noting that the number of books that a child has at home is a significant predictor of later outcomes. Free entry to public museums and art galleries may also have been a powerful equalizer, though the evidence from many cultural organizations is that most of their activity remains very skewed towards the middle classes, while the traditional bastions of working class culture – such as working mens' clubs – are close to vanishing. This decline might be of no concern if such clubs were being replaced by cultural activities that bridged across the class divide, but the evidence tends to suggest that cultural consumption is becoming more fragmented and privatized.

Of course, the cruellest effects are seen when many of these 'poverties' combine, and particularly their impact on the children in such households. When doing work on social exclusion, we sought to estimate the long-term impact on a 10-year-old child of experiencing multiple disadvantages on their outcomes at age 30. We found that around half of the children who came from the 5% of households with the most disadvantages had 12 or more problems or disadvantages by the age of 30 (such as poor educational attainment, unemployment, contact with the law and so on). In comparison with children from the top 50% of households, these children from the bottom 5% were more than 300 times more likely to end up with 12-plus problems as adults – an astonishing and shocking statistic by any reckoning.[20]

At the end of the chapter, we will turn to some of the kinds of policy ideas that might flow from a consideration of a broader range of inequalities. But first we need to ask, what is the appetite among the public for doing something about it?

Values and Sympathies

Before you turn the page and look at the next figure, reflect for a moment on what *you think* that people in different countries would answer when asked, 'Do you think that the incomes between the rich and poor in your country should be made more equal, or do you think that we need larger income differences?' You are asked to give your answer on a ten-point scale, where '1' means 'incomes should be made more equal' and '10' means 'we need larger income differences as incentives'.

You will recall that levels of inequality vary greatly between countries. On the one hand, the richest 20% of Brazilians earn more than 25 times that of the poorest 20% (and the richest 10% earn more than 60 times that of the poorest 10%). Similar high levels of income inequality are seen across Latin America, or countries such as South Africa, rooted partly in highly skewed land ownership (and the absence of land reform). In contrast, in countries such as Sweden or Japan, the top 20% earn less than four times that of the poorest 20%.

It took quite a while to put this graph together. I suppose I naively thought that people living in the breath-taking inequality of South America would want to see the gap between the incomes of the rich

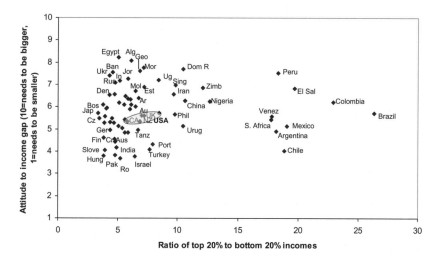

Figure 4.11 *Support for reducing or increasing income inequality versus actual income inequality by country. Remarkably, there appears to be no overall relationship. Income inequality is shown as the ratio of the top 20% of incomes to the bottom 20%. The attitudinal data is from the World Values Survey 2004.*

and poor reduced. On the other hand, I could well imagine – being a good Anglo-Saxon – that many of the residents of the high-tax, high benefit, low income inequality countries like Japan, Sweden, Norway, Denmark and Finland might feel more of a case for gently increasing income gaps to encourage incentives.

Of course, you've probably figured it out by now, and maybe you're a little less naïve than me: it turns out that there is no relationship between a nation's level of income inequality and the desire of its citizens to see the gap between rich and poor get bigger or smaller. The correlation is a non-significant 0.06 – effectively zero.[21]

It's not that there are no differences. People in high income-inequality Chile are quite keen on seeing a reduction in income inequality – yet people in equally high income inequality Peru say that the gap should be bigger. Similarly, people in low inequality Egypt or Bangladesh think that the income gap should be bigger – but people in similarly modest income inequality India and Pakistan want to reduce the gap.

There is some logic to where countries fall on the graph. For example, the citizens of recently economically liberalized countries such as Hungary, Slovenia and Romania would like to see income gaps closed – presumably a reaction to the harsh new wind of capitalism. On the other hand, the citizens of the relatively economically unreformed nations of Georgia, Ukraine and Russia, despite similar levels of inequality to their Eastern European neighbours, are much more keen on seeing income inequalities rise to support incentives.

There's not much relationship with overall wealth either, though there is a slight tendency for richer countries to favour reducing the gap between rich and poor.[22]

In the midst of this pattern, the UK along with other Anglo-Saxon countries can be seen in a tight cluster at the centre of the graph. Within the cluster, the USA has the highest level of inequality of the group, though Americans, if anything, lean towards favouring still more inequality relative to their Anglo-Saxon cousins. At the other end, the relatively low inequality Canadians lean, if anything, towards favouring still lower inequality relative to the rest of the group. The UK, Australia and NZ lie in between.

Other analysis shows that these value-based differences seem to have real consequences on how people feel about the world and about themselves. Hence we find that variations in income inequality have much bigger and more negative impacts on the happiness of Europeans than on North Americans – Europeans are literally unhappy about increases in inequality in a way that Americans do not seem to be.

I think these are remarkable and sobering results. In general, it looks like people get used to whatever level of inequality they have experienced – or that people get the society that they wish for. But there is a final hopeful twist to this story. Social attitude data show that during recessions, sympathy for the poor and unemployed tends to rise, and tolerances for the excesses of the very wealthy falls.[23] So if there ever was a time to revisit fairness and inequality, it is now.

Attitudes to Inequality in the UK

We saw earlier that levels of income inequality rose rapidly in 1980s Britain, and then flattened – as a result of extensive government effort – in the late 1990s and early 2000s. Did these changes impact on public attitudes?

The British Social Attitudes first asked Britons in 1987 whether they thought the gap between high and low incomes was 'too large'.[24] During this time of rapidly increasing income inequality and high unemployment, 79% agreed that the gap was too large. By 1991, after four years of further, but slowing, income–inequality growth, the percentage remained unchanged on 79%.

Under John Major, albeit partly as a result of problems with the economy, income inequality fell from 1991 to 1995, yet public concern about the gap between high and low incomes actually rose to 87%. By 1999, when Tony Blair pledged to halve child poverty by 2010 and to eliminate it within a generation, the percentage had dropped back to 81%, where it roughly stayed through to 2002. By 2004, it dropped a little further to 73%, and in the 2006 data had eased back up marginally to 76%. In other words, over the last twenty years, around three-quarters of the British public have typically felt that the gap between high and low incomes is too large more or less regardless of inequality. It moved up a bit in the years before the 1997 general election perhaps reflecting the profile given to it by Labour (since inequality wasn't rising much in that period) – and has since fallen back slightly, even though inequality again hasn't changed much.[25]

However, what is probably more interesting, and more relevant to policymakers, is what happened to public attitudes around what government should *do* about this gap. By the late 1990s when Labour came to power, a clear majority of the public – 64% – agreed that the 'government was responsible for reducing differences in income'. But by 2004, this had fallen to a minority of just 43%.

A similar story is seen in public support for the tools that governments have traditionally used to reduce poverty and inequality. The proportion agreeing that 'government should spend more on welfare benefits for the poor' fell from a peak of 58% in 1991 to 36% by 2004. And the percentage agreeing with the statement 'government should redistribute income from the better off to those who are less well off' fell from a peak of 47% in 1995 to 32% by 2004.

In short, while a large majority of the public still feel that the gap between the rich and poor is too large, only around a third now support doing something about it through the traditional tools of redistribution or benefits. This puts politicians in a difficult situation. It could reflect a public intuition that income support alone won't fix the problem (see multiple capitals argument above), or simply that the public, while not liking inequality, don't really want to pay the price to fix it.

What Do we Do? Between Weber and Laissez-faire

Peter Kenway has dedicated much of his life to the careful documentation of poverty and disadvantage. I first met him in 1996 at a small gathering in Oxford to discuss the potential policy programme in the event of a Labour government, along with several extremely young aids of the then Labour leadership. With funding from Joseph Rowntree Foundation – the living legacy of the same family that so prominently championed the issue more than a century ago – Kenway went on to track meticulously every trend he could get his hands on for the decade and a half since.

I saw Peter again recently when he was presenting to a conference in Cambridge on the big policy choices facing the UK today. Though very supportive of much of what the Government had done and achieved, his conclusion was that 'we are seeing the end point of a dominant paradigm on poverty reduction, social justice and inequality in the UK'. I was pretty surprised to hear him, of all people, put it so bluntly, but I can certainly understand how he has reached that conclusion.

The post-'97 UK experiment – a recap

In the first two years after being elected, the Labour Administration was hemmed in by a commitment to stay within previous Conservative spending figures. An early move was to create a Social Exclusion Unit to focus on some specific and high-profile issues, such as street homelessness and children who had been excluded from schools – focused rather than large-scale drives. Similarly, the 1998 Welfare Reform Green paper was mainly focused on getting people back into work rather than reducing poverty *per se* – noting that work itself was seen as a way of reconnecting people with the economy and society. A drive to improve the quality of state education, and particularly reduce the number of children – typically from more disadvantaged backgrounds – leaving school without basic skills such as reading and writing was also present right from the start, and has remained a prominent strand in policy ever since.

In 1999, Blair made his historic and ambitious pledge to end child poverty within a generation. From this point on there was a gear change in effort to do something about low incomes, with year on year increases in both benefits (notably child benefit) and in-work tax-credits – both to help 'make work pay' and to reduce poverty.

During the second term, the attack on disadvantage developed further attention shifting to the early years. This started with the offer of pre-school provision for three to four year olds, and was soon joined by the ambitious 'SureStart programme' to develop a network of centres to offer support for parents with infants. The gradual ratcheting up of child, pensioner and in-work benefits continued. Other programmes were also intended to ease the plight of the most disadvantaged, particularly the massive cash injections (and reform) of the public services. There was a major injection of cash into the National Health Service; spending on state schools continued to rise sharply with a programme of rebuilding and replacing underperforming schools (which were disproportionately in poorer areas); and there was a major programme of neighbourhood renewal spending targeted on poor areas. Even drives to reduce crime, such as through the expansion in the numbers of PCSOs, or the drive to reduce anti-social behaviour, arguably offered disproportionate benefit to the most disadvantaged, given that poorer areas tended to be most blighted by crime.

By the 2005 election, though overshadowed by Iraq, many of the same themes continued – ensuring a fair deal for the hard-working and aspirational poor and middle classes (but leaving the wealthy alone); continuing drives on crime and anti-social behaviour, notably the Respect agenda (see previous chapters); and investment and reform of public services. But with a tightening fiscal situation, and little public support for redistribution, Whitehall began to quietly lose enthusiasm for Blair's bold pledge to end poverty.

In the wake of the 'Respect' agenda, and in the final 18 months before standing down, Blair revisited the issue of the most disadvantaged in society one last time – specifically those families and individuals who came in contact with multiple public services at great cost but with little apparent benefit either to themselves or the community. We had a series of detailed discussions over how broad this 'social exclusion' drive should go, pouring over detailed analyses of the life histories, experiences and causes behind those who seemed to be doing worst in our society. It was as much a story about institutional and public service failure, with an added concern that our systems of performance management could be making the situation worse. In the face of many of our public service targets in education, health or benefits, many institutions were rationally focusing their efforts on the 'easier' end of disadvantage. Why spend great effort and expense on the most complicated and difficult cases, which often seemed doomed to fail, when the same amount of effort might turn around the problems of several easier cases?

Our models showed that around 2.5% of the population – drawn from less than 1 in 20 families – showed a pattern of deeply entrenched social exclusion. A typical case would be that of a child born to a poor and dysfunctional family, almost invariably with a background of low or absent educational skills in the family, with parents drifting in and out of the criminal justice system; problems with neighbours and often with a serious but undiagnosed mental health issue in the household. The life of such a child from such a high-risk background could often be characterized by what psychologists call 'heterotypic continuity' – problems manifested in different ways and at different ages, but nonetheless clustered around the same at-risk individuals. Warning signs tended to include: low birth-weight; educational underachievement; truancy; early contact with the police; early abuse of drugs and alcohol; early sexual activity; entry into the care system; teenage pregnancy; mental health problems; and entry into the criminal justice system. The response, published in the Social Exclusion Action plan in September 2006, was a shift to an unprecedented level of prediction and early supportive intervention. The emblematic policy was the piloting in the UK of the 'Nurse Family Partnership' model of pre-birth and first two years of life intervention focusing on the most at-risk first-time young mothers, resourced primarily by re-focusing the attentions of health visitors away from the more demanding to those most in need of support but least likely to ask for it.[26]

Reflecting back on this decade long experiment, and on where Blair finally ended up, there are several different stories you can tell.

First, you can tell a story about how the late Blair drive on social exclusion was rooted in the relative successes of the poverty reduction programmes of the previous decade. Compared with pre 1997 there were: 2.5 million extra people in work; 2.4 million lifted above the relative poverty line; a million pensioners lifted out of poverty; and more than half million children lifted out of relative poverty, moving the UK from highest levels of child poverty in Europe in 1997 to close to average by 2007. While it is true that much of this change has been about pulling a group of people from just below the poverty line to just above it, the investment in public services and even the indications that relative social mobility may have increased for the first time on record suggest that these changes were much more than cosmetic. One can argue that it was precisely against this background of progress on 'mainstream poverty' that the lack of progress of the most excluded stood out.

There was also a political twist to this story, elegantly espoused by my colleague Paul Corrigan within No. 10, and more publicly by Cabinet Office and Social Exclusion Minister Hilary Armstrong. Paul argued that a strong presumption of the left for decades had been that what you had to do to reduce poverty and make society more fair was to provide a variety of social benefits and to dismantle the barriers that acted to exclude a minority. This strategy had knocked down the 'deciles of poverty' like a row of dominos through the course of a hundred years. But the last domino had refused to fall. The left had found, much to its surprise and some discomfort, that it wasn't enough for those most deeply entrenched in poverty to dismantle the barriers to the mainstream. Rather, government and services had to actively pull, or even drag, the most excluded into the mainstream.

There is a second, and more negative story that can be told. It is rooted in the relative modesty of the New Labour drive to reduce poverty and the lack of a reduction in inequality despite the scale of spending and effort. Viewed through this lens, the late Blair revisiting of social exclusion is a story of retreat, if not despair. It is also a story of continuity, implicitly suggesting that inequality is deeply rooted – if not inseparable – in the nature of British, and perhaps Anglo-Saxon, society and economy. The Conservative Minister Peter Lilley had rehearsed very similar arguments about social exclusion, and the failure of services to grip the issue, more than a decade earlier. One could say that there was nothing new here – either in the nature of the problem or in the difficulty of doing anything about it.

One serious line of thought that follows from this account, quietly voiced on both left and right, is that we should change our ambitions. Rather than making poverty reduction and equality the measure of justice and fairness, we should instead focus on more realistic and culturally comfortable measures of justice, such as decency, mutual respect and universal access to decent – if not equal – services and opportunities.

The third story is more technocratic, but still important. The revisiting of social exclusion brought with it a deeper account of the causes of entrenched disadvantage, as well as a significantly broader account of what would have to be done to address it. Although building on an existing line of policy travel towards prevention rather than cure, it pushed the boundaries of prevention to a new level. It was also premised on an ability to predict; on a much broader and arguably more personal and relational intervention; a de-emphasizing of income *per se*; and on an extensive re-engineering of public services around the individuals and their families. The radicalism of this shift was graphically illustrated by the reaction of the BBC interviewer, Mark Easton, when interviewing Blair on the subject in September 2006 at Chequers. It was the first television interview of the Prime Minister after the Summer recess, and Mark was using the normal pressing questions to try and find a good line or soundbite. He started pushing on the idea that the way the PM was talking sounded like he thought you could predict who would end up poor, pregnant or in prison while they were still in nappies. Easton nearly fell off his seat when the PM not only agreed but said '. . . or pre-birth'. Of course the papers loved it, and the next morning the phrase 'FASBO' was born – fetal anti-social behaviour order.[27]

Was where Blair ended up the last gasp of a traditional big-spending state, or was it an early marker of a new kind of approach –

an 'authoritative' approach to social justice and poverty reduction in the decade to come?

National Differences

The policy responses to poverty, inequality and injustice will vary widely across countries. Citizenship – as famously argued by Marshall – consists of several elements which took centuries of struggle to develop in most industrialized nations. Civil rights, included both basic civil liberties such as freedom of speech as well as the right to own property, form and enforce contracts and access to a just process of law. Some countries – riven by conflict, war and endemic corruption – still lack these basic civil processes and effective legal institutions to deliver even the most rudimentary notions of justice and security to their people.

In other countries, political rights – the entitlement to participate in the exercise of political power – remains uneven or incomplete. The argument rages in the 'development industry' about the pragmatic compromises that might be necessary around political rights in relatively immature democracies, and especially where deep ethnic and social cleavages combine with limited basic protections of human rights or minority interests. But few seriously question the moral logic and deep human desire for some control over our own destiny and, for all its imperfections, the self-evident spread of democracy.

Social rights – Marshall's third category – he saw as the most recent and incomplete. He referred to them as:

> ... from the right to a modicum of economic welfare and security to the right to share in the full social heritage and to live the life of a civilized being according to the standards prevailing in the society. The institutions most closely connected with it are the education system and the social services.
>
> Marshall (1950), p. 11[28]

This chapter has focused most explicitly on this third area, but it is clearly not the only bit of the story even in mature democracies such as the USA or UK. There is also the question of what else we would add to Marshall's list of rights more than half a century ago – a time when rations were still in place and survival values dominated people's world views. For example, how would Marshall have viewed the 15-point differential in satisfaction with relationships across social classes in the UK today? And what of responsibilities, as well as rights, in an age when so many of the challenges we face are behavioural?

Policy Ideas for the Next Decade

The following discussion focuses primarily on the UK. It may be that some of these ideas are relevant to other countries, but that is something I will leave the reader to decide.

1. It's not only income, but . . .

It will be pretty obvious from the discussion above that there's more to the dynamics of inequality, and the question of fairness, than equalizing income. That said, we are clearly not anywhere near the end game of needing to provide income support for millions of people. As is well rehearsed, other kinds of rights don't mean much without the most basic financial means to take advantage of them, especially for the benefit of children and dependants.

Given limited public support for traditional redistribution, and genuine social and economic concerns about the incentive effects built into benefits, there is near consensus that future changes to benefits are likely to be highly differentiated. The rise of in-work poverty is a major concern and strongly suggests the need for continued expansions in in-work benefits and refinements to the Incapacity Benefit (IB) regime. The spectacular variations in IB claims across the country are a strong indication of the problem. It is perfectly understandable that there are much higher IB claims among the over 50s in areas of previous big industries such as coal mining, but it is much harder to understand the rise of even greater inequalities in IB claims in the under 35s.

The 'tough love' reforms of making work pay, together with continuing reforms around the incentives on, and competition between, service providers that are trying to get people into work – and to progress within work – will need to continue, not reduce.

2. Capital inequalities

The UK is not unique in terms of the rises we have seen in house prices and other fixed assets, but we are especially prone to this compounding with other forms of inequality to provide a powerful new driver of cross-generational injustice. I have a specific proposal about what we might do on inheritances (below), but we also need to fix the underlying problem of inflated land prices and restricted supply.

We need to change the underlying incentives in the planning system to increase the supply of housing in the UK. In essence this means channelling economic planning gains much more directly to nearby residents, together with taking a slightly more relaxed attitude to the 'green-belt' in the South East.

We have nudged in this direction, particularly with moves to allow Local Authorities to retain more of the planning gain in tax receipts. But we haven't gone anywhere near far enough. To paraphrase Steve Nickell, the residents of cities like Oxford and Cambridge – especially those close to green-belt sites – could be offered zero council tax for 10 years (or a cash auction between developers) for residents' support.

Politicians are terrified of this issue and the charge of 'concreting over the South East'. Leaving aside the bogus environmental arguments often employed (see also Chapter 1), a more rational set of mechanisms of compensation and incentives for residents most affected should essentially pass the real choice onto citizens. And since the value of land is highest in the most desirable areas, a properly constructed price mechanism built into our planning system should lead to development which is both efficient and just. Interestingly, when citizens are asked about whether we should build more houses so that our children can have somewhere to live, a majority do support development.[29]

Increasing the supply of land for housing is doubly redistributive. It should increase long-term affordability of housing so that the 30 to 40% of young people, who currently have no prospect of ever buying their own homes however hard they work, will gradually acquire the option. Secondly, the changes will halt the spiralling growth in asset values that is driving not only headline capital inequalities but also the polarization of neighbourhoods on the back of house prices.

There is also a case for radically expanding the idea of the 'baby bond' – the policy of trying to make sure that every child has a small financial nest egg when they reach 18. At present, every young person has in effect an invisible capital asset in the form of the State's commitment to part-finance their education at university or college. I think we should turn this into a formal capital endowment rather than concealing it and limiting it to direct grants to educational institutions.

We should consider radically expanding personal endowments to 18 year olds by channelling current student and skills budgets directly to individuals. These endowments could be partly means tested but would typically amount to around £10,000 per young person. These personal endowments could be spent at a pre-agreed list of educational establishments, in the UK and overseas, but could also be used for other purposes such as starting a business (or possibly buying a house) with the joint permission of a family and state 'trustee'.[30]

Some young people – such as those in the care system – should be given very much more substantial endowments, together with more robust trustee arrangements.[31] In the UK, only a handful of the 60,000 plus children who pass through the care system every year make it to university, though sadly they are hugely over-represented in our prisons and other custodial institutions. How can it be either morally, or economically, right that those who have been in care are 5 times less likely to get to university than other young people, but roughly 25 times more likely to end up in prison (which of course is a lot more expensive than university)?[32]

This system of endowments would also help address a number of other public policy issues, including the current inequities around how we pay for affluent students to go to prestigious universities, while often failing to pay for the development of skills for those who choose other paths or lack the intellectual talents for a traditional university education. An important sweetener for the relatively affluent would be the additional flexibility to use the endowment at a wider range of institutions, including universities in North America or Australia.

Endowments can also be usefully twinned with what we know about behavioural economics to allow students to pay for their first year at university outright, and only to borrow later on in their courses. The evidence is that poorer students and their families are most worried about debt and borrowing. The endowment system would allow them to try out the first year or two at college without debt. By this time poorer students will have become much more familiar with how debt can be structured – through their new middle class peers – and would be much closer to the end of the degree and the reality of extra earnings that will follow completion.

Finally, there is a strong case for reforming death duties and inheritance rules – not to try and eliminate inheritance, but to make it a little more progressive. Let me state the proposal, which may seem counter-intuitive at first, then explain why it would be progressive.

We should create simple 'descendents trusts' to encourage people to bequeath their assets to their grandchildren and great-grandchildren rather than leaving them to their children. These might be encouraged by favourable tax treatment up to a certain limit of trust value.

Here's why its progressive. Around two-thirds of people now have significant capital assets in their homes. When they die, the assets tend to be given to their surviving partner, then onto their children – typically by then in their fifties or sixties. The correlation between a father and son's income is about 0.5. But this relationship decays across generations: in rough figures the correlation with the grandchild's income will be around 0.25, and with great-grandchildren's income about 0.125. Each passing generation gradually regresses back to the mean – looking more and more like the general population. In other words, even if you are quite wealthy, it is very likely that at least some of your grandchildren and great-grandchildren will have dropped out of your social class, whereas your children are much more likely to be in the same class as you.

If even half of those who die with capital wealth passed on their assets into descendents trusts instead of straight to their children, within two generations the vast majority of the population would be covered by such trusts. There is a significant complication, however, which is assortive mating – people tending to have children with those from a similar social class background. This means that some people will tend to have more rich grandparents than would be expected by chance alone, and will end up with several descendent trusts while a few will end up with none. This slows the spreading effect, but does not eliminate it. The extent of this slowing depends on absolute levels of assertive mating – currently estimated at about 0.3 but with evidence that it has been rising. But it could be offset by some tapered tax arrangements on the recipient of the descendents trust. For example, we might say that it would be tax free below a certain threshold of total descendents trust capital received, but at very high levels – often resulting where an individual had several trusts from their eight great-grandparents – some tax would be applied.

It would still be the case in thirty or fifty years' time that some individuals will be unlucky enough to have had no great or great-great grandparents with the assets or inclination to set aside a descendants' trust. Society might judge that these individuals might have their personal endowments (see above) topped up at a higher rate. This could then be done at relatively modest cost, since they would only be a small proportion of the total population.[33]

Some people may want to build more elaborate conditions into their descendents trusts, and this should be made easy with a number of off-the-shelf options. For example, trusts could be designed to give extra help to any descendents with especially high needs, such as resulting from illness or disability. In this way, we would make it easy for trusts to act as 'micro-welfare states', further increasing their progressive impact. Others might want to vary the conditions attached to pay-outs, such as biasing them towards educational purposes. But some conditions might be ruled out, such as only allowing sons to benefit, or the excluding of beneficiaries on the basis of the ethnicity or religion of those who they marry.

How would a 'descendants trust' work?

Mr and Mrs Brown owned a house worth £180,000. When they died, after bills and the money they borrowed for care and a world cruise were paid off, the estate was worth £120,000. Of this, they left £40,000 to their two children – now in their mid-50s – and to a local charity. The remaining £80,000 was used to form a Brown family trust.

The Browns had four grandchildren ranging in age from their late teens to mid-twenties. The trust almost immediately paid out £10,000 to the oldest two grandchildren, one of whom used the money for a down-payment on a flat while the other used it towards college fees. The remaining money was reinvested. When each of the other grandchildren reached age 18, they were also given just over £10,000 each (the extra money from the investment ensures that they receive the same in real terms as their older siblings).

The trust investment now grows quietly for more than twenty years, by which time the Browns have eight great-grandchildren, but the fund has doubled in value in real terms. So as each of the great-grandchildren reaches 18, they can receive a payment equivalent in real terms to the £10,000 that their parents got. In fact, one of the great-grandchildren had mental health issues, so the trust held onto their money until they were 25 and were well enough to set up on their own.

At this point, more than 35 years after it was set up by the Browns, the trust was closed. However, several of the Browns descendants had in turn set up new trusts, continuing the new family tradition.

---

3. Human capital, more broadly conceived

Education matters for lots of reasons, including social justice. The restless drive to crank up educational attainment, and to squeeze out underperforming schools, is clearly a 'no brainer' both on economic and justice grounds. It was also right to extend the state offer of provision into the early years, given the strong evidence that social class attainment gaps were substantially in place by age five, and that access to high quality pre-school provision can greatly close the gap and improve long-term prospects.

There are ideas that merit further attention to improve the educational attainment of children from less advantaged backgrounds. For example, while class sizes have generally been found to have relatively modest effects on attainment, class sizes at key educational transitions have big impacts – notably at reception into primary school. Smaller class sizes at these key junctions benefit all children, but disproportionately benefit those from poorer backgrounds and those who are struggling. It would also make sense to ensure that the extra money that government assigns for poorer children in schools actually reaches them, and that targets move towards value-added measures and away from threshold targets that inadvertently encourage educators to focus on children close to the margins. When using such budgets, it is important to note that much of the educational gap between children opens up in the periods when children are outside of school, for example, it is during the summer school holidays that the gap in reading and other educational skills between children of different socio-economic backgrounds opens the fastest.

Reduce reception class sizes to 15 or fewer; introduce an individual child budget to be held in trust by school and parent that can be used for extra tuition or other support, including holiday activities; and move to value-added targets.

These types of interventions are likely to do more for closing the educational gap than, for example, the building of shiny new buildings or computer rooms to impress parents.

Yet human capital is about more than conventional cognitive skills, such as reading, writing and maths. We have known for some time that 'soft skills' are also very important, though rarely measured. Indeed, soft skills often mediate more formal educational attainment. For example, it has been found that measures of 'pro-social' behaviour in young children, such as empathizing with and helping other children, are often better predictors of subsequent educational attainment than early measures of cognitive ability.

If we shift our attention to a wider set of outcomes – such as getting employment, avoiding criminal offending and avoiding teenage pregnancy and early drop-out – social and emotional skills loom even larger. And as we move towards an ever more service-based economy, the importance of these soft skills, and the returns to having them, loom ever larger.

But policy focus on the 'softer' side of human capital has been a pale shadow of the effort focused on traditional cognitive skills, for several reasons. First is the widespread belief that soft skills cannot be measured. This is just wrong, though clearly there are challenges associated with using such measures in a formal performances assessment process for schools, since such scales will often need to be filled in by teachers or educational psychologists who may be employed by the school itself. Second, there is uncertainty over how such skills can be promoted. This is an appropriate concern, but there do exist a large number of techniques and programmes to start with. And third is nervousness that talking about soft skills could be an unhelpful distraction from the serious business of getting kids to read and write. However, since soft and hard skills are generally complementary – and no one is saying to give up on the latter – this argument doesn't feel very convincing.

Make hard measures of soft skills widely available, and put the same kind of effort into driving soft skills in the next decade as we did for literacy and numeracy in the former.

In broad terms, I think we are about ten or fifteen years behind the literacy and numeracy strategy in terms of where we are with soft skills. We sort of know it's important, but tell ourselves something like 'it's something that good schools and teachers already do, and it's not something you can teach the rest'.

The UK has introduced the SEAL programme for primary schools, which is a significant step in the right direction. However, there are questions about the evidence on which the programme is based, as well as its emphasis on self-esteem. There are a number of approaches out there, such as the Canadian 'Roots of Empathy' programme or the Seligman Pennsylvania programme (the latter being trialled in a handful of schools in the UK). Cross-age classes and mentoring also look promising. Such forms of teaching and activities can allow older children to develop maturity, nurturing and responsibility (even if they may be academically struggling) and also helpfully disrupt some of the problematic same age dominance rivalries that can undermine same-age classroom settings.[34]

We need to carefully evaluate these programmes, as well as other approaches that although not explicitly designed to promote social skills may be better at it than programmes that have such skills as their main focus. For example, the 'Teens and Toddlers' programme in which young people do voluntary work looking after an infant in a childcare setting while also receiving personal development and counselling may be much more effective than conventional class-based approaches to developing empathy, self-awareness and other soft skills. Similarly, we should investigate variations in the social skills of young people across schools and identify any patterns in school practices that help to explain them. We could then use this information to inform and shape better practice.

Just as it took a few years for the evidence for synthetic phonetics to filter through to practice, it will take a few years for us to refine our approach to soft skills. But even a cursory inspection of some of the most successful – and equitable – educational systems in the world, such as Finland or Canada, shows how they go to great trouble in the early years to nurture the social and emotional well-being and skills of their young people. After all, as developmental psychologists have long since told us, it is the child's entry into the social world on which all future learning and development is premised. From the early meshing of parental babble with their new-born infant, through to the endless negotiation among young children over what to play, getting along with other people is the true foundation of successful individuals and societies.

4. Social capital

Social networks and mutual trust have value, both to individuals and societies. Whether you can get a job or not; how much you get paid; how much things cost you; how well you do in school; whether you smoke or drink; how long you live; and whether you end up as the victim of serious crime all depend heavily on your social capital. Unfortunately, it also turns out to be highly unevenly distributed. If you come from a well-connected family and background, the chances are that this will take you where you want to get to in life. If not, you'd better work twice as hard at school, and instead hope that your human capital will make up for the difference.[35]

Generally speaking, the most difficult social capital to build, but also the most socially valuable, is what researchers call 'bridging social capital' – that is links between people of different social classes, ethnicity, religion or age. The most well-rehearsed policy lever is to try and stimulate socially mixed schools and neighbourhoods. For example, it is better to avoid large tracts of social housing, and instead mix small pockets inside more affluent areas (at least for the benefit of the children who live in such housing).[36] Similarly, there has been much controversy over the years in the UK and elsewhere about the selection methods employed by schools. The politically tough finding is that everyone benefits from being with the most able and affluent children or students. Hence while social (and ability) mixing greatly benefits students from poorer backgrounds, it tends to have a small negative effect on the most able and affluent who otherwise might have clustered together.

My own reading of the literature is that your best bet is to go hard for social mixing but be a bit more relaxed about selection or clustering on the basis of ability. On the old British question about what to do with Grammar Schools (schools that select the most able), the evidence suggests that disadvantaged kids who get into these schools do indeed do much better than equivalent kids who stay at mixed ability schools.

The real problem is that far fewer children from poor backgrounds, despite their ability, end up going to such schools.[37]

Consider requiring schools to take a socially representative intake of the larger catchment area within which they are situated (not just the immediate few streets).

There is a case for creating a positive incentive for mixing, such as the talented 20 scheme in the USA within which the top 20 students of every school are guaranteed a place at university. This would create an incentive for some middle class parents to stay in their local school rather than abandon it, and might get some extra young people from low performing schools to university. However, the same objectives can probably be more efficiently delivered through a combination of a premium payment for poor or high need students; school-adjusted selection by universities (i.e. adjusting applicants' grades for the average grades in the school they studied at); and requiring schools to draw a socially balanced intake from a wider catchment.

Creating socially mixed residential areas has been the good intention of successive governments, with only moderate success. Residential sorting by wealth – a key driver of why the world is tending to get 'spikier' – shows little sign of reducing, and growing capital inequalities are making it more of an issue, not less. We can at least try and avoid some of the more obvious errors, such as geographically concentrated social housing, as many social landlords already try and do – and of course, try and do something about capital inequalities in the medium to long term (see the proposals around capital inequalities above).

There are a whole range of things that can be done to boost social capital and the current growing inequalities within it. One important prerequisite and linked idea is to boost social and emotional skills, as noted above. I have documented social capital-building proposals elsewhere, but let me highlight a couple that I think are especially promising because of their ability to provide 'bridging' across social groups.

Local and central government efforts should be focused on building social capital across social cleavages such as the work-rich versus work-poor, or across ethnicity or class. Examples include using ICT to support local collective action (such as neighbourhood pledge-banks); compiling neighbour directories; and supporting complementary currencies and Local Exchange Trading Schemes. There is also a strong case for supporting 2 to 6-week voluntary programmes or service by young people, taking care to ensure a high degree of social mixing.

I think we have genuine grounds to be concerned about the extent of social disconnection at both the top and bottom of society. As discussed in the previous chapter, I think that there is a case for expecting all able adults in society to have to make a non-financial, time-based contribution to society. There are a lot of important details about how this might work, including how to ensure that contributions are not gamed or 'misspent', but I think it is a road that we need to explore.

We should consider whether all able adults should be expected to contribute a minimum number of hours of community or local service, such as six hours a year, or 350 hours over a lifetime. Contributing hours might include, for example, for the care of non-kin; mentoring or coaching in school; or the supervision or maintenance of local communal spaces or parks.

What about sanctions for those few who don't want to do any service? I suspect that positive sanctions – such as publishing local or neighbourhood lists of contributions should do most of the heavy lifting. It's essentially about creating a positive dynamic, rather than punishing a lack of contribution. But it is possible you could have some stronger sanctions, such as a periodic reckoning – say at age 50 and on death – resulting in a thank you in recognition of contributions made for most, but a fine for those who did nothing.

Finally, we might note that families remain the key building block of social capital as well as much more. Both left and right have come to recognize that the state may have to intervene in the support of families though much uncertainty remains as to how. A key statistic is that a child born outside marriage will on average spend a far longer period of their childhood with only one parent present: 7.8 years for those born outside a live-in partnership; 4.7 years for those born in cohabiting unions; but just 1.6 years for those born in marriage. In raw social capital terms, let alone in terms of emotional development and household income, these are big differences with substantial consequences.[38]

More active policies to support stable family formation must be a high priority for future policymakers.

Interestingly, research shows that relationship failure can often be highly accurately predicted even from a relatively short 20-minute observation of a couple by a trained psychologist. For example, the ratio of negative to positive comments made is a key predictor. For every negative comment made about a partner, there needs to be about three positive comments to make up for it (see Chapter 1). Fall below this level, and the relationship is probably doomed.

There are a myriad of practical and political problems about the state getting involved in such personal relationships, but if you are interested in equitable outcomes for kids, someone will have to. Free, evidence-based advice (we should all take the negative-to-positive test if we had any sense!); parenting classes; and intensive support pro-grammes such as the Nurse Family Partnership for the most at risk are all strong candidates. There may also be more structural interven-tions that could help, such as ensuring greater symmetries in earning power across genders or even seeking to avoid gender imbalances in population numbers.[39]

5. Cultural capital

The spreading of cultural capital is perhaps the most difficult and controversial to get a policy handle on. This is partly because it feels much more inherently value and preference based. Who is to say what constitutes the basic cultural needs of the typical citizen? Do we all need to have a basic working knowledge of opera, football, and the main TV soaps? Isn't it enough to equip citizens with the other types of capital and leave them to decide what aspects of culture to acquire or consume?

Interestingly, despite these concerns, we do spend a lot of effort and resources to make sure that citizens – and especially young people – have access to and acquire cultural capital. In the UK, for example, we have made access to most museums free, and have an extensive system of public sector broadcasting (financed largely through a not especially equitable TV licensing fee). Most countries have some kind of core cul-tural curriculum in schools which teaches children about their nation's cultural and institutional traditions, as well as equipping them with a set of shared cultural reference points in the form of stories, metaphors and histories.

I am personally a little wary of state-based prescriptions or lists of cultural experiences that all children or citizens should have. For the most part, it feels like schools, families and communities should figure this out for themselves. That said, I think we should make sure that all young people have got sufficient resources to be able to experience a range of cultural activities, even if they are not all the same. This is one of the arguments behind individual budgets for young people from poorer backgrounds, and indeed for personal endowments.

I also suspect that economists are apt to miss the social, and even economic, value of shared cultural experiences. Does it matter, in a multi-media age, that fewer and fewer people watch the same TV shows, or that public sector broadcasting activities, such as the news, get squeezed out?

6. And finally . . . political empowerment

One of the biggest, and growing, class differentials is around the exercise of political power. Traditional forms of political engagement, notably voting, show significant but not overwhelming social skews – affluent and older voters turning out in greater numbers. But this social skew is modest in comparison with that in non-traditional, or alternative, forms of engagement such as going on marches, writing letters or signing petitions. As traditional forms of engagement fall, and alternative forms rise, this is bringing with it a big underlying shift in political empowerment.

The institutional implications of this shift are picked up in the next chapter, but since they have such a strong 'fairness' strand behind them, let us at least outline the main concerns. If we rely on the 'accident' of who engages in political action or who takes office, we inadvertently accept a serious and growing inequity in the distribution of power. In principle, anyone can go on a march, become a councillor or a charitable trustee. But in practice, many cannot afford the time, the cost or lack the know-how and familiarity to do so.

Some of this is once again just a function of financial resources and other capitals. For example, it was only very recently that the UK's Charity Commission made it legal to pay trustees of charities, and culturally it remains very much the exception. This is of course a recipe to ensure that being a trustee is seen as something only for the great and the good. Similar issues apply to the holding of unpaid offices in local government that ensure that only the affluent and the retired can consider it as a serious option.

But money is not the only factor. We need to have political institutional mechanisms that actively ensure that democratic practices are statistically representative of the population, not just representative in the sense of Burke. This does not necessarily imply social, gender and ethnic class quotas for our Parliaments, Councils and Parties – though it is an important issue to keep an eye on. But if we don't want to go that route, it does imply supplementing these traditional democratic mechanisms with alternatives that are strictly representative, such as random sample deliberative polls or the use of paid citizens' juries in relation to key local and national issues.

Conclusion

There are powerful long-run forces driving inequalities and potentially deep inequities within and between countries. These are not only income inequalities, but are increasingly around other forms of less obvious or 'hidden' financial, human, and social capitals that policies and official statistics have been less focused on. At the same time, in nations such as the UK – but also in countries of very different levels of inequality – there is little public appetite for much more traditional redistribution.

This combination of causal and political forces suggests that we need to look much harder at the wider range of factors that drive inequality and inequity. We have to look at the darker sides of the hidden wealth of nations. In my view, a key characteristic of the next generation of these policies is that they will need to harness people's personal affiliations with those in their extended families and communities more effectively that current Weberian, or rational welfare states. And yet I don't think laissez-faire will work either. We might call this new model, the 'affiliative welfare state'.

Some readers will have noticed a fair amount of behavioural economics creeping into the proposals in this chapter too – lots of 'nudges' to help us do the right thing for those around us but without too much pain. The inheritance tax proposals are a good example of this approach. It doesn't seem like much of an effort, once suitable descendents trust vehicles are conveniently at hand, to give our assets away to our grandchildren and great-grandchildren, but it proves powerfully progressive (albeit it takes a few years). It's not the formula a perfectly rational Weberian welfare state would prescribe. Instead it harnesses our natural feelings of affiliation for our kin, stretching them gently an extra degree to create a myriad of overlapping micro-welfare states. The resulting gaps in capital inequalities then represent a much easier and more acceptable challenge for wider communities and the state to address.

There is one final point we should note. The time frame over which the inequities discussed in this chapter build up, and over which they can be ameliorated, must be measured in decades or generations, not in four or five year Parliamentary cycles. It's not a project that an Obama, Brown or Cameron can take on alone. Instead you need to secure a degree of cross-party consensus and create a project that will last across the cycle of a single government.

But there is good news. Modern democratic societies have under their belts some historically extraordinary achievements in terms of fairness and equal opportunities across races, genders and classes in relation to our systems of justice, politics, and welfare. There is also clear evidence that government policy affects inequality and the distribution of wealth. So we should approach the remaining, and some new, inequities that we see around us with a sense of optimism, not despair. We have an unprecedented level of understanding into the dynamics of cross-generational inequity. With a little imagination, patience and goodwill, we can address these too.

5

Power and Governance

The solution does not lie only in power sharing, as if power is like a cake
that should be shared . . . If the democratic process has to be followed to
that end . . . then we shall never have peace because there will always be
unsatisfied and dissatisfied parties.
    Alpha Omar Konare, speaking on the prospect of ethnic clashes
                                              in Kenya, August 2008.

What is Government For?

The practice of government has been around for at least five thousand
years. If we count the micro-governance and conflict resolution of
families and tribes, the essential ideas of government have probably
been around for as long as humanity. Libraries have been written on
what government is for, what constitutes good and bad government,
and how it has evolved over time. For the purpose of this chapter, let
us distinguish three threads of thinking about what government is for,
including how these might boost, and tap into, both the hidden and
overt wealth of nations.

- **Justice – the classic state.** Through Locke and Rousseau, a core idea
  of the modern state is the protection of citizens from the tyranny
  of arbitrary power. A key challenge is to create a system with a

balance of powers to ensure that government itself did not become the tyrant.

- **Public goods and the framework for prosperity – the practical state.** A core function of government is to solve collective action problems around common or public goods. Challenges range from preventing the 'overgrazing of commons', to the building of public goods such as roads, clean water supplies and modern public services.
- **Anticipation, planning and the promotion of a way of life – the paternalistic state.** Governments have traditionally had a big role in seeing the bigger picture and in orchestrating or directing the activities of citizens for the greater good (or at least for the greater good of the ruling elite). Many of these activities have historically had a strong cultural component, such as the promotion of mass religious activities and beliefs, or the building of the great monuments and institutions of antiquity. This, in some ways, has become the least fashionable aspect of what our predecessors built the state for, though – as we shall see – it is undergoing something of a renaissance.

The Classic State

Sir Richard Wilson was Cabinet Secretary, Britain's most senior Civil Servant, from 1998 to 2002. He was almost a perfect model of what people across the world think of as a British public servant: quietly-spoken, modest and considerate, but also brilliant and a skilful manipulator of wheels of power.

Before he left office, he gave a remarkable one-off seminar on 'the nature of power'. At its heart, Wilson reflected on the curious paradox of how those who had risen to the highest positions of power in our government often felt frustrated and powerless, while some of the seemingly humblest of officials seemed to wield power beyond that of even the most senior Ministers. For example, even a relatively junior immigration official had the power to lock someone up for 24 hours – something no Prime Minister could do. Indeed, Prime Ministers would frequently bemoan that many of the formal levers of power that they thought they had often didn't seem to work – it was like the levers weren't connected.

This sentiment of frustration and constraint among even the most senior Ministers is a very striking aspect of a modern democracy, and certainly one I often saw in Government. Sometimes this frustration might be rooted in disappointing results of a policy or action, or

Rank	Voice & accountability	Stability	Effectiveness	Regulatory quality	Rule of Law	Control of corruption
1	Denmark	**Iceland**	Singapore	Denmark	**Switz**	**Iceland**
2	**Switz**	**Lux**	**Switz**	**Lux**	Norway	**Finland**
3	Neth	**Finland**	Denmark	Hong Kong	**Iceland**	Denmark
4	Norway	**Switz**	Norway	Singapore	Denmark	**Sweden**
5	**Lux**	Aruba	**Sweden**	UK	**NZ**	NZ
6	**Finland**	Andorra	**Iceland**	Ireland	**Sweden**	**Switz**
7	**NZ**	Kiribati	Australia	Neth	**Austria**	**Lux**
8	**Sweden**	Liechten	**Finland**	**NZ**	**Finland**	Neth
9	Belgium	Tuvalu	Canada	Australia	Canada	Singapore
10	**Iceland**	Vanuatu	**NZ**	**Finland**	**Lux**	Canada
11	Ireland	Malta	Liechten	**Sweden**	Singapore	Norway
12	Germany	**Sweden**	Neth	**Austria**	Australia	Australia
13	**Austria**	NZ	Hong Kong	Canada	Germany	**Austria**
14	UK	**Austria**	UK	**Iceland**	Ireland	UK
15	Canada	Norway	**Lux**	**Switz**	Neth	Germany
16	Australia	Brunei	**Austria**	Germany	UK	Ireland
17	Andorra	Barbados	Germany	Estonia	Anguilla	Hong Kong
18	Liechten	Anguilla	Ireland	Belgium	USA	Belgium
19	France	Cayman	USA	Chile	Malta	USA
20	Puerto Rico	Martinique	Andorra	USA	Belgium	Bahamas

Figure 5.1 *Which are the 'best' governed countries? The top-ranking 20 countries on the World Bank measures of over 200 nations, 2007 data. The World Bank uses a combination of indicators, surveys and expert views to estimate national government performance on the six indicators. Shading indicates confidence interval from the top performing country (i.e. countries that have essentially similarly outstanding scores). Countries that are in the top 20 across all six indicators are marked in bold.*

sometimes in genuine uncertainty about what to do. But most often it would be because other powerful players did not agree with you, or because you simply lacked the resources or powers to do what you wanted to do. This frustration could be expressed in many different ways – in smouldering anger and dark threats; in sighs of exasperation; or occasional crockery smashed against the wall. But, of course, it is a frustration built into democracy itself – a balance of powers born of a thousand years of experiment and struggle. Even Prime Ministers know they often don't get their way.

Shifting power and engagement: myths and problems

There are a series of widely accepted truths about the state of modern democracies that are largely, or completely, wrong.

In the UK, it is widely accepted that there has been a massive 'collapse in trust' in politics and politicians. Yet trend data show that trust in politicians or Ministers has remained largely unchanged for more than half a century. Today, around one in five of the public trust politicians to tell the truth – but this is a marginally *higher* figure than twenty-five years ago. There has been a decrease, in the proportion of the public who think that the politicians or Government put 'national interest' above Party or personal interests – falling from around 38% in the mid 1970s to around 20% in the mid 2000s. The expenses scandal pushed this figure even lower, such that by May 2009 only 12% thought MPS put the national or constituency interest first, with a record 62% saying they put their personal interest first, and 21% saying they put their party first. But in general – as the current Cabinet Secretary is fond of reminding people – the British have never been very trusting of their governments. In a Gallup poll conducted more than 60 years ago, and in the context of a post-war government of national unity, only 36% of Britons said they trusted the politicians 'to do the best for their country'. In contrast, a clear majority – 57% – said they thought politicians were just out for themselves or their party.

There has been a dramatic fall in political interest, we are often told. Yet trend data show that expressed political interest has remained essentially flat for at least 30 years. In 1973, 60% of Britons said they were 'very' or 'fairly' interested in politics. In 2001, the year of lowest general election turnout since the First World War, political interest was essentially unchanged at 59%. Similarly, periodic tests of political knowledge show 'depressingly' low levels of public political knowledge, but again these figures remain largely unchanged over time.

Finally, it is widely held that political engagement has fallen. This is based heavily on declining voter turnouts, not only in the UK but in a number of mature democracies. Yet, with the arguable exception of

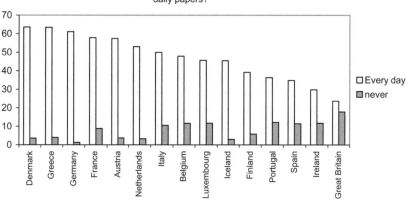

How often do you follow politics in the news on television or on the radio or in the daily papers?

Figure 5.2 *Day-to-day interest in politics across countries (WVS, EU nations, 2004). Britain may be the home of democracy, but that doesn't mean Britons are very interested in it.*

the US, other forms of political engagement have generally been rising, such as going on marches; signing petitions; writing to local newspapers or other media; and taking political action through consumer choices, such as boycotting a product or buying 'fair trade' produce.

Levels of trust in politics and politicians in Britain are low, but we are quite mistaken in thinking that our parents and grandparents felt very differently. But if the decline in political trust, interest and engagement are overstated, does this mean nothing has changed? No. There have been a number of significant changes in the nature of politics, government, and our engagement with it – just not the ones that the media tend to focus on.

- **There has been a collapse in the membership of mass political parties**, and personal identification with the parties has also fallen. Falls in party membership have occurred in most industrialized nations, but with particularly marked falls in the UK, Denmark, Sweden, France the Netherlands and Italy – all of which saw party memberships more than halve in the four decades after 1960. A small number of countries, notably Greece and Germany, have seen rises in party membership but from unusually low starting levels.
- **The relative salience of politics has changed.** While it is true that expressed interest in politics has not moved, the *importance* placed on it relative to other domains of life has changed. For example, there have been marked increases in the importance that people place on friends, leisure, and even work. In contrast, the importance placed on politics – which was already low – has if anything

fallen. This pattern has led some leading theorists to characterize our relationship increasingly as that of spectators – we're interested in politics, but just don't think it's very important.[1]

- **The social composition of who is involved in politics has changed.** Across countries, and across time, the more educated and affluent tend to be more likely to vote, though it is only a modest difference. Across countries, turnout tends to be about 10% less among those with limited or no educational qualifications compared with the more educated. In contrast, there is a large social skew in engagement in alternative or 'protest' activities. For example, in the UK, those with a degree are more than twice as likely as those without qualifications to have signed a petition; more than three times as likely to have contacted their member of Parliament or have got involved in a campaigning organization; and are more than five times more likely to have gone on a protest or have contacted a government department. The combination of falling voting (less skewed) and rising alternative action (more skewed) is leading to an overall shift of political engagement towards the affluent and the educated, and a rising tide of the totally unengaged. In the UK, despite the steady rise in the total volume of alternative political engagement, the proportion of adults who are totally disengaged rose from around 16% in 1973 to 21% in 2001. Among lower socio-economic groups (D's and E's) the proportion of totally disengaged rose from 21 to 33%, or from 1 in 5 to 1 in 3 over the same period.
- **The nature of what government does, and the balance of power with citizens, has changed.** This has become a hackneyed phrase, but it does seem to be true. In contrast to earlier phases of industrial development, where state planning and even ownership of industry could sometimes bring comparative advantages, the economic argument seems to play out very differently in the contemporary knowledge economy. In terms of the economy, the state often does not seem to know best, and citizens have access to the same information. With the exception of modest regulation, most modern states stay out of the day-to-day management of the economy and instead focus on promoting the conditions for growth and well-being, such as ensuring good basic educational skills. Many of the challenges the state faces are 'wicked problems' that are more about everyday behaviour than classic limitations in the capacity of public services. This issue will be returned to in more detail in later sections.

These issues are relevant to all aspects of the state, but they are especially critical to its 'classic' core. The balance of power in a democracy rests on citizens' engagement, preparedness and ability to kick out the ruling elite. And the power of the state rests on the legitimacy with which it is viewed by its citizens.

Turnout

Turnout in elections has been drifting down, albeit jerkily, across the mature democracies. Across the OECD, turnout in general elections fell through the 1980s and 1990s by around 8% on average. The fall was seen across electoral systems, though was marginally larger in First-Past-the-Post (FPTP) systems.

Crudely put, it seems that enthusiasm for voting tends to rise in younger democracies, then levels off, and eventually drifts down outside of close contests. In younger democracies, a mixture of enthusiasm and a sense of a duty to vote drives turnout, but tends to fade away among later generations who take democracy for granted. Immediately after the Second World War, around 86% of Britons thought that someone was 'seriously neglecting their duty' if they did not vote, but by the turn of the twenty-first century, this had more than halved to around 40%.

Older people tend to be more likely to vote. The low turnout among young people is often considered especially troubling as there is evidence that turnout early in life is predictive of turnout in later years.

Voting is 'compulsory' in more than 20 countries, and some commentators have argued that this should be pursued in countries with falling turnout. Models suggest that compulsory voting can boost turnout by 8 to 15%, depending on the severity of sanction. But the political dilemma is that it is most likely to be supported in countries which still have a strong sense of the duty to vote – generally least likely to be ones with a problem. There is an argument that compulsory voting is a way of addressing the social skew in voting, though this implies significant winners and losers across parties. For example, compulsory voting in the USA or UK would probably disproportionately boost the prospects of the Democrats and Labour (and probably BNP) respectively.

Other ideas for boosting turnout include expanding postal voting (the evidence suggesting this can boost turnout by 5–10%); making voting easier by holding elections on weekends or over several days; and making polling stations more appealing places to go to (such as with refreshments or music). Models also indicate that electoral systems based on proportional representation also boost turnout – though not political trust.

I have to confess that I hold something of a heretical view, which is that absolute turnout doesn't matter much as long as the result is what

the electorate wanted. By 'what the electorate wanted' I mean something quite specific – that the result was statistically representative of
what people would have wanted had they all voted. From this viewpoint, the lack of representativeness of elections across social groups
stands out as the major problem, not the turnout.

From a numbers viewpoint, arguably the biggest demographic
concern is the gulf in voting across age groups. For example, in the
2004 US presidential election, which was noted for its relatively high
youth turnout, only 47% of 18–24 year olds voted compared with
more than 73% of those aged 64–75. The youth vote is estimated to
have risen again in 2008 to 52% – the highest since 1972 (at 55%) – but
still more than 20 percentage points below that of older voters.[2] These
raw numbers have significant distorting impacts on US politics, such
as around debates over spending on medicare (of particular concern
to older voters) versus the environment (of more concern to younger
voters). In contrast to this 20–30 point difference, the gender gap in US
voting is about 3 points (women vote more) and between non-hispanic
whites and African Americans is about 7 points.

In the UK the age gulf in voting is even larger – and still growing. In
the 2005 general election, just 37% of 18–24 year olds voted compared
with 71% of those aged 55–64 and 75% among the burgeoning 65+
group. Strikingly, turnout rose across most age groups in 2005, reflecting the closeness of the election compared with 2001, but fell among
the 18–24 year olds.[3]

Lowering the voting age could help. First, by simply increasing the
absolute size of the youth vote it would help to correct political and
statistical imbalance against the young. Secondly, there is evidence
from trials in Germany that 16–18 year olds given the opportunity to
vote did so in considerably higher numbers than 18–24 year olds. If
the theory is right that a person's voting is anchored to the turnout in
their first opportunity to vote, then boosting turnout among the young-
est voters will lead to a knock-on effect that will boost voting for the
whole cohort. A final reason to offer the vote to under-18s is that it can
transform the nature of citizenship education into something which has
an immediate and real meaning – as well as encouraging politicians to
visit schools and engage with one of the most captive audiences they
will ever get.

A handful of countries already allow voting from 16, notably Brazil
and, most recently, Austria. Though the idea has been toyed with in
the UK and elsewhere, many politicians are wary that it would be seen
as a stunt.[4] Maybe it is easier for me to propose, not being an elected
politician, but I think that – at the very least, the idea should be trialled
(or put to a citizen's forum – see below). In fact, we could go further,

and extend a right to vote by proxy to people as young as 14 or even 12.[5] Under this proposal, parents or guardians of young people would cast the vote of the young person 'in trust'. The strong expectation would be that the parent or guardian would discuss the choices, how their son or daughter would like to vote, and would generally cast the vote in a way that respected these wishes.

Ethnic gaps in turnout are generally being closed by a combination of normal competition between parties, and the value and behavioural convergence that tends to happen across generations (see previous chapters).

The social class and, more markedly, educational gaps in turnout are trickier. In some countries, notably the US, this gap has become very substantial. In the 2004 US Presidential elections, only 40% of those without qualifications voted compared with 80% of those with bachelor degrees or above. Compulsory voting is one way of addressing this gap, but generally not a popular one as mentioned above.

The scale of this gap, and the relative lack of concern about it, is striking. It is difficult not to suspect that there is some tacit acceptance by commentators and politicians that it is OK for the more educated to have a bigger say in democracy. This idea has deep roots in the classical democratic thinking of Burke and Locke that representative democracy is not about the slavish expression of the average view of the public. Rather, representatives – and even voters – should preferably be of exceptional character and judgement, reaching considered views that may often be at variance with those of the majority. For reasons that we shall see through this chapter, the grounds on which this tacit acceptance has rested has shifted, creating a powerful drive for democratic innovations to address the asymmetry in political engagement across social and educational groups, and these innovations extend beyond boosting turnout.

Parties

The decline in mass political parties is probably the single biggest change in the political-institutional landscape of the past half century. It is not an issue that many people care about, but it does seem to raise fundamental questions for our core institutions of state that are based so heavily on the existence of such parties.

The UK has seen a particularly large collapse in political party membership, but the overall trend is common to many advanced democracies. In the Britain of 1945, around 1 in 10 were members of a political party. Today it stands at less than 1 in 50. The main exception to this long-term trend were those countries – and their political parties – that were most shattered by the Second World War. In the post-war years in these countries, in their party structures had to re-grow, but the most recent evidence suggests the trends they now face are also of decline.

The trends in party identification across countries tell a similar story, though much less dramatically. Across Europe, in the 1970s around 30% of people reported having no party identification, but by the 1990s this had risen to over 40%. There has been only a gentle decline in the sub-10% who strongly identify with a political party, though a more marked decline in the numbers who see themselves as 'sympathizers'.[6] In the USA the pattern has been less clear. Identification with the Republican party fell in the post-Nixon era, but subsequently recovered. Identification with the Democrats looked like a slightly more steady decline, but has been reversed by Obama, especially in the young.

However, a more careful analysis suggests that party identification is not quite what it used to be. Across the mature democracies, voters have become more fickle. They have become far more likely to switch between parties from one election to another, regardless of overall levels of identification.[7]

At the same time as overall party memberships have been falling, there has been a marked increase in the overall numbers of political parties – a pattern again seen across countries. On this measure, many democracies have never been more vibrant. The large political parties have adapted to life without mass memberships and a more volatile electorate, often by fighting more aggressively for the growing middle ground of floating voters. This has created new political opportunities for regional and issue based parties to differentiate themselves by appealing to minority political views neglected by the big parties fighting for the middle ground.

The growth in the number of parties, and in voter volatility, has been especially marked in countries with proportional representation such as Italy, Germany, and New Zealand. In contrast, the dynamics of FPTP systems have slowed the process in countries such as the USA and the UK. However, as scholars such as Russell Dalton and others have noted, it is striking that the underlying trends seem to be expressing themselves very widely across countries. While there is a tendency for politicians and commentators in each country to attribute the trends to domestic and national party issues, the wider pattern suggests a much deeper seismic change across nations. Two questions arise: does it matter, and what might we do about it?

Party decline clearly matters for practical reasons around how we organize our Parliaments and our institutions that presume the existence of effective, functioning parties. Most Parliamentary systems are based on meaningful value distinctions between parties, with sufficient discipline within them to ensure that governments are stable and predictable. More fundamentally, we look to parties to articulate key cleavages of ideology, approach and group interests in society. If they fail to do this, there is a real risk that our institutions will fail to address these cleavages risking other forms of conflict as well as political disillusionment on the part of the public. There are also practical questions around where tomorrow's politicians and leaders will come from if the parties from which they were drawn are disappearing, and how will elections be organized in the absence of mass party members to canvass, deliver leaflets and get the vote out?

On the other hand, mature democracies have proven themselves quite flexible institutions, and well able to survive the rise and fall of individual parties. Indeed, contrary to popular opinion, satisfaction with democracy in general has increased in most of the mature democracies over recent decades, even if we don't necessarily trust the politicians that populate them.[8]

Most countries have begrudgingly moved towards some form of state funding for the major parties. These moves are fraught with difficulty, as it feels like a case of special pleading on the part of the parties. I think that a version of 'participatory vouchers', proposed by Bruce Ackerman, could be an elegant solution for the party funding problem. This involves channelling state party funding through giving every citizen a low value cash voucher – for just a few dollars, euros or pounds – that they can assign to any party from an agreed list. To be on the list, a party would need to have polled a certain minimum number of votes in a national or regional election. The mechanism for assignment would vary from country to country. Where all citizens have to fill in a tax return by law (such as the USA), this could be where vouchers were assigned. But it could also be done at elections themselves, or through some other mechanism such as through banks, web-based applications or other assignment. Of course, citizens could also choose not to donate their voucher to any party.

One of the attractive features of the Ackerman proposal is that it creates a new and powerful incentive for political parties to reach out to large sections of the population. Party members often associate mainly with other party members. This cannot be right, especially when this group is becoming ever more atypical and smaller in number. Participatory vouchers would drive parties to knock on doors and hold events to encourage citizens to donate their voucher to the relevant party – not as members but as loose sympathizers – state funding from the hands of citizens themselves.

We could also look for ways of lowering the barriers to citizens, including public servants, being able to engage in political life. The very mention of this idea causes shudders down the spines of some constitutional experts in Westminster systems, though it is much less of an issue in many Northern European systems. Political party membership is often treated like a modern-day form of leprosy. In a whole range of public service and private activities, membership of political parties is often frowned on or even seen as an explicit reason for exclusion from service. In the days of mass party memberships, lifelong and rigid party identification, and bitter class or ethnically-based inter-party battles, it made sense to ensure that these deep political cleavages were left outside many domains of life. But today, with these cleavages a shadow of their former selves, these restrictions seem bizarre, inappropriate and unhelpful. We should make room for party political expression, albeit in its more varied and softer shades, in any walk of modern life. I even think we should be prepared to allow it in our Civil Service – though for many, this will still be seen as a step too far.

There is an important sense in which the public are absolutely right not to trust political parties and politicians, for their role is precisely to be partisan. It is a bit like lawyers in a court of law whose job it is to clearly articulate one side of a case, and it is for the court and judicial process as a whole to reach a balanced judgement. Similarly, political parties – and especially in a PR system – are there to articulate a series of viewpoints, and we look to Parliament and the other institutions around it to meld these viewpoints into a balanced view. In FPTP systems, the parties generally try to form a broadly balanced overall view within their offer to the public, because they expect to go on to form the government by themselves and must compete for the average voter.

In either system, we look to our political institutions to put together the competing interests and viewpoints of us as citizens. This can happen at various levels, as long as it does eventually happen.

But voters have an alternative to political parties. They can give money and support to special interest and lobby groups (SIGs) that will promote their interests and concerns in a narrower way. Such SIGs today often boast memberships much larger than those of the traditional political parties. These special interest groups allow citizens, through cheque-book membership, the ability to support several causes all at once leaving their distant advocates to fight it out. Of course, unlike in political parties, these advocates aren't trying to offer a balanced overall view – they are just there to get the best possible outcome for their particular cause.

If this is the shape of our politics – and citizens – to come, then our institutions have to do more of the heavy lifting of political balancing and negotiation. To some extent this is already happening behind closed doors inside the parties. Party conferences and memberships are increasingly dominated by professional political lobbyists.

Viewed through this lens, low and falling levels of public confidence in Parliament are a much greater concern than low levels of confidence in political parties or politicians. Confidence in the UK Parliament has roughly halved in a generation – a much bigger change than that in trust in politicians. We can't have it both ways. It's fine for us all to become more politically promiscuous and fickle, as long as we have institutional mechanisms that we trust to 'put Humpty back together again'. What we can't do is go our separate ways then refuse to accept the inevitable compromises that Parliaments will have to form.

Parliaments based on proportional representation (or mixed models) do not, on average, attract higher levels of public confidence than FPTP models. The key seems to be when PR systems are mixed with a consensual style of government and interaction. As usual, it is the blending of the soft and hard aspects of institutional practice that makes all the difference.

An old colleague of mine, Matthew Taylor, lays much of the blame for public disinterest in the trade-offs of living together in a democracy at the feet of the media. He compares the situation to a therapist (the policymaker or politician) trying to explain to an angry patient or teenager (the voter) that several of the things they are demanding are incompatible, like wanting lower taxes and better services. Matthew argues that it's a doomed process as long as there is a third person in the room (the media) who, whenever the patient might be close to recognizing the tensions in what they're asking for declares 'yes, you can have it all!'

Matthew may be right – the UK media in particular doesn't seem to see its role in life to offer nuanced views of difficult tradeoffs – but it is also true that Parliament hasn't made a great fist of presenting or reforming itself. Its language and habits are arcane; it goes to great trouble to keep the public out of affecting its processes; it is opaque about what will be debated and when it has been shown to be out of touch on Members' expenses; and its debates are dominated by the party whip (the obliging of members of parliament to vote along party lines). It has also been too hesitant, in my view to embrace democratic innovations.

Box 5.1   What to do about the media?

Trust in the press in the EU
Proportion who tend to trust the press, by country

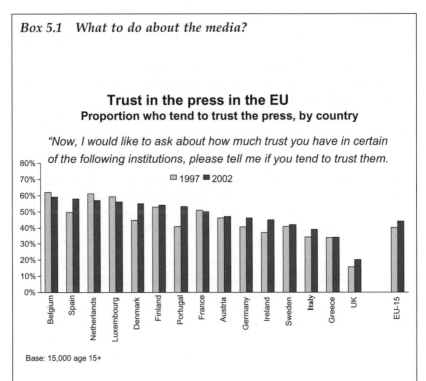

"Now, I would like to ask about how much trust you have in certain of the following institutions, please tell me if you tend to trust them.

Base: 15,000 age 15+

The UK has by far the least trusted print media in the EU-15. There is a credible argument that trust in the media in a country reflects the economics of how it is distributed and sold. In many countries, the print media is characterized by dominant regional papers, like the *Boston Globe* and *Washington Post* in the USA. Freed from the necessity to compete on the basis of screaming headlines, these papers seem more inclined to explore difficult trade-offs. There is also evidence that the particular way we buy and sell newspapers in the UK – mainly through a fleeting decision on the way to work – reinforces the logic of headline-grabbing competition. In countries such as Japan, where most people have their newspapers delivered, their competition is driven more by reflective content than headlines.

The good news is that this suggests that, in principle, the character of the media reflects structural and economic factors that can be subject to change or even direct policy intervention. However, it may be that we don't need to introduce regional licences or subsidies for paper-boys and girls, as the steady rise of web-based news may change these factors anyway.

However, whether web-based, print or broadcast, it would be good to have a media that was more effectively self-regulating. Ministers have periodically toyed with imposing change, such as forcing the press to give factual corrections occupying the same space (or time) and prominence as the original article. However, it would be a brave Minister indeed that tried to push this through Parliament and the Courts. A more politically practical idea would be to hand the issue to a high profile public deliberative event to rule on the future shape of the Press Complaints Commission and on the development of a more public-driven regulatory system. For example, the social-internet entrepreneur Tom Steinberg has proposed a web-site that allows readers to indicate and track the factual errors made by individual journalists. This, tied with some modest reforms to the PCC, might succeed where politicians fear to tread.

New institutions and ways of working: social skew and behaviour

We have several basic facts that we need to square:

- Most people don't want to spend their time discussing politics.
- There is a strong social (and age) skew in most forms of political engagement.
- Many key issues can only be resolved with the active support and involvement of the public.

Classic representative democracy, as articulated by Burke and others, solved the first problem. A small group of elected representatives would wrestle with the issues in detail using their judgement and more detailed knowledge to figure out what the nation should do. However, this conception of democracy – where we elect our leaders and leave them to get on with it in peace until the next election – is running into increasing difficulties on the second and third points.

Direct democracy

Many governments are seeking to plug these democratic gaps through various forms of consultation with the public between elections. The UK central government, for example, has run on average more than 600 'consultations' over each of the last few years. Many of these consultations are rather thin affairs, merely inviting interested parties to make their views known to the Department or Bill team concerned. In some cases, hundreds or even thousands of submissions are received. However, these tend to be dominated by special interest groups, and not a representative sample of the public.

A few countries have constitutional provisions that require more extensive and direct forms of democracy. Of these, Switzerland stands out as the closest nation to a true direct democracy with a constitution that requires almost all significant government decisions to be ratified through a direct referendum. Consequently, more than half of all the referenda conducted in the entire world to date have been within Switzerland. Of course, there are problems with the Swiss model. First, decision making can be very time consuming, and many decisions – such as the right of women to vote – have happened much later in Switzerland than in any other comparable nations. Burke would surely have been appalled. Second, perhaps ironically, the Swiss system does not necessarily address the issue of social skew very well either, as mass referenda are no guarantee of a socially representative sample. Both problems are further aggravated by the inevitable and rational action of lobby groups who target the cantons and populations most likely to say no in order to ensure that a proposal is blocked. This, of course, is why no one ever expects Switzerland to join the EU.

Similar problems plague most other forms of direct democracy. For example, California has a relatively full form of direct democracy in that a referendum can be triggered if sufficient citizens petition for it. Sadly, this largely comes down to money. A corporate or special interest group can usually get enough signatures for a given petition by employing an agency to get the requisite number of signatures. It then faces a harder battle to get the referenda passed and into law, but it is a battle that can often be won and leaves the government crippled with endless and sometimes contradictory constraints.

These examples are enough to persuade most governments and reformers to steer away from the excessive use of referenda and direct democracy in general.

Abrogative referenda and trigger powers

A number of countries have given their citizens the power not to make laws or policy through direct referenda, but to block or throw back legislation passed by government. Italy is a prominent example. The details of the mechanism varies, but typically it works such that if enough citizens petition and/or vote against the measure in a citizen-triggered referendum, the legislation is stopped or thrown back to Parliament to reconsider. Often there is a specific time period, such as six months after the legislation is passed, within which opponents to the bill must mobilize opposition or else the legislation passes into law.

Abrogative referenda have the advantage of empowering the public to intervene if they feel strongly enough, but without the problems associated with fuller forms of direct democracy. They also fit well into a world of 'spectator' and special interest politics, where most of the time the public are happy to keep one eye on political life while they get on with the rest of life. Such referenda also have a secondary advantage, often missed by the political classes of countries that lack them, that referenda provide an important new role for political parties. Given the thresholds normally required to succeed, political parties turn out to have a critical role in mobilizing sufficient numbers to trigger and win such referenda. Referenda also require parties to engage much more directly with the public, so provide a powerful line of reconnection.

There is a mechanism which lies somewhere in between direct democracy and abrogative referendum, which is where the public is given the power to trigger action in Parliament, central or local government. In some US states, for example, large scale petitions of referenda can trigger an obligation on the state government to act on an issue without specifying the exact legislation or action to be taken. A milder variant – gradually spreading through many nations – is that large petitions can trigger an obligation for Parliament to have a debate on an issue. The Scottish Parliament now incorporates such a mechanism, and Westminster is looking at a similar proposal.

Similar trigger powers now operate at local government level in a number of countries. In the UK, perhaps the most striking example is the ability of citizens to trigger a local referendum on whether the area should have a directly elected mayor. As Vernon Bogdanor, the constitutional expert, has approvingly noted, these trigger powers are probably one of the most important constitutional innovations of recent decades, and there is a strong case for them to be applied to a host of other issues. Vernon may get his wish, for there are a host of new areas where government proposals point in the direction of citizen 'calls to act' which will place an obligation on local government and other public service providers to respond should a sufficient number of local citizens request action.

Deliberative forums and juries

Trigger powers and abrogative referenda still don't guarantee that decisions are made by a statistically representative sample of the public. More damningly, particularly to proponents of classic representative democracy, such mechanisms still rest heavily on relatively unconsidered judgements by the public, often with the issue presented in a narrow context.

Another recent set of additions to the family of democratic innovations is designed to address these deficits, and interest in their use is growing steadily across the democratic nations. These innovations include citizens' juries, deliberative polls and deliberative forums. The common thread across these mechanisms is that a sample of ordinary citizens are brought together to deliberate at length over an issue; are presented with a broad range of evidence and views; and are then asked to reach a considered view. In principle, these mechanisms combine the best of all worlds – they offer a carefully considered view (not just that of an opinion poll); they directly address the problem of social skew; and they are respectful of the fact that most of us don't want to spend our lives weighing up the finer points of policy choices. That said, although these mechanisms are often lumped together, there are some important differences between them that senior policymakers need to consider.

The citizens' jury works much like a legal jury. A sample of around 10 to 20 citizens are brought together to discuss a policy issue, or budget, in depth for anything from a day to a week. Background briefings are usually provided to the jurors, evidence presented, and conflicting views heard. Juries are normally able to ask for further evidence or advice and can call back experts or 'witnesses' for points of clarification. For example, a three-day citizens' jury was used to help design the UK's new regulations around parental leave around the birth of a child, a process which was considered by officials and outsiders to have considerably improved the quality of the subsequent provisions.[9] Citizens' juries are also an increasingly familiar part of local decision-making, such as around the provision of local government services or even the prioritizing within budgets (see box).

Porto Alegre and participatory budgeting

Porto Alegre in Brazil is probably the most famous application of deliberative democracy.[10] From 1989, an annual process of meetings in each of the 16 districts of the city has brought together citizens and officials to discuss and vote on budget priorities. In a typical year, around 50,000 residents take part in these meetings, with individual meetings sometimes having as many as a 1,000 participants. The budget agreed through this process is substantially binding, and although the Mayor can in principle veto it, this has yet to happen.

The participatory budget process has successfully involved residents in the large slums around the city, and has led to substantial improvements in the conditions of the poor, notably through improved sewerage, water, health care and education. For example, there was roughly a quadrupling in the number of schools within the first decade of the process. The process has been credited with encouraging citizen engagement and boosting support for taxes and the provision of public goods. Porto Alegre has been praised by the World Bank, and the process has now been adopted by more than a hundred other Brazilian cities and copied in other parts of the world.

That said, criticisms have also been made. Though many people get involved – including from poorer districts – the process still only involves around 3% of Porto Alegre's population. It has been noted that participation is strongly skewed towards militants and party activists, and is not a strictly representative sample. Some cities that have adopted a version of the process have been disappointed that citizens have tended to choose 'the lowest common denominator' – i.e. to cut taxes – though sometimes this has been linked to the thinness of the consultation process or the non-representativeness of samples.

Citizens' juries have two important weaknesses, however. First, because of the small numbers of people involved, they cannot make strong claims to be statistically representative. Like real juries, they can also be skewed by the presence of one or two particularly strong personalities (though this can be partly dealt with through effective facilitation). In technical terms, this means that their conclusions may not be especially robust, in that a different sample might have reached a different view. Second, their public visibility tends to be relatively low, making it easy for policymakers to ignore their conclusions. Ironically, this may sometimes make them more popular with policymakers, since they can be heralded if they give the 'right' result, and otherwise ignored.

The issue of statistical representation is taken head on by 'deliberative polls', an innovation linked to Robert Fishkin of Stanford. A deliberative poll takes a true random or representative sample of several hundred people and brings them together for a day, weekend or more to listen to evidence and discuss an issue. Participants are asked their views on the issues at the very start of the process, and then again at the end (hence 'poll').

It is often found that the views of the sample in a deliberative poll move quite significantly after they have had the opportunity to think about and discuss the issues under consideration. For example, in a deliberative poll on Europe conducted by Channel 4 in 1994, views were found to shift quite dramatically away from the anti-European instincts of a standard poll of the British public. The percentage agreeing with the statement 'If we left the EU Britain would lose its best chance of real progress' rose from a clear minority of 40% to a majority of 53% afterwards, and those agreeing that 'Britain is better off in the EU than out of it' rose from 45 to 60%. Clearly, 10 to 15 percentage differences can change history, as illustrated by public referenda on Monetary Union, the EU constitution; and on the Lisbon Treaty.

The 'deliberative forum' at first glance looks very similar to the deliberative poll. A sample of the public are brought together to hear evidence and reach a view. However, a small but important difference is that the forum is often asked to reach a collective view, rather than simply being re-polled at the end of the process. This puts more pressure on participants to discuss and negotiate with each other.

The policy-maker, and especially an elected politician, faces a dilemma when the conclusions of a deliberative event differ significantly from that of a standard poll. To go with the answer offered by the deliberative event is to go against the views of the wider public who have not had an opportunity to reflect on the issue in detail, and could lead to electoral unpopularity or even defeat. But in most walks of life, we would consider the considered answer to be the 'better' one. In this sense, the deliberative mechanism reposes the challenge of classic representative democracy: should the elected representative do what they think is right, having considered the case in detail, or do what the electorate who haven't reflected on it want?

Yet there is a key difference – the members of the deliberative event, at least at the start, were genuinely a representative sample of the public. In other words, the implication is that any randomly chosen group of the public would have reached the same conclusion had they gone though the arguments. So, as a member of the public, if I understand the mechanism, I should trust the result on the basis that I would have reached the same view.

There is a familiar and highly trusted mechanism that has these characteristics – the legal jury. It is noteworthy that even the most venomous newspaper editor will rarely ridicule the verdict of a jury, even if they will happily criticize the judge or the legal process. Public trust ratings of legal juries are in the range 80 to 85% – far in excess of that of judges, politicians or Parliaments. Similarly, while only a third of the public say they would trust a group of local councillors to make a difficult planning issue, two-thirds say they would trust such a decision made by a sample of twelve members of the public.[11] So the strong indications are that the public like the idea of at least some difficult decisions being made by other members of the public.

If these mechanisms work well and are trusted, then why do we need politicians? Why do we even need Parliaments? Understandably, these questions bother senior politicians. If a bureaucracy can employ these kinds of democratic innovations to test ideas with the public, and enable the public to shape policies and priorities themselves, then we may face 'legitimacy races' between different democratic mechanisms – and it is not clear that Parliaments and Ministers will necessarily win. This issue has been a concern, for example, in Canada where a number of relatively high profile deliberative mechanisms have been used, including around the question of whether to change the voting system. Senior politicians worry that once such mechanisms begin to be used, there will be calls to use them in every domain and the power of government and Ministers to act could become compromised.

A balance of approaches

There is a genuinely appropriate concern about legitimacy races and conflicts. Imagine a controversial but everyday policy issue, such as at what age should children receive sex or drugs education. The bureaucracy, hopefully guided by expert opinion may reach one conclusion (say age 10) but Parliament and the elected Government reaches another view (say age 12). But it is pretty clear who is sovereign – the democratically elected government – and their view wins out. But let us suppose that the bureaucracy conducts a large and methodologically sound deliberative forum, and this comes down in favour of age 10. Elected ministers now have a much more fragile claim to insist on a different age. Why should Ministers' views trump the considered view of a representative sample of parents, adults and perhaps teenagers whom it directly affects?

Now consider one more twist to the story. Let us suppose that rather than the bureaucracy or Ministers that initiated the deliberative forum, it was a third party such as a TV network. A simple poll can be shot down, but a full scale, rigorous deliberative forum within which a sample of the public carefully considered the views of experts and each other before reaching a view would be much more difficult to dismiss.

We have already begun to see these kinds of democratic legitimacy races. In one sense, they are simply a new extension of the well-established democratic legitimacy races that have long gone on between central, regional and local elected governments, and between upper and lower houses of Parliament. Indeed, one of the main arguments against shifting to elected upper chambers is that enhancing their democratic legitimacy greatly increases the frequency and effectiveness of their challenges to the lower house.

Yet the beauty of democratic mechanisms, when carefully assembled, is that they are not a zero-sum game. This is the biggest misconception around the use of new democratic innovations (as well as some of the public sector reforms discussed later). Power is not like a cake that has to be cut. Rather, democratic mechanisms can increase the total pool of agency and power – expanding the 'cake' not just cutting it.

This is clearly illustrated by the 'wicked issues' that are increasingly dominating policy concerns, such as climate change, obesity or anti-social (and pro-social) behaviour. Passing a law in Washington, Westminster or Brussels may have little direct effect. What we are trying to do is change citizen behaviour, typically through a change in the prevalent social norms. Affluent, educated and informed citizens are powerful agents in their own right, and if they don't buy into the need and desirability for change in their behaviour then it is a very tough ask to expect laws and even economic signals to do it for you.

Many of the new generation of democratic innovations show their greatest promise in areas where the legitimacy of the classic state is weakest. In most nations, citizens don't want to be told by central governments how to parent their children or how to live (see below). In contrast, one of the most powerful messages that comes from citizen deliberation is not an instruction to government, but a message to fellow citizens. In this sense, democratic innovations are a powerful new tool that elected governments can employ in areas where their own legitimacy is weak, and yet where important dilemmas and decisions lie for us all. In short, their results can give government permission to act in areas where otherwise they would fear to tread.

The experience so far is that citizen participants are happy to respect the brief that a given forum is about. But what matters most is that citizens feel that what they are doing will have some impact, and their views respected. This is also important for media coverage and wider public interest. As it becomes clear that these events have real significance, news coverage and public interest will build to create a positive circle of profile and impact, remembering that a key function of the Forums is to encourage communication from informed citizen participant to citizens around social norms. Topics might include: smoking bans and other 'lifestyle laws'; budgetary dilemmas; and issues around the sharing and use of personal information by public and private providers.

One idea is that upper Houses of Parliament might incorporate deliberative forums within them. The problem with this idea is that there could be severe tension between how you would arrange a debate for a group of experienced representatives versus one for a random sample of the public. However, it may be worth experimenting with links between deliberative forums and Parliamentary debates. For example, one could design a deliberative forum to be wrapped around a Parliamentary debate. Hence a three-day forum could be structured such that the first day involves listening to the evidence, the second incorporates listening to a Parliamentary debate, and the third involves reaching final conclusions. The Parliamentary debate might itself be structured such that a second session was held sometime after the Forum had concluded so as to respond to it.

In short, a new generation of democratic innovations can address the three big challenges that were identified at the start of this section: citizens' twin desires to be listened to but not to spend much time on politics or dull deliberation; the social and age skew in engagement; and the need for citizen engagement and acceptance around behavioural issues. The real challenge and opportunity for Parliaments and Governments is to build these mechanisms into existing institutional frameworks rather than shutting them out. The worst of all worlds is what a number of governments are doing, which is to use these mechanisms in an insincere way to bolster existing policy positions or rubber-stamp decisions that were going to be made anyway. This latter approach will undermine the power and legitimacy of the new mechanisms without doing anything to help the government itself.

Conclusion: the classic state revisited

The key idea of the classical democratic state is that we cede power to government to pass laws, regulate and protect us, while at the same time the public retains the power to remove the government from office. Mature democracies offer their citizens unprecedented opportunities to exercise democratic leverage over their governments, and citizens have unprecedented levels of education and information to utilize this. But these democratic opportunities are used highly unevenly across social and age groups; voter turnout is drifting down; elected members are viewed with suspicion; and there has been a collapse in political party membership and identification (with the possible exception of the USA). Policy responses could include:

- Lowering the voting age to 16. It may even be worth considering lowering the voting age further, or giving young people a vote which is cast 'in trust'.

- State funding for political parties through 'participatory vouchers' that citizens can assign to a party of their choice, or not at all, and lowering the barriers for the expression of party positions in office and everyday life (in the UK).
- Adjust institutionally to the realities of a more volatile electorate, probably including the further spread of proportional representation.
- Parliaments and Governments to hold regular high-profile deliberative forums, such as one a month, which Departments would bid to use, with a refreshed sample of the public for each event.[12] A Parliamentary or Ministerial Cabinet Committee would judge whether topics were suitable for the forum.
- Expand the range of trigger powers given to citizens, including the ability to trigger debates within Parliament.

Box 5.2   *What issues might be referred to Government sponsored deliberative forums?*

Forums are expensive, and will need to have their legitimacy built over time. Criteria that the Parliamentary or Cabinet Committee might use to judge a Department's bid to use one of the forums might include:

- The Department was seeking a genuine public deliberation, not just a 'consultation' – in other words, it was genuinely open-minded around the options.
- The issue encapsulated a difficult dilemma for citizens – where the public would have to choose or strike a balance around a key trade-off (such as the pain of more taxes or restriction in exchange for a greater public good or reduced harm).
- The issue rested heavily on public acceptance or changed citizen behaviour.
- The proposed sample for the Forum was appropriate for the issue to be discussed.[13]
- The Department must subsequently and publicly explain how it has followed the forum's recommendations or if not then why.

Across nations, democratic accountability and effective governance tend to go together. The Scandinavian nations and Switzerland top both indicators, with the Anglo-Saxon nations not far behind. In the short term, nations can develop well under 'benevolent dictatorship'. Singapore, for example, scores poorly on measures of voice and

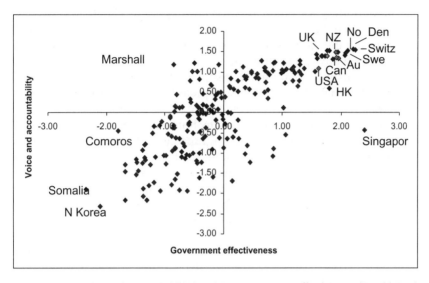

Figure 5.3 *Voice and accountability against government effectiveness (World Bank indicators, 2007). The two measures are strongly correlated (r = 0.76).*

accountability, yet is the highest scoring nation in the world on effective government (see Figure 5.3).[14] But the best justification for the use of new democratic innovations – including what we might call 'direct democracy-lite' – is not just because power corrupts, and therefore needs a democratic check, but because power is not a zero-sum game. The democratic innovations discussed above have the capacity to simultaneously increase the power of citizens *and* the state, increasing our ability to address collective problems and build prosperous, empowered and meaningful lives.

The Practical State

For all the talk of democracy and empowerment, we also want our governments to get on and deliver, or facilitate, some practical stuff. We look to the state to ensure that we have the public goods that we need and that it makes no sense for individual citizens to build for themselves, like roads, vaccination programmes, or national security. If the division of power (the classic state) is the foundation on which government is built, the 'practical state' is the structure that we build on it.

There has been a dramatic evolution in the nature of the practical state over the last hundred years. In the early part of the twentieth century, the state stayed out of most aspects of life. Health and welfare was left largely to citizens, charities and the private sector. Education, apart from the most basic provision, was generally up to families and church to fund and provide. Mass transport, mainly railways at that time, was a private sector enterprise. The state, much as it had for millennia, concerned itself mainly with national security through armies and navys; with the rule of law including enforcing property rights and criminal justice; and with rudimentary regulation of public goods such as building and fire regulations, rudimentary sanitation and water supply, and sometimes the planning of cities.

The twentieth century saw a massive expansion in the role of the state. This was driven partly by the experiences of the world wars, but also by the rise of socialism and the changing economic logic of industrialization and mass production. From the production of food, machines, transport and houses, the state seemed to be able to solve problems that markets were stumbling over. Small and inefficient farms could be scaled up though mechanization and subsidy. Squabbling private rail networks could be nationalized into integrated transport systems. With state planning and funding, road networks and quality mass housing could be built. And health and welfare systems offered the prospect of mass wellbeing, an end to extreme poverty, and a fitter population (such as to fight when needed). Across many nations, the 1930s to 1960s was an era of largely undisputed big, practical states.

In many European countries, this period was associated with the nationalization of large sections of the economy. The public sector effectively expanded to include not only health, education and transport, but power, communications, and much of industry.

By the 1980s, not only the fashion but the underlying economic logic of nationalization had changed. States had been effective at creating the scale and integration necessary for big industry; driving investment around sectors where there was a strong advantage to a national monopoly (such as communications and power); and rebuilding shattered war-time economies. But states were less effective at providing the differentiated consumer offerings that citizens now wanted, and big nationalized industries were often a recipe for difficult industrial relations – the power of monopolies worked more than one way. Technology, market sophistication and changing modes of production were also making it easier to break previous monopolies into separate business units.

By the 1990s and 2000s, the talk was of the state as an 'enabler' rather than direct provider. But where should the line in the sand be drawn? If private companies could provide previously public utilities like electricity, water and transport – albeit with state regulation – could this same logic apply to other traditional public services?

Public services: what are they for?

There is question we often asked candidates applying to join the Prime Minister's Strategy Unit (PMSU): 'why do we have a national health service, but not a national food service?'[15] Most candidates would struggle to answer this question, but those who had a good shot at it generally got employed. What we were after was not just a historical account, but one rooted in the logic of 'market failures' (who would insure those with high risk of genetic illness); informational asymmetries (you know to eat when you're hungry, but how do you know if you need an expensive medical procedure?); and the nature of public goods (if everybody else gets vaccinated, I don't need to bother – but everyone thinks that).

The best candidates will realize that the answer is not black and white. The state continues to regulate the food market with (controversial) subsidies to ensure supply; ensuring safe and sanitary food production; deciding whether genetically modified food can be grown or sold; and regulating the competition of food retailers. On the other hand, even in countries with well developed health services, non-state actors play a big role in provision too. Private pharmaceutical companies develop and supply many of the drugs used; the private sector are contracted to provide support functions and services (and sometimes core medical services themselves); and citizens invest much of their own time and money in health related activities, such as joining gyms or eating healthier diets.

It also turns out that most of the goods produced by 'public services' aren't really public goods in the true sense. If we calculate how much the average person will pay to the state over their lifetime in taxes for public services, and how much is then spent on those public services for the average person, we find that around 90% of the money gets spent as a 'private' gain for that individual. For example, the typical state might spend US$100,000 on the education of a typical citizen, of whom the primary beneficiary is the individual citizen themselves through a lifetime of higher earnings and a better quality of life. Similarly, most healthcare expenditure is not on 'public health', such as vaccinating against infectious diseases, but on the 'health of the public' – treating and ameliorating ill health that mainly affects just the individual concerned.

Both health and education are associated with significant externalities, which are often a strong indicator of the need for state involvement to achieve more optimum outcomes. Employers will be wary of investing heavily in the skills of workers if other firms can simply hire those workers to get the gain without the costs. An educated person can be more productive when working with others who are skilled (a positive externality, making the case for marginal extra investment). And in health – unless we are happy to leave citizens and their families destitute – the state ends up picking up the tab where people are too sick to work.

This makes for a complicated landscape within which to judge the appropriate role for the practical state. Within the PMSU this issue was wrestled with repeatedly through the Blair years as we struggled to draw out a general analytical story from case-by-case efforts to drive improvement in public services. One lesson screamed repeatedly from every area and cross-national comparison we looked at: money alone wasn't enough to drive improvement, even though it might be necessary to build capacity.

Eventually, and after many laboured iterations, an overall model of reform and improvement did emerge (see Figure 5.4). It stood in contrast to the early reliance of the Blair years on 'top-down' targets and direct reform. Instead the approach sought to create a self-improving dynamic of bottom-up pressures from users of services; of contestability and challenge between public service providers; and capability-improving measures aimed at the public sector workforce itself. In this model, the state was envisaged as having a more hands-off and strategic role. The state should stay out of day-to-day service provision, but retain a role in setting overall direction and objectives, intervening where services were failing while leaving good providers alone. As Michael Barber, father of the earlier regime of top-down targets, remarked, 'you can use targets to drag up underperformance, but top-down targets don't deliver excellence'.

The PMSU model – or 'the washing machine' as it was known in-house due to its graphic representation – has gone on to be widely borrowed by other departments, governments and private consultants. But it was not without critics, both inside and outside of government. Within government, the Treasury under Gordon Brown tended to dislike the emphasis on competition and choice, and preferred to emphasize the role of state as a builder of capability and capacity. Indeed, the 'washing machine' itself was to some extent a compromise between these sometimes conflicting views. Purists in No. 10 would have been happy to leave the right of the diagram out entirely, on the basis that capability and capacity building should flow from the combination of bottom-up or user pressure; horizontal competition and learning; and limited top-down pressure.

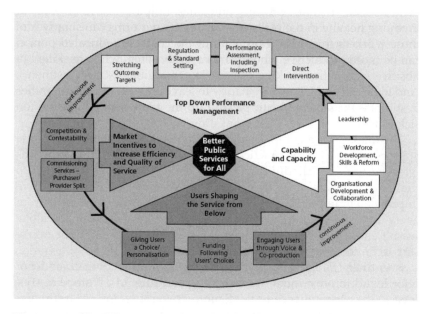

Figure 5.4 *The UK government's model of 'self-improving' public sector reform (PMSU, 2006).*

Outside government, critics felt that the 'washing machine' and language of endless reform was overly technocratic and potentially undermining of the public sector ethos. The imagery itself gave a sense of public services under attack from all sides – not a comfortable and trusted place to be. A sensible technocratic model, primarily designed to set out the appropriate role of central government, doesn't necessarily make an attractive or engaging offer to citizens or public servants.

Interestingly, over the same period that this approach to reform was developing, public service ethos in the UK strengthened. In 1997, there was only a relatively small difference between the proportions of private and public sector workers who said that it was very important to them that their job be 'useful to society': 17% of private sector workers and 22% of public sector (a 5-point difference). But by 2005, this proportion had dropped slightly to 15% in the private sector, while rising to 32% in the public sector (a 17 point difference). This gap grew especially among younger workers: among the under 35's in 2005, 19% of private sector said it was very important that the job is useful to society, compared with 49% in the public sector (a gap of 30 points, up from 12 points in 1997).[16]

Public sector ethos and motivation, and how the citizens feel about them, is not incompatible with the late Blair and PMSU model of reform, but the model is relatively silent on it. In this sense, the model fails to speak to something important about what public services are about.

Lessons from public sector reform: what worked and what didn't

This section cannot be more than a cursory overview of the lessons learned from a decade of public service reform. The lessons learnt draw mainly from the UK, but where possible are cemented with parallel evidence from elsewhere.

Getting money where it matters

Arguably the single biggest achievement of the Blair administration was to drag UK spending on public services away from basic USA-style levels to which they were drifting and back to a European-style level. Nowhere is this illustrated more powerfully than in healthcare spending, which by 1997 had slumped to a little over 5% of GDP – well below that of other European nations, and priming the conditions for a massive expansion of private, insurance-based provision. A little over a decade later, public health spending has nearly doubled to more than 10% of GDP.[17]

A similar story can be told for education, and less dramatically for transport. It is difficult to confidently separate the effects of this extra expenditure from other reforms, but there can be no doubt that both public sector outputs and outcomes have improved markedly. The public appear to have noticed these improvements too. Whereas in 1997 and 2001 public services – particularly health and education – dominated public concerns, by the late 2000s these concerns had dropped away (see Figure 2.1). Though Ministers and policy-wonks are still very much talking about improving public services, to use Donald Winnicott's phrase, the public seem to think that public services are 'good enough'.

There is hot debate as to whether this money could have been more effectively targeted. In many areas, substantial sums of money had to be used simply to crank up the raw capacity of the system, such as to increase the numbers of doctors, teaching assistants or to build more roads. But a lot of money went on increased salaries for public servants. This largely eliminated the severe recruitment problems that had plagued public services in the previous decade, and led to significant improvements in the quality of staff intake, such as teachers. Yet there were also dead-weight costs where the salaries of whole occupations or sectors were increased with only modest gains in output.

An important lesson for public policy is how marginal cash can be harnessed more effectively to marginal gains. Programmes intended to reward the most productive public servants, aimed at individuals but run by central government, do not seem to have worked. Schemes designed to link pay increases to individual performance in teachers, for example, were in practice administered by peers with the vast majority of those applying up-rated at great cost to the Treasury and little gain to students. Similarly, crude mechanisms to pay-by-results are intuitively appealing, but often difficult to apply. Leaving aside the gaming and measurement problems payment-by-results throws up, such mechanisms have a tendency to entrench the position of the best and worst performers. For example, a poor performing school or hospital would find itself losing income, and spiralling further into difficulty whereas the best would get even more. Furthermore, since Ministers and the community rarely want to see public sector failure, interventions and further cash almost always follow.

We shouldn't give up on payment-by-results, and certainly not in mature sectors with strong and larger operators (see further below), but there are a couple of other mechanisms that we might be wise to use more extensively to squeeze extra value out of our public services.

One such mechanism is to put marginal extra spending into a pot to reward *improvements* in outcomes, such as over the previous year, rather than absolute outcomes. This might sound similar, but its incentive effects are very different. Suppose you have £100m extra per year that you put aside for a school 'excellence' award. This money gets given to the schools that make the largest improvements in grades in that year, or even better, in 'value-added' (i.e. grades taking into account the student population's social background and previous grade performance). Schools that are already performing very highly won't have much chance of getting this extra money – their kids are already getting excellent grades. The schools with the best chance are those that have relatively poor grades or that are 'coasting' – with adequate grades but that are low relative to the quality of their intake. These schools would have an extra incentive to improve their grades, with the prospect of winning a prize say from £50,000 to £1 million for doing so which they could then use to build a new playground, re-furbish their labs, or pay a bonus to staff. But since this prize is for improvements, it does not lock the underperformers into a vicious cycle nor entrench the position of those at the top.

Such improvement-based grants could also create a very helpful dynamic between schools. The best way the highest performing schools

might get access to a prize is for them to look around for underperforming schools to help (for a chunk of any prize that is won). The prize
thus effectively puts a 'bounty' over underperforming schools, and
directs each marginal pound to where it will have most impact. Such
incentives could also work for hospitals (around clinical outcomes),
police command units (around public confidence and victimization
rates), and most measurable public service outcomes.

Commissioning, choice and contestability

Another way of getting the marginal pound, or dollar, to where it will
have most impact is to put it in the hands of a discriminating purchaser
or, arguably, in the hands of the user themselves.

Anybody who spent any time in No. 10 or the Cabinet Office during
the late Blair years would have heard the three 'C's – commissioning,
choice and contestability. The one that tended to get most attention in
the world outside was 'choice', as it was both easy to understand and
politically controversial.

Choice was promoted both as a means to improve better services,
and as an end to empower citizens to shape the provision they wanted.
Controversy surrounded several aspects of choice in public services.
The three principle debates concerned: Does choice increase inequality? Is it efficient? And does the public really want it?

In brief, the story on inequality is complicated, but international
evidence shows that provided choice is structured carefully, it does not
worsen inequality and can reduce it.[18] The Swedish school system, for
example, is characterized by a strong element of parental choice, but
also high equity and performance. Those with more resources can often
take more advantage of choices, including 'bussing by Volvo' when
parents drive their children to better schools in other areas, or making
better use of information to make a better choice of hospital.[19] This
means that support and advice is often necessary to ensure that all can
take advantage of choices. Critics often forget that even where there is
not overt choice, large inequalities exist in the quality of service provision, and those with more resources tend to get access to better options.
Affluent parents buy houses next to the best schools, driving up house
prices as they do so; and better connected middle class patients and
their families find out through their networks who are the best clinicians for given conditions and get themselves referred to them. Structured choice, especially with access to suitable advisers, can extend
these kinds of choices to all, and can drive up quality at the same time.

The question on efficiency revolves around whether, for choice to
be real, there needs to be slack in the system and therefore ineffi-

ciency. Without this slack, choice can be illusory, such as when popular schools in effect choose their students and parents, rather than the other way around. This is clearly about balance, but generally speaking the gains from service providers feeling under some pressure from 'market forces' are enough to more than cover the slack needed in the system to allow some element of choice, not least because the marginal cost of provision is much lower than the average cost.

The question of whether the public want choice is arguably the least clear cut. Most survey data suggest that choice in public services is a relatively low priority for the public. They are much more concerned about having a good service. Where expert judgement is involved, such as over which hospital to go to or treatment to have, the public often prefer to 'let the professionals decide'. But the public also want public services to become increasingly responsive and personalized. In other words, people want choices when they want them – not necessarily all the time. We shall return to this issue of 'choice architecture' later in the chapter.

Even the most vigorous proponents of choice generally concede that there are many services that are not amenable to a simple model of user choice. As of yet, there has been little serious discussion about whether citizens should have a choice of police services, ambulances, or fire services (though some of these choices have existed in the past). However, such services can still be subject to 'contestability' – that is, alternative providers can compete to offer services in a given area. Like choice, contestability can provide a mechanism through which good service providers can expand while poor providers are squeezed out.

Both choice and contestability can be thought of as different ways of sharpening up the commissioning of services. Across the public services, there has been longstanding interest in how various kinds of purchaser-provider splits can help drive service quality and value. In many countries, local government plays a large role in commissioning decisions – it is unusually weak in the UK – as do other local and regional commissioners of services. Local commissioners of services are often better placed than central government to know both the needs of their local populations and the strengths and weaknesses of the local providers.

One role that central and regional government can help with is to facilitate and put in the hands of commissioners well-evidenced but easy to understand guidance about alternative service providers (see also Chapter 1 on the role of government in providing information). There is little sense in hundreds of commissioners separately trying to compile their own 'what works' or 'which provider' guides.

Commissioners can also be individual citizens or lead-practitioners. Individual budgets can be a powerful tool to drive personalization and the improvement of services. Individual budgets have been tried in a number of countries and for a number of different public service needs, but most commonly for social care and for adult skills (see also Chapter 4 on educational endowments). The evidence is particularly encouraging for social care. Citizens with long-term conditions given individual budgets often choose to make extensive but sensible changes in the care they receive, such as employing carers who will come in at the start and finish of the day to enable them to take up work, or using the budgets to make physical changes to their homes so that they need less care. Such cases often involve moving stories of everyday empowerment, as well as improved outcomes at the same or lower cost.

For some vulnerable groups, such as children in the care system, such budgets may be better held by an intermediary or lead-practitioner who purchases care tailored to the individual's need. For example, when working on social exclusion we were shocked to discover that many child mental health services would only visit a troubled young person at a fixed address, and often with long waiting times. But the intensity of the child's problems – partly rooted in their lack of treatment – often led to frequent residential changes. A number of carers said that if they held the budget, they would prioritize buying in such expert psychological help, and bring it to the child wherever they were.

One thing you find – at least within the UK – is that new policy ideas get talked about a lot, and commentators then write about them as if they are already widely in place. This can create a large gap between the rhetoric and the reality of reform. For example, individual budgets for social care have been much discussed for several years in the UK, with real excitement over the results of the early trials. But a recent assessment concluded that only 3,500 people had actually received an individual budget against an estimated 1.3 million for whom they would be well suited.[20] Sometimes the results of reform are disappointing simply because it hasn't happened yet.

Maturing public service 'markets', networks and innovation

One of the biggest tricks that governments often miss is nurturing and maturing the markets around public sector provision. This may be down to the deep-seated, and admirable, tradition of probity and concerns about corruption. An irony of the 2008–9 banking crisis is that it dragged many governments back into assertive private-sector market shaping at the same time as such governments had become nervous of market-making in the public sector.

Innovative sectors and areas have a number of well-documented characteristics. Businesses within an innovative sector often cluster together in a dynamic of 'cooperation' – competing over business and products while simultaneously cooperating through shifting collaborations, the movement of staff, and the 'borrowing' of ideas. Big firms, such as Proctor and Gamble, BT and IBM have learnt these lessons too, restructuring around more open product innovation and greater collaboration with suppliers and customers.

An optimum structure for an innovative, learning and effective 'delivery chain' is unlikely to be thousands of separate and disconnected delivery agents (such as schools or general practitioners); a single monopoly (such as central government); or a single local monopoly (such as a single local government provider). A better structure is likely to involve a diversity of providers of different scales, many with a geographical spread outside of a single area and contesting or competing for services within areas. Supermarkets are sometimes cited as an example of such networks – both by supporters and sometimes by opponents. They achieve economies of scale and organization but, with the help of a little competition regulation, compete hard with each other within local areas, borrowing the best new ideas from each other and working closely with their suppliers to improve prices and quality.

If there is an outstanding school or hospital, we should want it to do more than grow modestly in its own area. We should want it to grow into a network of such schools or hospitals bringing those same benefits to a much larger population. If Thomas Telford school, or Great Ormond Street Hospital, are able to perform so well, can't we help them grow into 'networks' or hard federations of 50 plus outstanding schools or 10 children's hospitals?

Larger networks have a number of advantages. They can achieve scale benefits around purchasing and service development. They can extend the reach of the best leaders, a precious and expensive resource. They can create more opportunities for staff development and training within the organization. They can spread innovative practice more rapidly. They can give local commissioners more choices for the benefit of their local citizens, such as around failing services. And larger providers can often provide more personalized and flexible provision. For example, teaching Cantonese, high level gymnastics, or car mechanics would be difficult for an individual school, but a federation of 50 schools could employ specialists in all three.

In conclusion, prudent and strategic central governments should not shy away from active 'market shaping' in relation to public sector providers. Such a new generation of larger, less geographically based providers does not necessarily mean handing public services over to the private sector or losing the public sector ethos that we so value. Nor does it mean the elimination of small providers. Providers can be, and often should be, third or public sector organizations. Such an ecology of providers will probably eventually emerge on its own – it's a question of whether we wait for 100 years for it happen, or help the process along through incentives, facilitation and a few nudges.

Satisfaction

Readers who have made it through the rest of this book will realize that I'm quite big on the value of citizens' subjective experiences. This applies to public services too. Indeed, the growing use of subjective satisfaction measures may prove to be the single most important innovation in public services of the last decade.

In the PMSU, and OPSR[21], we were strongly influenced and impressed by the way in which the Canadians started to use subjective satisfaction measures as a tool to drive service improvement from the mid 1990s. The Canadians made what seemed like a very rash commitment – to increase public satisfaction with public services by 10% over a decade. What's amazing, is that they did it (see also Chapter 1).

The Canadians implemented a survey of the users of public services called 'Citizens First'. This survey asked users about their satisfaction with various specific services, and the data analysed to explain the variations. An early – and politically helpful – surprise was that Canadians' satisfaction with public services was as high, if not higher than, that with private services. This helped to put to bed the myth that private was always good and public bad, and helped secure support for the survey among public sector workers.

The survey put in the hands of public servants very useful feedback about what the public liked about particular services, and what they didn't like. A handful of factors tended to show through repeatedly, like timeliness and staff who went 'the extra mile' (see Figure 5.5). As those behind the survey explained, 'most public servants get out of bed in the morning wanting to do a good job, and don't want to feel that people who use their services are unsatisfied.' The Canadians were also careful to build up a sense of ownership in the survey by public servants, which made them more open to its critical findings. Armed with feedback, public servants could adjust their behaviour and how they were working in order to address points of public dissatisfaction.

In the decade since these Canadian surveys started, the headline average score for the 26 services that have appeared in all studies

Drivers of Citizen Satisfaction. *Citizens First 2000.*	
1. Timeliness	*"I was satisfied with the amount of time it took to get the service."*
2. Knowledge, Competence	*"Staff were knowledgeable and competent."*
3. The Extra Mile, The Extra Smile	*"Staff went the extra mile to make sure I got what I needed / I was treated in a friendly, courteous manner."*
4. Fairness	*"I was treated fairly."*
5. Outcome	*"I got what I needed."*

Figure 5.5 *Key drivers of satisfaction with public services from the Canadian Citizens First survey.*

of Citizens First has risen from 64 in 1998 to 72 in 2008 – an 8 point increase (or a 12.5% increase). This is despite increases in citizens' expectations of many service areas, such as how rapidly mail should be turned around. There is also clear evidence that these increases in satisfaction have helped raise public trust in state and central government too.

In the UK, we have sought to apply these lessons with the introduction of satisfaction surveys into most of the main public services. In several of these, a focus on public satisfaction is replacing a host of process and outcome measures (see also the discussion on targets below). The Italians have also recently moved in this direction, introducing an 'ebay-style' system of feedback on citizens' satisfaction with service transactions.

One of the reasons why satisfaction measures are so powerful is that they prompt an investigation of what the public really does care about, and often this turns out not to be what central government, or the service provider, thought it was. Merseyside police, for example, was early to pilot the use of satisfaction surveys. It had previously had as one of its key targets getting response times down: if someone called to say they had been burgled, the police would try and get an officer there as soon as possible, though this might still take several hours. However, once their focus shifted to public satisfaction, it became clear that the public were much less concerned about response times *per se*, than that the police turned up when they said they would. Most people were OK about the police turning up 4 hours after the call rather than 2½ hours, provided that they did show up at the time they said they would. These kinds of insights allowed the police to re-engineer how they worked with the public, and satisfaction rose.[22]

Satisfaction measures can also be a source of controversy precisely because they can imply a refocusing of effort and attention. In healthcare, public satisfaction is dominated by the sense of being treated with 'respect and dignity'. To caricature, a hospital might seek to drive up satisfaction through more attractive reception areas, better food, and by staff holding the patients' hand. But clinicians might argue that resources are better focused on more operations or better medicines, not 'cosmetics'. Similarly, it is found that satisfaction is strongly affected by familiarity. Hence one of the simplest things that local government, and other services, can do to boost satisfaction is simply to send users lots of information about what services exist, where they are, and when they're open. However, in most service areas, there is no great tension between what you would do to drive up satisfaction versus improve other 'hard' outcomes.

In fact, one of the best aspects of the use of public satisfaction measures is that it gets government, administrators, frontline public servants, and citizens all on the same page – the satisfaction of the citizen-user. What most deeply undermines the morale and satisfaction of public servants themselves is when they feel that activity is being driven by a managerial agenda that doesn't relate to the person in front of them. Satisfaction measures fundamentally change this dynamic. At the same time they create a powerful feedback loop direct between the user and the practitioner that can transform the relationship.

Let me close this section by giving a personal example from when I used to be a full-time lecturer at Cambridge.[23] Universities were relatively early adopters of the use of satisfaction surveys. In my Faculty, we had a rather forgiving qualitative set of feedback forms that students rarely bothered to fill in, and that lecturers didn't take very seriously. We revised these scales to include simple quantitative satisfaction scores, along with space for students to express more specific concerns, and strongly encouraged students to fill them in. These new scales revealed shocking variations in satisfaction between lecturers, and – without any sanctions – led several lecturers to overhaul and update their teaching.

A simple conclusion from a decade of work and experimentation with satisfaction surveys will be familiar to social psychologists – practitioners generally mean well, but often don't realize how the interaction looks and feels to the citizen in front of them or at the other end of the phone. It is not the professionals' fault. We all think that our perspective on the world is more representative than it is. Satisfaction surveys provide us with a mirror and reality check, giving us insights that we can often easily accommodate to increase both the citizen's satisfaction and our own.

Targets

The UK government has been a pioneer in the extensive use of targets in public services. Indeed, critics would say we went 'target mad'. Lessons were learnt along the way, some of which will be of interest to governments in other countries and within the UK.

The Labour Government came into power partly on the back of a small set of public service pledges that it promised to achieve, such as smaller class sizes for 5 to 7 year olds, cutting the numbers on health waiting lists, and halving the time from arrest to sentencing of young people. The Prime Minister's Delivery Unit (PMDU) was subsequently created to ensure the government's targets were delivered, and headed by Michael Barber after his early successes post-'97 in education.

Initially, the PMDU had 17 key targets that it monitored on a regular basis, with monthly stock-take meetings between the PM and the relevant Minister. Over the years, the number of targets rose. This arose both top-down, as the PM and Chancellor added new priorities with a corresponding expansion of the coverage of the PMDU, and bottom-up – or at least middle-up – as officials and other layers of government added their areas of concern to the targetry framework. Spending reviews were also a major source of the growth of targets, as the Treasury sought to link settlements with specific objectives embodied in 'Public Service Agreements' (PSAs).

As the targets multiplied, and complexity grew, Barber and others sought to clarify that many of what people were calling targets were really just indicators (giving important information about what was going on, but not necessarily a government priority or 'target') or measures (data that was administratively gathered but not necessarily either a key indicator or a target). There were also inevitable concerns about gaming. Goodall's Law became widely quoted: that when a measure was turned into a target, much of its value was destroyed. There was the nagging concern, particularly in the Treasury, about the lack of consequences for failing to meet targets. If a Department failed to meet a key target, did this mean that they should have their funding cut, or that they had to be given more?

It was the question of how many targets, or indicators, that local government was supposed to be responding to – perhaps more than any other – that brought the issue to a head. By the mid 2000s, no one seemed very sure how many targets or indicators local government was supposed to be delivering on, but it was widely believed to be more than 1,000. Everyone agreed that this didn't make much sense – 1,000 priority indicators simply meant that you had no priorities at all.

At the same time, as illustrated by the PMSU model of reform, there was widespread recognition of the limitations of a system of public administration that relied heavily on top-down targets as opposed to a host of other tools to drive improvement.

These lessons had been, or were being, learnt in other countries (and the private sector) too. New Zealand, for example, pushed much further than perhaps any other country in creating a host of delivery agencies contracted to deliver specific public service outcomes. The Chief Executives of these delivery bodies duly set about delivering their targets, but often to the exclusion of wider public service objectives, and sometimes in direct conflict with each other. The conflicts and complexity, twinned with the problem of 'incomplete contracts' where it is difficult to fully encapsulate or sanction the range of activities involved in a public service role, forced New Zealand to revisit the structure and responsibility of these Executives.

On the other hand, something very attractive remains about the idea of an explicit target. In principle, it makes clear for all the actors involved in an area what the priority should be. The classic business example is of a Las Vegas casino where the two core elements of the business – the hotel and the casino itself – would sometimes appear to have conflicting priorities. A hotel manager would normally want to ensure maximum profit through full occupancy, while a casino manager wants to maximize profit on the tables and machines. But a key dilemma is whether the hotel should always keep a few rooms available just in case a high spending gambler comes into town. In this case, most casinos have reached the view that keeping rooms available for high spenders is more valuable than full occupancy, and this is made clear to everybody, including the hotel manager. Maximizing the gambling spend is the priority.

Targets can, in principle, serve as the core element of a performance management system. Ministers, senior civil servants, and even front-line staff could be rewarded or side-lined on the basis of whether they had met or missed their targets. In democracies, targets can also offer a clear set of yard-sticks by which the public and electorate can judge the performance of the government. Of course, the harder these consequences, the more gaming must be expected, and the greater the pressure to get the targets and their technical measurement right.

Needless to say, the UK subsequently re-engineered its targetry regime, and it is a system that continues to evolve. The most recent round of Public Service Agreements (PSAs), which came into force in April 2008, are both smaller in number and at a higher level of abstraction than the previous generations of targets. At the same time, there has been a slashing in the number of targets applied to local government, and an expansion of what are called 'Local Area Agreements' (LAAs). These LAAs consist of a cluster of around 30 priority targets that are agreed between local delivery partners, led by Local Authorities, and central government (typically brokered by regional government offices). These targets are drawn from a longer menu of around 200 local indicators that are gathered but are not necessarily considered a priority for the area. This process is intended to allow local areas to emphasize issues that are of particular concern to them, but also for central government to impose others that are of concern to it. The early indications are that there is generally around 80 to 90% agreement between the centre and locality as to what should be the local targets, and a healthy discussion over the remainder.

Some regard the latest round of targetry and performance management in the UK as a radical and sophisticated evolution of a system that is rebalancing power and 'changing the DNA of government itself'.[24] Others point to continuing areas of concern. Critics argue that the new generation of PSAs lack the visibility necessary to really shape the day-to-day prioritization of large public sector organizations or the political judgements of the public, yet are generally not specific enough, or linked to enough sanctions, to be built into a hard performance management system.[25] Departments retain separate budgets and their own strategic objectives, and the day-to-day reality is that these often loom larger than the messy shared responsibilities of PSAs.

The conclusion on targets seems to be something like 'you can't live with them, and you can't live without them'. Within the public sector, perhaps the best way to view them is as part of a process, not as an end in themselves. They force key stakeholders to make priorities explicit. They encourage deeper enquiries about what drives these indicators; what interventions might affect them; and whether they are as consequential as we think. As targets and performance management mature, they facilitate judgements around the cost effectiveness of interventions, and can sometimes throw up new ways of thinking about old problems.

When assessing the legacy of Michael Barber, and the UK experiments with targets, it is worth understanding what really made Michael tick and what made him so valuable to the Prime Minister. As well as being an affable and pleasant man, he had a profoundly deep-seated 'can-do' attitude. Anyone in policy and public services who looks across a range of local areas, delivery bodies, or countries will come across wide variations in outcomes that can't be explained away by exogenous factors and population characteristics. But within those underperforming areas, there will almost always be some who simply accept these poorer outcomes as inevitable. Michael couldn't bear this, and would always throw himself with a passion and impatience into driving up standards.

The ultimate answer is not a target and PMDU probe in every aspect of life – a public sector equivalent of the control rooms at Boeing or Rolls Royce that track the performance of every engine ever made in real time (to use a recent metaphor of Michael himself). But we should want a streak of Michael's impatience with underperformance, and passion for delivery, in all of us. The trick is to harness the piles of data that we now gather, the evidence on what works, with a wider dynamic of peer comparison, incentives and public pressure to squeeze out underperformance and promote excellence. Governments need priorities, but not necessary targets.

Joined-up services

One of the great challenges – and slogans – of recent years has been the idea of 'joined-up government for joined-up services'. This issue has arisen in many if not all countries. The basic problem is that large bureaucracies and services have evolved to 'deliver' services that are efficient and rational from the viewpoint of the provider rather than being moulded around the particular and often complex needs of the 'user'. This is sometimes termed the 'letterbox' model of delivery – the service is delivered in a pre-packaged form regardless of the user's personal circumstances.[26] The user receives a series of such parcels and it's up to them to see if they can put them together into some sort of meaningful whole.

The classic example is what happens when someone dies. Relatives find themselves having to notify literally dozens of different agencies – both private and state. Already distraught relatives end up feeling immensely frustrated with different public services that seem unable to inform each other of the situation, and who rely on citizens to repeat the same information again and again.

Numerous approaches have been used to help overcome this failure to join-up, which we can loosely divide into 'front-stage' and 'back-stage' approaches. 'Front-stage' approaches seek to create a single shop-window for services, even if the processes behind it remain separate. One-stop shops are a common example, where multiple service providers co-locate so that the citizen can complete all their transactions in one go. Another is the use of single emergency telephone call-centres that identify the nature of the caller's concern and channel them directly to the right person or service. Many countries have long had this in place for the emergency services, and several are seeking to extend this principle to non-emergency services. New York's 311 number, introduced by Bloomberg, has led the way. It now handles more than a million calls a month, 24 hours a day in 170 languages, and directing them to over 80 separate agencies. It replaced a system of more than 4,000 separate phone numbers directed through 45 different call centres.[27]

Some countries and local governments have introduced a two- or three-person 'pass rule'. This states that public servants are not allowed to 'pass-on' a citizen query more than a certain number of times. In more than one case, this rule was established after a senior policy-maker – trying to get some fairly standard transaction completed in their 'normal life' found themselves passed from one person to another, often going round in a time-consuming circle.

The use of individual budgets and lead practitioners can be a way of forcing joining-up, with the user or practitioner assembling services like items from a menu – the users doing the joining-up for themselves. Another approach, with particular relevance to tax and benefits, is to require both services and citizens to use a single transparent account into which payments are made (an approach pioneered by the Danes). This enables those administering different and interacting benefits to see other payments that have been made and to make adjustments without the citizen having to provide the same information repeatedly (see also Chapter 2 on social exclusion).

More fundamental, or back-stage reforms, involve a re-engineering of services or bureaucracies themselves. The creation of 'super-departments' is periodically discussed and occasionally tried – such as creating a department for children or older people in local or central government, instead of separate departments of education, health, social services and so on. The creation of 'Children's Trusts' in local government have proven to be a reasonably successful example of this in the UK context, helping to bridge across earlier divides in responsibility. But wherever these departmental lines are drawn, new cleavages tend to appear (such as between child and adult services for the young person leaving care, or across child and adult mental health services).

Joined-up targets, such as the new generation of UK Public Service Agreements (PSAs) and Local Area Agreements (LAAs) are a way of potentially joining-up big Departments, while cross-cutting Cabinet Committees are a way of joining-up at a Ministerial level. Satisfaction measures again have a role to play, as they tend to involve more holistic assessments of service quality and often highlight inadequacies around handovers and junctions between services. However, the brutal reality remains that money – i.e. separate budgets – and old habits often overpower good intents to join-up across boundaries and services.

For this reason, more radical options have been tried by a number of countries. In the UK, there have been experiments with double- or triple-key budgets that require the mutual agreement of more than one Department for their release. These merit wider use, including in relation to future generations of PSAs. In Finland, Ministerial responsibilities have been restructured so that senior Ministers hold responsibility for cross-cutting objectives, while more junior Ministers take responsibility for individual Departments. In New Zealand, this approach is taken one step forward in that Ministers physically sit together up in the 'beehive', as their building is known, rather than being based in the Departments. This arrangement changes the normal gestalt and loyalty of Ministers to Departments. Instead, Departments and officials have to get together and approach Ministers as a collective group, with a focus on the problem in hand rather than the convenience of the individual Department.

Joining-up departments and services remains an often elusive goal of policymakers. Few have faith in the capacity of big structural reorganizations to deliver this goal. On the other hand, the capacity of better information technology, more sophisticated budgetary arrangements and more savvy and educated citizens gives good reason to think that public services can be increasingly joined-up. In the UK, a nice everyday example is the way in which citizens can now renew their car tax online. This used to be a very clumsy and bureaucratic process requiring citizens to manually compile their car insurance, MOT (a certificate of car roadworthiness from a garage), and their ownership documentation and taking it all to a post-office to buy a new annual car tax disc. This process can now be done online, with automatic checking of the relevant documentation from different sources, and is a much easier and more efficient experience for the car owner.

However, even if joining-up can be done from a technocratic point of view, an unexpected barrier has emerged in the form of public concerns, and consequent Parliamentary wariness, over data-sharing by public services. This has been aggravated further by high profile losses of data or security breaches. This may have to be resolved through restricting direct data sharing by government departments or public services while helping citizens to instead use intermediaries to pool their data, with citizens granting access to their profiles to selected services. A younger generation familiar with Facebook and Amazon may simply make this happen, while older bureaucracies fumble. Data sharing services, with some state regulation and strong and transparent consumer feedback, may prove to be a key ingredient in the joined-up services of the future.

Professional responsibility

As a result of the unpopularity of targets, there are calls in the UK that much greater responsibility should be handed back to front-line professionals and to the services themselves. The reduction in the number of PSAs and the introduction of LAAs are a step in this direction. But critics who want to see a bigger shift of power would be right to view Whitehall with suspicion: the instincts of central Departments and the shifting priorities of Ministers will always mean an imaginative search for new ways to get leverage over public service providers, such as offering 'ring-fenced' funding for a particular objective or placing obligations on providers through legislation.

Yet a complete handing over of control and responsibility to public service providers and professionals is very unlikely and undesirable. The public have legitimate and sometimes different priorities to that of any particular professional group. We, as the public, may want more services, but we don't want to pay too much for them. We respect expertise, but we are the experts about our own lives and communities. And the history of totally self-regulating professions is not a happy one, with a great reluctance of professionals to sanction their peers except in the most extreme cases of failure or abuse.

There is an echo here of the false zero-sum game of the division of power of the classic state. Effective public services rest on a genuine partnership between professionals, citizens and the state – albeit one in which there is room for specialization in this sharing of responsibility. This is expressed in the latest, softer expression of the approach to public service improvement in the UK – the successor to the 'washing machine of reform' and in the idea of centrally enforced minimum 'citizen entitlements' (see Figure 5.6).

As a final example, let us illustrate this balance and shared responsibility with the example of information, the lifeblood of service improvement and delivery. Understanding and mapping citizens' experiences and outcomes is critical to all actors. Citizens – as parents, patients, students, welfare recipients and so on – want to know what their options are, not just to choose between them but to shape them too. This information can come in many forms, including league tables to much more personalized information on choices, options and outcomes. Often the most valuable source of this information is other citizens, including the experiences and outcomes that they have had. In this sense, TripAdvisor and Wikipedia are a glimpse of the future of public service information.

We look to professionals to provide expertise and guidance, but the relationship is clearly symbiotic. Professionals get to be better at their jobs when their practice is based on systematic evidence and feedback

Figure 5.6 *The characteristics of world-class public services (Cabinet Office, 2008).*

from those that are seeking help. This evidence can be drawn both from classic academic studies, but also the natural variations that occur in practice and across populations.

The state can play a role in facilitating the gathering and exchange of all this information, especially if we wish its benefits to be widely and equitably spread. Information has strong public and private good aspects. Knowing which school or doctor is most effective is valuable information that some will pay a good price for. But we don't want this to be just a private good. We want to harness it for the widest possible benefit. Similarly, though the information about the citizen's experience or outcome is of great potential value, it represents a cost to the citizen to document and share it. This combination suggests a *prima facie* case for market failure and a role for the state to ensure that such information is gathered, pooled and shared most effectively. This doesn't mean that the state has literally to gather the information itself. It may just need to incentivize and facilitate intermediaries, public services and citizen organizations to perform this role.

The practical state: a few conclusions

The role of the practical state, and our expectations of it, have grown enormously over the last half century, and the world recession of 2008–10 may only increase expectations further. Charlie Leadbetter has characterized the change in citizen expectations of services from one of 'I need' (such as the postwar need for housing, basic healthcare and benefits); to one of 'I want' (such as the growing demand for expensive medication or specialist schools); to one of 'I can' (in which citizens increasingly shape services for themselves). Leadbetter has also pointed out that public services are in a game of catch-up across these shifts in citizen expectations. Governments are struggling to move public services built in an age of 'needs' to one more suited to an age of 'wants', just as the population itself begins to move into an age of 'cans'.

However, there are a number of tools that policy-makers, public service professionals and citizens can use to foster improvements in public services almost regardless of whether viewed through an 'I want' or 'I can' lens.

- Using money as a lever. Powerful but underutilized tools include: using incentives or prizes for improvement, effectively putting a bounty on underperformance; using multiple-key budgets that require providers or purchasers mutually to agree to the release of funds; and the wider use of individual budget holding by users and lead practitioners.
- Market making and networks. Innovative and efficient sectors and markets have distinctive structural characteristics. Policymakers have been too hesitant, and unclear, about how to actively culture such characteristics. In particular, priority should be given to the nurturing of networks, chains or hard federations of non-geographically based public service providers, though also taking care to ensure than none become dominant regional monopolies. The state's role in regulating private markets will also continue, and probably grow.
- A new generation of mutual targets or key indicators. Top-down targets have gone out of fashion, but this does not mitigate the need for a degree of clarity between providers, citizens and central government about what services are trying to achieve. Satisfaction measures, local area agreements, citizen entitlements and Ministerial level (non-Departmental) objectives are all good examples of being explicit about priorities and using these to foster improvement. In the context of more dynamic and flexible public services, with informed and informing citizens, the improved flow of information around these indicators will often be enough to transform services and outcomes.

There can be no doubt that, like it or not, there will be more of a blurring between public and private services in coming decades than there were in the previous ones. A number of Ministers have found the concept of 'public value' a helpful tool in navigating this shifting landscape.[28] It draws attention to the broader bundle of yardsticks by which public services must be judged – not just by outputs, but by outcomes and the justice and compassion of processes themselves. In many areas we will see the state acting as more of a facilitator and commissioner, rather than direct deliverer, as we already begin to see in healthcare, education and benefits and workfare programmes. We may also see it in new areas too, such as policing.

The redrawing of this line in the sand is often characterized as one of retreat. But it is important to see that the same logic is extending the reach of the state and communities into the regulation of the public good aspects of the traditional private sector. For public value applies to the private sector too. The practical state should not stand by where consumers are being ripped-off in sectors with strong asymmetries of information, such as car repairs or financial products. It should not stand by where large sections of the public find themselves unfairly disadvantaged by market dynamics, such as when poor consumers find that they have to pay more for everyday goods because no supermarkets or banks operate in their area. And it should not stand by when poor quality providers drag down a market to ultimate detriment of all – including where short-term market incentives lead banks and whole countries to the edge of bankruptcy.

Finally, it is worth noting that many of the areas that we traditionally think of as 'public services' will be the great growth 'industries' of the twenty-first century. A number of respectable economists take the view that the industrialized nations could well be spending more than 20% of GDP on healthcare alone by 2050 – and for the USA, this could be as much as 40%. Education too is likely to be an area of increasing spending, both for practical economic reasons and as a consumption-good. So getting the practical state right is not just a matter of public goods in the traditional sense – it is also a new battleground of trade and comparative advantage between nations.

The Paternalistic State

The concept of the paternalistic state revolves around ideas that have become rather unfashionable in recent decades. This includes ideas such as the state might make better choices than citizens; that forward or master planning and building in resilience is sometimes better than letting the market figure things out; and that the state has a role beyond protecting us from the tyranny of the strong (the classic state) or ensuring the provision of public services (the practical state). In short, the paternalistic state revisits the idea that the state might sometimes know best, after all.

In many mature democracies – and certainly in the UK – the suggestion that the state or government might be capable of 'wisdom and foresight' would prompt a wry smile or open derision from many citizens – and even from policy-makers. But in relation to a number of the key problems our societies face, a dose of wisdom and foresight seems to be what we need – yet what would this mean?

The traditional justification for the activities of the practical state is around the provision of public goods, the addressing of market failures, and action around activities characterized by strong externalities. This leaves large swathes of life as *not* the business of government. In this respect, it is worth noting that governments – often as a direct result of public pressure – have actively removed state controls from many areas of public and private life. Most governments (but not all) have made it easier for people to get divorced; removed laws outlawing homosexuality and other private sexual practices; relaxed measures around gambling and prostitution; eased restrictions on when shops may trade; and cleared away measures once aimed at restricting the rights of different religious, gendered or ethnic groups. Many of these measures give a glimpse into an earlier age of state action, when state and religion were closer and governments frequently mandated the behaviour of citizens in a distinctly moral and paternalistic way.

The 'wicked problems'

A clear illustration of the new dilemma is the rise of obesity across Western nations. Contrary to popular opinion, there is plenty of food in the world. While it is true that over the last 40 years the world population increased by just over 90%, world agricultural production over the same period rose by nearly 140%. At the same time, levels of physical activity and corresponding calorific needs have fallen. The real problem, and tragedy, is that while around 850 million people in the world are under-nourished, around 1 to 2 billion are overweight (see Figure 5.7).

As we all know, obesity isn't good for us. It greatly increases the risks of diabetes, respiratory difficulties, chronic musculoskeletal problems, skin problems, infertility, hypertension, heart disease, stroke and cancer. In analyses carried out for the World Health Organization in

Prevalence of obesity, males, aged 30+, 2005

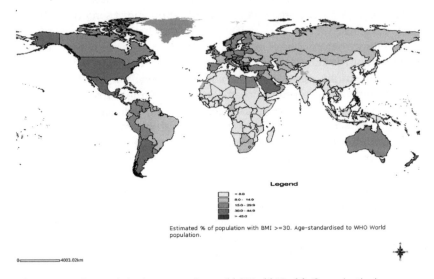

Figure 5.7 *Rates of obesity across the world (World Health Organization).*

2002, it was estimated that approximately 58% of diabetes, 21% of ischaemic heart disease and 8–42% of certain cancers were attributable globally to having a body mass index (BMI) above 21 kg/m^2. Both the absolute levels of these medical problems, and the proportion attributable to obesity, are set to rise further.

Rising obesity rates, in both adults and children, are not limited to the industrialized West. Obesity rates are estimated to have tripled since 1980 in large areas of North America, the United Kingdom, and Eastern Europe – but also in the Middle East, the Pacific Islands, Australasia and China. This is not just a Western issue. In the USA 36% of men and 42% of women are obese – and 21% of men and 24% of women in the UK – but there are already several nations that have obesity rates in excess of 50%.[29]

The question is, is this really the responsibility of the state? The costs of obesity are primarily private, and so are its proximate causes – eating too much and not exercising enough. This does result in some costs to publicly funded health care systems, but these costs are only a few per cent of healthcare. There are welfare benefit costs too but, to put it brutally, these are at least partly offset by lower pension costs resulting from premature deaths.[30]

Obesity is not the only contemporary policy challenge with these characteristics. Faced with ageing populations, the funding of pensions has become a major issue. We are living longer than ever, with higher expectations of our quality of life than ever, but we aren't keen on saving money for our retirements. Again, one might argue that this is primarily a matter of private costs and benefits. If an individual chooses not to save and instead enjoys their money while young, why should their impoverished old age be the concern of anyone else?

There are other more extreme (literally) examples that illustrate the same point. There is a growing fashion for all kinds of extreme sports and activities from bungee jumping to parkour (moving as rapidly as possible between two points over a series of difficult obstacles), with a strong element of thrill-seeking and danger to the individuals concerned, but not necessarily to other people. But once again, why should this be a concern of the state, particularly if the individuals or instructors are insured?

Personal responsibility

There is a strong moral and economic logic that individuals should take responsibility for the knowing personal choices that they make (see also Chapter 4). In contrast, the state's role is more appropriately focused on attenuating bad 'brute luck', such as mass unemployment or genetically linked illness. The 'polluter pays principle' follows this logic, as does some paternalistic legislation such as to protect children or strangers from the effects of passive smoking.

The emphasis on personal responsibility runs especially deeply in Anglo-Saxon countries, but is also a strong strand of thinking in many Scandinavian and other countries too.[31] When it comes to welfare-to-work, anti-social behaviour or immigrants taking advantage of publicly funded services, both politicians and public are apt to take a pretty tough line on personal responsibility. But how does this principle apply to issues such as obesity, pensions or even extreme sports?

When the public is asked 'who is at fault for obesity?', 79% blame parents, 48% blame food and drink manufacturers, and 22% blame the individual.[32] Only a very small minority – 12% – blame the state. But when asked, 'who is responsible for dealing with obesity?' a whopping 69% say 'the state'. Food and drink manufacturers also get mentioned by 40%, but only 31% say parents, and only 30% 'the individual'. So even though the public think it's parents' fault, a clear majority want the state to sort it out.

We – as the public – and hence politicians too, are deeply con-
flicted and contradictory about our position on personal responsibility. For the most part, we are very big on personal responsibility for
other people and when things are going well for ourselves. But when
things go badly in our lives, regardless of the cause, we go off the
idea of personal responsibility pretty fast. Unfortunately for policymakers, we hold both these positions quite strongly and at the same
time. When we drive too fast or aggressively in heavy traffic, it is
because we're in a hurry to sort out an important matter. But when
other people drive too fast it's because they are idiots and ought to
be fined.

There are two strong arguments in favour of a paternalistic state,
and one that seems rather dodgy. All concern personal responsibility.
The first, and most traditional argument for a more paternalistic state
is a literal one. The state should act as a proxy parent for children and
those who lack the capacity to make reasoned and informed decisions.
Hence we have little problem with the idea that the state should require
children to go to school and be educated, regardless of whether they
would rather stay at home and watch TV. Similarly, the state will often
take a particularly strong interest in protecting the rights of those who
have lost their mental capacities, such as through illness or physical
trauma.

The second strong argument concerns the distinction between 'task
responsibility' and 'causal responsibility'. Our starting presumption
tends to be that moral responsibility should follow causal responsibility – you made the mess so you should clear it up. But we also recognize that sometimes the person or actor best placed to address the
problem or prevent it happening again may not be the person or actor
who caused it. For example, consider a dangerous mountain road with
a perilous drop on one side. We might fairly say that it is up to drivers
to take extra caution driving along it, and the 1 in 100 who drive off the
edge do so primarily because they are not being careful enough. But in
practice, it is not that difficult for the highway authority to put a safety
barrier up. The provision of public services often rests on this logic, but
where should the line be drawn? To take a real example, in most countries people sort out their car insurance with private companies with
the state simply requiring people to be insured to drive. But there is a
case that it would be administratively simpler if the state just took on
the function directly. We could still keep some personal responsibility
in place, with a differential charge according to previous claims and
so on, but it might be administratively easier and more efficient for
the state to run the system, just as it does for basic 'insurance' against
unemployment.

The third is often considered much more morally and politically shaky: that we are rubbish at making decisions. Furthermore, we are plagued with self-serving attributional biases that make us bad at judgements about personal responsibility itself. The first part of this argument – that we are rubbish at making decisions is increasingly well-rehearsed, with a new book published on the subject every other week. We look at the errors we tend to make in decision-making and the policy implications in more detail below, but let us look at the second part of the argument now.

There is a long-standing branch of psychology which looks specifically at how we reach judgements about the responsibility of, and intention behind, the behaviour of other people. It is called attribution theory, and it goes back to the work of Heider in the 1950s. It explores our very human curiosity about what other people are *really* up to. Why did that guy just smile at you in the elevator? Do you have something on your face? Did one of your kids stick a label on your back saying 'I am as dumb as I look' like happened last week? Was he making a pass at you? Or maybe it was nothing to do with you – he was just thinking about the holiday he'd just booked, or just passed wind? Maybe he wasn't even looking at you at all.

Humans are really concerned about this stuff, partly because a huge amount of our adaptive advantage and evolutionary history comes from being able to read the intentions of other people in a social group. When the action concerned is more dramatic and consequential than a smile, our attributional brains really go into overdrive. When we hear a large crash and come out to find our neighbour's car smashed into our front fence, our brains start spinning. We aren't just interested in what happened – the direct causes of how the car got there – but in the intention of the neighbour himself. Apart from asking, 'What happened to my fence?' Did their brakes fail? Is that my neighbour in the car, or is someone trying to steal it? we also start asking: did he do this on purpose or was it an accident? Did he want to smash up my fence? Is he trying to hurt me? Did I cause more offence than I thought when I told him I hated the colour he painted his house? Maybe he knows that I fancy his wife?

You're at it now. You're trying to piece together the story, to figure out what each of the people concerned are up to. First of all, maybe you thought the neighbour's foot had slipped on the accelerator, or maybe there's something wrong with them. Maybe he's angry. I mean, you're ogling his wife!

So it turns out that we're obsessed with attribution. But we're also strongly prone to 'self-serving attributional biases'. Many of these revolve around what's known as the fundamental attribution error.

Basically, we tend to over-attribute the causes of other people's behaviour to their own personal abilities, personality and intentions. An everyday example of this is that we tend to think that the questioners on game shows must be very intelligent.[33] Lab experiments show the effect very clearly. Subjects are arbitrarily assigned either to be questioners, which involves thinking up some tricky questions, or answerers, and others are then asked to rate their intelligence. What happens is that people consistently rate the questioners as being of higher intelligence.

Why? Well imagine yourself as an impromptu questioner. The chances are that you can think of some tricky obscure question that you know the answer to, just because of your personal history or interests, but that most people won't know. But then, of course, other people could think of some obscure questions that *you* don't know the answer to. So in this situation, it is almost inevitable that the questioners look smart, and those trying to answer don't. It's the situation that is explaining the variance, not the individual characteristic, but our bias to attribute causes to people trips us up.

There is one big exception to the fundamental attribution error, and that's when it comes to explaining the causes of our *own* behaviour. When it is us struggling to answer the difficult and obscure question that our fellow subject has asked us about seventeenth-century chamber music, or what LASER stands for, the situational factors loom very large indeed. We certainly don't race to the conclusion that it's because we're stupid. Similarly, when we get a parking ticket, we'll tend to grumble about how unclear the signs were, that the meter must have just clicked out, that it was the fault of the dry cleaners for being so slow, or even that it was unfair and small-minded of the warden to have noted when the meter was going to run out and check at exactly that time. What we probably won't want to dwell on is that we should have put more money in the meter, or that we shouldn't have spent 30 minutes in the bookstore trying to decide which book to buy.

In sum, we tend to over-attribute the behaviours of other people to personal factors, and over-estimate the importance of situational factors when it comes to ourselves, especially when something bad happens to us. In contrast, when good things happen to us, like being well paid because we're smart, or living in a big house because our parents gave us money or a good start in life, we are more than happy to overlook the situational context and take the credit personally.

This combination of factors helps make sense of our seemingly contrary attitudes to personal responsibility. When it comes to all the annoying things that other people do, like anti-social behaviour, we want them punished (see Chapter 2). But when it comes to bad things happening to us, even if they are our own causal responsibility, we're pretty keen on the state stepping in to help us out. We want a bit of paternalism after all.

Behavioural economics

Unless you've been living on the policy equivalent of the moon, you will by now have heard of behavioural economics. This is all about understanding how people actually remember, weight, judge and predict as opposed to how we – or at least economists and political scientists – think we should.

Curiously, I used to lecture on behavioural economics before it got to be popular. I got to read Tversky and Kahneman's now classic book when it was still an obscure cognitive psychology text back in the early 1980s.[34] It was very cool, new and exciting. On the other hand, I don't get to feel *that* smug because it took a host of popularizations to get policymakers to think about, though within UK our strategy unit paper did help raise the profile.[35]

It turns out that there are literally dozens of different kinds of mental shortcuts that, at least some of the time, can lead us into making decisions that seem to be irrational or non-optimum. In crude terms, we are prone to three linked types of error, which often work to compound each other (see Figure 5.8).[36] We misremember our own past experiences, which means that we go on to repeat past mistakes or fail to learn as much from them as we might hope. Partly this is because remembering isn't a neat and tidy process, but one that is active and interpretive. Second, we tend to be prone to errors of judgement arising from mental shortcuts – or 'cheats' – that we use in the present. Though we're great at lots of things, maths, stats and figuring out our own emotions aren't among them. So we often prove rather poor at interpreting the data in front of us, and make the wrong choice compared with that an economist or statistician with a calculator would have made. Finally, we're often amazingly bad at predicting what would be good for ourselves in the future, and this gets us in no end of trouble. This last type of error partly follows from the previous two – misremembering the past compounded with errors in the moment don't make a great platform for prediction. But these errors are further compounded by biases that specifically concern the future, such as overly heavy discounting costs and benefits in the long versus short-term, and our general tendency to be over-optimistic about our own abilities and likely future.

In a nutshell, behavioural economics uses this knowledge to make more accurate predictions about how people are likely to behave and,

Remembering	Judging in the moment	Predicting
Recency effects: lead us to overweight our most recent experience. We vote for governments that cut taxes before elections, and forget earlier tax rises.	**Anchoring**: leads us to stick close to an initial estimate, even if completely irrelevant. Our answer gets biased towards an openly wrong 'illustrative example' given before.	**Hyperbolic discounting**: future gains and losses are overly discounted. Investing in a pension is something we will always do tomorrow.
Peak effects: unusual or extreme experiences are more prominent than more constant experiences. We prefer the dentist that gave us three hours of steady hell over the one who gave us sharp pang of pain.	**Framing effects**: the context makes us zoom in on one factor or dimension. We buy speakers that don't fit in our house because we chose them in comparison to the sound of others in the shop where the issue of size didn't occur to us.	**Presentism and focusing**: we are poor at predicting how we will feel in the future. We think losing our legs or our child would make life not worth living, because we fail to see the pleasures our future selves would still enjoy.
Consistency: we blot out and embellish experiences to make them fit with our beliefs. We don't recall fouls committed by our own football team but remember those of the opponents.	**Loss aversion**: losses have higher salience than logically equal gains. We're more likely to insulate our house when told about the $200 we're losing through not insulating than the $200 we'd save if we did.	**Representativeness and simulation**: we overestimate the chance of that which we can easily recall. We think airplanes are dangerous because we can easily recall examples of when they crashed.
Suggestion: the questions others ask us about an experience can reshape our memory. The details in a lawyer's cross-examination get incorporated into our own memory of the event.	**Social proof**: we follow the crowd. If everyone else is buying it, it must be good.	**Over-optimism**: we think that better things will happen to us than others. We never think it will be our marriage that fails.

Figure 5.8 *Examples of common mental shortcuts that lead to 'errors' in thought.*

in the hands of a new generation of policy wonks, gives strong clues about how behaviour might be shaped for better outcomes. For now, it is right to say 'strong clues' rather than exact tools because behavioural economics remains more a craft than a science. This is because, although there are literally hundreds of studies documenting the various errors and influences on our decisions, there is often great uncertainty over which one will spring into action in any given situation, or which will predominate. The best you can do is look for a study on a decision that is very similar to the one that you are interested in, take a punt that it will apply in your case, then experimentally try it out. Even if it doesn't work, you can probably still get an academic paper out talking about the limits of the particular heuristic, or maybe the new mental shortcut that you have uncovered.

The conflicted citizen: higher versus lower brain

Within this literature, and its policy applications, there are two very different approaches jostling with each other. These correspond to a kind of battle going on in our own heads, and perhaps within our politics.

Much of what behavioural economics is concerned with is what Robert Cialdini refers to as 'click-whirr' reactions. You put someone in a particular situation or dynamic and, almost like clockwork, they respond in a certain way – at least on average across a population, if not in every single case. For example, people seem to have a very strong tendency to reciprocate. If I give you something or some help, then ask for something back, you will be strongly inclined to do so. An everyday example of this is a subtle form of 'aggressive begging'. You are at the station looking for your train on the departures screen, and someone hands you a tiny sprig of flowers. You look at them slightly baffled, but before you have time to think they put their hand out and say something like 'it's for the little children'. For added effect, there might even be a little child in tow, looking forlornly at you. Even as half you brain is saying 'wait a minute', the other half has reached into your pocket and taken out a dollar or a pound. You've been stung. But what slightly grates is that you weren't caught by a great criminal, but by the collusion of your own brain.

A milder version of the same trick is when charities give you something then ask for money. The typical example is a pen (so you can fill out the form or write the cheque), but it can be 'free Christmas cards' or a book. Even more effective, of course, is if the gift comes from someone in your social network. Hence charity dinners or events where you are invited to dinner or a drink, then afterwards there is an auction or some other contribution is asked for. In the latter case, the chances are that you know what's going on and are happy with it. But this doesn't stop the dynamic of reciprocity pulling you along (together with social comparison) to make you give more than you intended.

But there is a secondary dynamic, which is to bring in our thinking brain to stop the 'click-whirr' reaction and to arm ourselves with the tools to resist these influences. We might think of this as 'higher' versus 'lower' brain; automatic versus reflective thinking; or 'click-whirr' versus the use of 'commitment devices'.[37] The latter concern techniques that we can employ to protect ourselves from our 'weaker' or automatic selves.[38] The classic example and metaphor is how Odysseus had himself tied to the mast of his ship, and his crew's ears plugged with wax, so that he could hear the voices of the sirens and yet not hurl himself into the sea, or steer the boat onto the rocks. He knew his own weakness and the nature of the trap, so he pre-committed himself to be tied to the mast and to the wisdom of his higher brain.

It is no surprise then, that in parallel to the marketers' handbooks messing with our heads and our wallets, we find a host of other advice telling us how to resist these dark arts. Stores figure out how to sell us highly profitable extended warranties at the moment we are most attached to our brand new TV and sensitive to how much it cost. But consumer groups warn against these bad deals and governments introduce obligatory two week 'cooling off' rights to change our minds. It's an evolutionary arms war between influencers, with our brains split down the middle. Even Cialdini's increasingly famous book has evolved over time, becoming not only the marketers' handbook, but also offering tools to the consumer in how to resist.

The policymaker faces difficult choices across this divide. Does the policymaker join the marketers and the behavioural economists, albeit in a benevolent way, and 'nudge' the citizen towards 'better' choices? Or does the policymaker arm the citizen with the tools to resist the 'behavioural predators'? Whose side of the citizen's brain are we on?

The answer is that the policymaker could be, and probably should be, on both sides – especially since the two brain-sides will themselves often be in conflict. If the policymaker acts as a regulator of the excesses of behavioural manipulation by other actors, perhaps partly by arming our citizens themselves to take on these influences (a sort of Swiss approach to possible attack), they can argue that they are well within the jurisdiction of the classic state. It is simply a new form of tyranny that the state is protecting us from. But if the state chooses to use the dark arts of manipulation itself, then it needs to justify this new and potentially powerful form of paternalistic action.

Libertarian paternalism and 'co-production-lite'

Many senior policymakers, and citizens, are wary about the idea of the state as a subtle but powerful manipulator of behaviour. 'It's just not cricket', we might quaintly say, in that it violates some tacit rule of democratic government. When we brought Cialdini into No. 10 for a seminar a couple of years ago, I asked him about this concern – the appropriate wariness that citizens and policymakers should have of the state as a super manipulator. His answer was that we should think about it in terms of the state being an 'effective rather than fumbling communicator'. If the state had the legitimacy to act in a given area – such as around public health and obesity (see above) – then it might as well do it well, particularly when up against food manufacturers and others who had very different agendas.

Cialdini's answer offers a sort of 'dog eat dog' world justification. A more nuanced and arguably acceptable account is that of 'libertarian paternalism', as proposed and popularized by Richard Thaler and Cass Sunstein. The basic idea is that the state should set up important everyday decisions so that the default, or psychological line of least resistance, is set as one that is sensible and fair. This is the 'paternalist' bit, shaping choices up with an eye on our lower brain or 'click-whirr' selves. The 'libertarian' bit is that these defaults should be set it up in a way so that the citizen retains the ability to override or opt out of the choice – leaving room for our higher brain or reflective selves to take over.

For many policymakers, libertarian paternalists have got a 'killer argument' up their sleeves. Libertarian paternalists point out that whatever you do – even deciding to do nothing – it is not a neutral option. All action, or inaction, affects the ecology of behaviour in some way or another. The policymaker is a 'choice architect' whether they like it or not.

The policy application that has most powerfully made the case for libertarian paternalism is pensions. Across countries, whether in state or privately administered systems, we don't seem to save enough. Partly because we discount the future relative to the present, and partly because we don't trust the state or pensions companies not to do the same as we would and spend the money now, we don't want to pay more taxes or contributions for the prospect of a comfortable distant retirement. Hence average savings rates rarely rise above 3% when they really need to be perhaps double this rate.[39]

In an innovative intervention based on behavioural economic principles, employees in a firm of 80,000 had their pension contributions restructured.[40] A change was made so that when employees got a pay rise, a slice of this rise would automatically go in their pension contributions. However, they could opt out at any time. This seemingly simple change led to a remarkable result: within a three-year period, savings rose from the normal 3% to over 11%. Once savings rates reached these higher levels, employees began to opt out of further rises, but maintained their higher levels of savings.

How did it work? The scheme flipped around the normal problem of 'pain today for gain tomorrow' by ensuring that the saving was also in the future, and therefore psychologically discounted (it only kicked in when you got a future pay rise). This ensured that the employee never suffered a psychologically painful cut in income (note asymmetry of loss and gain in Figure 5.8). Social proof helped too, since everyone was doing the same thing. And finally, though employees retained control, the barriers associated with joining – a major up-front psychological cost – were removed. In everyday speak, we're a bit lazy, so we take the easy option – in this case to do nothing and opting in.

One can argue about which ingredient made this scheme so successful. Much of the 'heavy lifting' is done by the automatic enrolment. Sunstein and Thaler elsewhere highlighted the huge differences in motor insurance cover between US states that seem entirely attributable to the setting of the default. Whereas only 20% of motorists in New Jersey opt to pay for the full right to sue other drivers in an accident, in Pennsylvania, where the default is that premiums cover this right, 75% pay the premium and retain the right.[41] We're not sure exactly how much social pressure and future discounting also add.

Libertarian paternalism opens the door to what we might call 'co-production lite'. Co-production refers to the concept that goods and services are more efficiently and better produced jointly between service 'providers' and citizen-users. In such a model, citizens are thought of as co-producers rather than 'users', and professionals as facilitators rather than 'providers' (see also Chapter 3 for discussion of Edgar Cahn's thinking). Hence co-production fits well with the Leadbetter notion of a new generation of 'I can' citizens, busy not only choosing between services but actively shaping and co-creating them.

Yet a problem with full models of co-production is that they imply a lot of work for the citizen. The much beloved examples of proponents of full co-production models are the development of Linux, the computer operating system developed by a world-wide community of programmers; Wikipedia, the on-line encyclopaedia with entries built and amended by users; and even a medical textbook written by a community of sufferers of a disease. These are wonderful, interesting and inspiring examples, but like direct democracy, they are quite a big ask of busy citizens. Do I really want to spend my evenings as part of an investment club for my pension, or would I rather someone else does all that?

Libertarian paternalism makes it easy for citizens to do their own thing but stops short of a fully paternalistic state, leaving plenty of responsibility in citizens' hands to take over the controls anytime they feel like it. In their most recent work, Thaler and Sunstein have become more ambitious in their claims for libertarian paternalism, arguing that it is a 'third way' between state and market, and between left and right.[42] The level of interest from politicians on both sides of the Atlantic suggest that they may be right, at least in the context of politicians wishing to offer more in the context of a public that is wary about the state doing more, and in a situation when money is tight.

We shall return, in the final discussion, to whether libertarian paternalism does indeed offer an important new model of the state. But for now, let us put this bigger question to one side and look at some of the practical suggestions that behavioural economics might suggest to reluctant, or enthusiastic, paternalists.

'Nudging' the lower brain

This section explores proposals that are broadly based on gently tilting, or 'nudging', citizens towards choices and behaviour that are likely to be better for both them and the community.

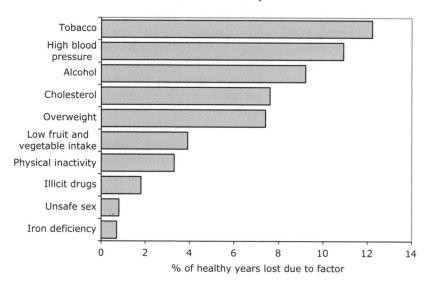

Figure 5.9 *Behavioural factors explain the majority of years of healthy life lost (leading ten risk factors in developed nations, based on World Health Organization estimates, 2002).*

Setting defaults: pensions, insurance, organs and schools

As we have already seen, the early success of the Libertarian paternalists was in relation to pensions. The UK is now moving to a system of pensions based on opt-out principles, as are a number of other countries, such as New Zealand. Indeed, moving to an opt-out default in employer or state top-ups for pensions can be so successful that it can lead to strain on budgets.

Organ donation is another area often cited as a prime target for changing the defaults.[43] The basic idea is that rather than carrying around a card to donate, the default would be reversed. In the event of an accident, the presumption would be that you were happy for your organs to be donated *unless* you carried a card saying you didn't want to, or had given instructions on your medical records to that effect. It is estimated that countries moving from opt-out to opt in systems would see rises of around 50% in donations, saving thousands of extra lives a year.

Defaults are already set in many other areas of public policy already, and the question is sometimes about whether they are the right defaults. For example, most educational systems and schools require children to study certain subjects until at given ages and, of course, that children will go to school. But in some places the arrangements are more flexible, though still with defaults clearly in place. For example, in some Canadian provinces there is support available (including financial) for parents who wish to home-educate their children. Another simple change to educational defaults – at least in the UK – would be to shift to a presumption of permission for children to go on school trips unless the parent requests otherwise, getting away from the heavy bureaucratic burden of having to get the written permission of every parent for every trip.

Another example could be a presumption that children will walk or take public transport to school. Schools might automatically plan routes and charge for children to be picked up, unless parents explicitly opt out of doing so. This would help to address the familiar problem of every parent deciding to drive their kids to school because of worries about safety from other traffic (caused by other parents), with consequences for congestion, safety and emissions.

Many areas where choice or individual budgets are used could benefit from well-structured default options. Patients offered a choice of hospital or treatment may often prefer to have a clear default. Similarly, in social care or education, many people may prefer individual budgets with the comfort and convenience of defaults already in place.

Defaults can also be used to drive political or structural change. Earlier it was mentioned that the UK has introduced trigger powers such that if a certain percentage of citizens sign a petition, a local referendum is then held on whether to introduce a mayor. A number of senior political figures feel that mayors have worked well, but they remain rare as citizens tend not to use their trigger powers to create them. The default could be reversed to one where there will be a referendum in the local area on a given date unless a certain minimum number of citizens sign a petition to block it.[44]

A common theme to all these examples is that there is clear evidence that the default would benefit and be favoured by the majority of the public. It is possible that more sophisticated defaults could be developed. For example, on pensions it may be that for people below, or above, a certain income threshold the presumption of opt-in would be wrong. A more sophisticated series of defaults tailored to particular population segments is a likely future development.

Structuring choices and the salience of incentives

One of the ways in which our choices are guided, as supermarkets and other stores know well, is through the physical layout of the options. Thaler and Sunstein give the example of 25% differences in the selection of different foodstuffs in a school canteen according to height and position. Many would feel that it would be reasonable that schools might use this information to encourage students to take healthier options, such as salad and fresh vegetables (put up front) instead of high fat, low vitamin foods like French fries (put later on and lower down). Similarly, one could imagine that supermarkets might be obliged to avoid putting especially unhealthy foods, like sweets, right next to the checkouts.

Just like swapping the sweets at the checkout for health bars or fruit, many fiscal incentives can be reshaped at no overall cost to make one option more attractive than another. In Chapter 4, it was proposed that young adults should be given substantial personal endowments or grants which they could use to pay for further or higher education. It was mentioned that such grants could be made more effective, in terms of attracting less traditional students to go to university, by shaping them using behavioural economics. Rather than having student grants paid evenly across a three or four year course, it would be better to allow students to spend the money up front, so that the early years of university could be tried 'for free'. At the same time, concerns about debt would be discounted by its pushing into later years of study. By this time, the non-traditional student would have formed relationships with their new peers, and the default presumption will have shifted to completing the course even if this meant taking on some debt.

Another example is in relation to fuel and green taxes. Fuel duties are theoretically a very efficient tax. The more you drive, and the more fuel inefficient your car, the more you pay. The problem is, by the time you're paying all this tax, you have long since made the decision about which car to drive, though it might affect whether you take an extra journey or not. At the point at which you bought the car, the future fuel costs were discounted in your head, and you weren't focused on the extra £5,000/$10,000 that the turbo would end up costing you, let alone the damage to the planet. For this reason it would be better, from a psychological viewpoint, to apply a big up-front tax differential on cars proportional to their emissions or fuel use. The extra £5,000 up front would definitely cause pause for thought.

Another way of cranking up salience is to harness the 'simulation' heuristic. One of the reasons why every lottery organizer in the world wants to have giant jackpots is because these make us buy far more tickets than lotteries that distribute the same proportion of funds more evenly. Indeed, so effective is the lure of the big jackpot that most nations strictly regulate the size of jackpots in gambling to stop us all becoming addicts. Is it possible that we could use some of the same psychological effects to promote more publicly useful behaviour? For example, most countries are reliant on voluntary declarations of earnings for tax purposes. It is interesting to reflect on what would be the overall incentive on declarations if we said that for 1 in 10,000 tax returns, we would pay back the tax ten-fold? Economists would say this is nuts: any rational economic citizen would realize that they should cheat on their taxes, at least at the margin, and this prize is irrelevant. But that's just the point – that isn't how we think.

An even more controversial idea is how behavioural economics might shape punishments. If a key objective of punishments, such as prison, is to put people off offending because of how unpleasant it is, it's designed completely wrongly. If you want people to remember prison as being an unpleasant experience, it should be characterized by a few memorably unpleasant events with the worst bit being just before you came out. But generally it is exactly the reverse – prison is boring and monotonously unpleasant, and generally gets better towards the end as privileges and freedoms are increased. To caricature, a much more memorably unpleasant prison spell might involve shorter sentences, would deliberately break the monotony (take TVs away for a few days along the way) and would culminate in prisoners having to walk through burning coals or naked through the streets to get out. Obviously, the detail is not a serious suggestion, but you get the idea.

Harnessing declarative norms

One of the most powerful forces on our behaviour is the clues we pick up from other people about how they are behaving, and how they think we should behave.

Littering provides a familiar and well-evidenced example. People will rarely drop a piece of litter on the ground in an environment that is clean and litter free. However, they are quite likely to do so if there is already litter on the ground. Experiments have repeatedly shown that the more litter already on the ground, the more likely someone is to drop the piece of litter in their own hand.[45] It's not that people decide that littering is a nice thing to do, they just figure that everyone else is doing it so . . . 'oops!' We tune into what psychologists call the 'declarative norm' – the unwritten rules of the situation.

Decades of experiments have found that people tune into the behaviour of others around them to figure out 'what goes' – or, in Wittgenstein's phrase, 'how to go on'. Otherwise well-behaved students will rapidly join in the vandalism and destruction of an apparently abandoned car once one or two others start to do so. Subjects in waiting rooms slowing filling with smoke will sit quietly and for longer in a group of eight strangers than when in smaller groups, as they look for clues in those around them whether or not this is really an emergency. People will go along with the blatantly wrong answers of a panel of other people who agree with each other, and their own perception will be changed by the answers of others. Even in Milgram's famous compliance experiments, where the majority of subjects would obey the commands of an authoritative instructor to electrocute another subject, peer influence and declarative norms were shown to have major impacts. When Milgram ran the experiment such that the subject was in a pair where one refused to take part, the other subject would almost invariably also refuse to comply.[46]

So, if you think others are cheating on taxes, getting drunk every night, carrying knives or sleeping around, you become much more likely to do the same. Similarly, if you think that most other people are paying their taxes, are recycling, or are picking up their own litter, then you will also follow suit. Unfortunately, we are often not very good at estimating how prevalent behaviour is.

For example, college students tend to greatly overestimate the amount that other fellow students drink, do drugs, or have sex. Given that we judge frequency by how easily we can think of examples, it is not surprising that a student would think that his fellows are often drunk. A couple of drunk students stumbling through college in the early hours of the morning make a lot more noise than the hundred reading books or trying to sleep. Similarly, rumours of wild sex make better gossip than tales of dull nights in with your friends.

The power of declarative norms, and the unreliability of our estimates of actual behaviour, provide many opportunities for policy intervention. Simply telling college students the actual incidence of alcohol abuse and sexual activity can help reduce subsequent alcohol and sexual health problems (as well as causing quite a bit of relief).

Unfortunately, politicians, public officials and the media often do the exact reverse, inadvertently inflating estimates of problematic behaviour. It's what Cialdini calls 'the big mistake' (see also Chapter 3 on crime). In order to raise the profile of an issue, it is often tempting to say that it has become very widespread and cause for grave concern. If you want to get attention, you talk about the terrible problem of young people carrying knives; the epidemic of gun crime; widespread teenage pregnancy; school drop-outs or whatever. However, if you want to change behaviour, it is better to say 'the vast majority of young people just carry mobile phones and resolve their conflicts in non-violent ways' rather than 'lots of kids are carrying knives (so it's what you do)'. It's very difficult to resist this temptation, especially when there is the political danger than an opponent will make the claim and will accuse you of complacency. But it is worth trying to re-frame the problem in terms of the positive, prevalent norm – if you actually want to change behaviour.

Cialdini gives an example from his nearby national park in Arizona, where visitors were greeted with a big sign along the lines of 'please don't take petrified wood from this forest as it is destroying this natural resource'. Psychologically this sign actually reads 'everybody's doing it, so you'd better take a piece before it's all gone'. Re-wording the sign to emphasize that the vast majority of people left the forest intact led to a marked drop in people removing the petrified wood. Similarly, an effective recycling campaign showed images of people recycling, and posed a single non-recycler as the exception, not the rule.[47]

The influence is particularly powerful if the clue about behaviour relates to other people who are like you, or that you particularly care about. Hence hotels experimenting with different messages to encourage guests to re-use towels and avoid unnecessary washing found that the most effective approach was to emphasize that 'previous guests in your room' – i.e. people just like you – chose to re-use towels to save resources. Similarly, if you are a teenager, what you really care about is what your friends and peers are doing, not the wider community. Hence having two or three peers who smoke raises risk of a teenager smoking by more than 1,000% – whereas smoking in the family has a much lesser effect.

A good practical example of using these effects is in campaigns about sexual health. Most such campaigns contain a lot of factual information that has limited impacts on behaviour. Much more effective is to talk about what other people think about the use of protection – i.e. that your peers and potential partners think it is cool to use a condom and will respect you for it.[48]

Many statutory changes aimed at behaviour change get much of their behavioural power from social proof. Raising the school leaving age; banning smoking in public places; and the wearing of seat belts lead to a self-reinforcing shift in the declarative behavioural norm. Most other people are adopting the new behaviour, so you do too. This is a tool that could be used more overtly by policymakers, focusing effort on shifting the social norm within a whole network rather than focusing on a few individuals at a time.

For example, if you want to reduce drug abuse, it may be more effective to focus all your efforts on one location at a time, seeking to sweep up all the addicts in one go and driving sellers out of town. The standard argument against this type of approach is that it merely causes displacement; that the problem will soon come back; and that you should instead focus on the most problematic users and sellers wherever they are. But if the behaviour is being maintained by a social norm, you are better off harnessing social proof and getting all the users in the area in treatment at the same time and thereby seeking to change the declarative social norm.

The same is probably true of alcohol abuse, energy use, recycling, speeding, and so on. If you want to make a change, you really need to get everyone's behaviour to move at the same time, such as by a pre-announced campaign that runs from a specific time, and then reflect back to the public the prevalence of the new behavioural norm. Reflecting back the new social norm needs to be part of the campaign, whether this is through subsequent adverts, or through glowing orbs on our roofs showing our neighbours that we are using less energy.

There is one more trick, but it is a dangerous one for the policymaker. Almost all the examples above revolve around making the public more aware of the prevalence of a behaviour to reinforce the norm already held by the majority. It is much harder if the behaviour you are trying to move away from is the majority behaviour. If you are cheeky, you can try to persuade people that the majority behaviour is different, thereby dragging them into line with a false sense of the majority position. Clearly, this is what political candidates do when they tell you that there is a swing their way – the new social norm is 'vote for me'.

This is a trick which is normally left to politicians and marketers ('the nation's most popular airline/party/shampoo'), but occasionally bureaucracies try it too. My favourite example is the way in which American official infant weight curves – the tables against which parents judge how well their young offspring's weight is progressing – no longer contain the actual weights of the general population. The problem was that everybody wanted their child to have an above average weight and height. You don't have to be a master statistician to figure out where that will end up. If every parent tries to get their child above average, then that average is going to get dragged up. So instead the figures now published are what experts consider *should* be the distribution – closer to that of several decades ago – rather than the *actual* weight distribution today. This means that most parents can succeed in having 'above average' weight children, at least removing the pressure to drive up weights even higher.

I guess, in a way, that's what many health professionals are trying to do when they tell us that we should 'eat five a day' (fruit). Ben Page, director of Ipsos MORI, has argued that maybe we should up this figure to the Danish 'six a day', as anchoring would help drag up behaviour. I'd bet that more effective than this would be to try and convince us that most people like us, or that we care about, were already eating five a day – or at least four a day. I guess that means we need to see our Olympic heroes, rock stars or the cool kids at school with an apple in hand.

Authority

Although we all like to think of ourselves as independent minded souls, and that we wouldn't fall for Milgram's experiments of the 1960s to electrocute some middle-aged guy because someone in a lab-coat told us to, the evidence is against us. When people are asked which kind of car they would be more likely to honk at if it failed to go on a green light – a scrappy old car or a smart limousine – most say the limousine. But experimentally, it's the old car we honk at, and leave the limo in peace. Similarly, if a pedestrian in a smart suit crosses the road on the stop signal, we are much more likely to follow him across than someone less smartly dressed.

A practical policy application is to ensure that advice and guidance comes from the most authoritative figure possible. This will generally be someone who the public respect as having real expertise on the issue, and who they trust to tell the truth. Unfortunately for politicians, this generally isn't them. More likely it is a senior doctor, scientist or economist, depending on the topic. It is even better if the message comes from someone you know and like, like your own doctor or someone you respect in the community. Hence letters to encourage people to get health checks are much more effective when they are signed by a doctor you know than by an administrator you don't.

A fascinating but repeated finding is that even fake cues of authority can have marked effects on behaviour. For example, the police in more than one country have found that wooden cut-outs of policemen on busy junctions or dangerous roads can greatly improve traffic and other behaviour. It is not that the figures are especially realistic, so that you think it is a real policeman standing there about to give you a ticket. Rather the cut-out seems to remind you at a very automatic level about the rules of the road, and the need to drive carefully.

Uniforms and other such cues help to perform some of the same functions. Interestingly, they not only change the reactions of others to the person wearing the uniform, but change the behaviour of the person wearing the uniform itself. This has been notoriously demonstrated in experiments where people are asked to play the role of a figure in authority, and especially if the uniform allows a degree of anonymity too.[49] But these effects can be used for good too. For example, neighbourhood watch type schemes can be successfully augmented by volunteers being given a rudimentary uniform, such as a fluorescent vest with a suitable official title on the back.

Certainly in the UK, there is considerable interest in how we might repopulate public spaces with figures of authority, though not necessarily from the state. Neighbourhood wardens are an interesting half-way house – funded by the state, but working very closely in the community. There may even be useful ways of co-opting new forms of authority, such as respected figures in gangs or local communities, to exercise more leadership and control to reinforce prevalent social norms of acceptable or pro-social behaviour.

Helping the higher brain

Much of current policy interest around behavioural economics focuses on how government might join battle against other behavioural predators to bend public behaviour to more beneficial outcomes. But there is another strategy which is to arm the citizen with the tools to fight off these behavioural predators – and sometimes their own instincts – for themselves.

Information and incentives

The '101' of behaviour change, and co-production of outcomes, is information plus incentives.

Americans Demand Increased Governmental Protection From Selves

NEW YORK—Alarmed by the unhealthy choices they make every day, more and more Americans are calling on the government to enact legislation that will protect them from their own behavior.

"The government is finally starting to take some responsibility for the effect my behavior has on others," said New York City resident Alec Haverchuk, 44, who is prohibited by law from smoking in restaurants and bars. "But we have a long way to go. I can still light up on city streets and in the privacy of my own home. I mean, legislators acknowledge that my cigarette smoke could give others cancer, but don't they care about me, too?"

"It's not just about Americans eating too many fries or cracking their skulls open when they fall off their bicycles," said Los Angeles resident Rebecca Burnie, 26. "It's a financial issue, too. I spend all my money on trendy clothes and a nightlife that I can't afford. I'm $23,000 in debt, but the credit-card companies keep letting me spend. It's obscene that the government allows those companies to allow me to do this to myself. Why do I pay my taxes?"

Figure 5.10   *A spoof article from the US publication the Onion. Is this the future of libertarian paternalism?*[50]

I won't restate the arguments here (see Chapter 1 and above), but just want to note that from a behavioural economics viewpoint, information by itself is often not enough to effect significant behavioural change. Most smokers know that cigarettes aren't good for them. The overweight know that they shouldn't eat that extra piece of chocolate cake. And the urban driver knows they really should get a bike. Other factors, such as those documented above, tend to overpower the influence of information alone.

Raw incentives matter too. People generally do respond to prices, especially if there is an alternative option available. Drivers switched from leaded to unleaded petrol within a very short time, and with only a modest price differential between them. For years in the UK, a 1% increase in the price of cigarette duty led to roughly a ¼% drop in smoking (until price differentials became too large with France, and a thriving black-market was born). Bottles and cans in the USA got recycled when a few cents deposit was added. And consumers in Ireland greatly reduced the number of plastic bags they used once supermarkets starting charging for them.

Of course, we know there are lots of examples where consumers don't seem to respond to price signals the way they are 'supposed' to. If we were better at math, we'd never buy another iridescent light bulb – we'd only buy long-life bulbs and save a fortune. But we're not, so governments like Australia and Canada end up proposing to ban them. Similarly, we should all insulate our homes; take advantage of employer contributions to our pensions; and no one would leave school without a qualification – but that's not how it is.

Generally these failures in price signals are to do with the effects discussed above, particularly hyperbolic discounting. Sometimes they are more complex. In an Israeli nursery which started fining parents for picking up their children late, it led to *more* parents picking up their children late. The fine served to make parents feel less guilty about late pick-ups, as they were now paying for it.

The current fashion for behavioural economics sometimes seems to imply that we can forget these more conventional tools. The real trick is combining information and incentives with the other kinds of techniques. The literature sometimes makes the distinction between 'conversion' and 'compliance'. You can often use behavioural techniques to get people to comply, but if you want to achieve conversion, you need to persuade people that it is rationally something that they want to do.

Give your reflective self a chance

One of the ways that the state can help the citizen barraged by other behavioural predators is to give the citizen a little time to think. Cool-off periods built into consumer law are the most obvious example. Another is to require the seller to give information or warnings in a way that makes it easier for consumers to make rational comparisons.

There is, however, a problem with many of these types of consumer-power tools, and especially those that involve the citizen getting a pile of small-print telling them about their rights. Citizens rapidly come not just to ignore it, but to take comfort from the fact that its presence must imply that a regulator somewhere has checked it all over. Ironically, therefore, many of these measures that pure libertarians favour as a way of addressing consumer abuse end up creating a greater appetite for a more directly paternalistic state.

Another take on the same issue is to give people the skills and experience to resist unwanted behavioural influences, and to know the traps their own thinking is inclined to lead them into. Once you have been stung by the aggressive reciprocity trick, especially if you've had a chance to reflect on it, you generally won't fall for it again. One can imagine that a balanced education of the future will equip young people to recognize their own cognitive blind spots, and the tricks that can take advantage of them. You can think of it as a kind of psychological inoculation, but also as a form of self-knowledge.

A wackier, but intriguing possibility, is that there may be ways of increasing the power of people's reflective selves in the moment too. For example, experiments have shown that subjects' behaviour is more consistent with their previously expressed beliefs when there is a mirror present. It seems that catching sight of yourself makes you more self-aware, and this drives the increased consistency. Maybe we should encourage financial advice and other key decisions to be made in rooms with prominent mirrors.

Earlier we discussed the idea of 'co-production lite'. There's also still a strong case for co-production 'full'. This implies re-casting the public service 'provider' into a facilitator or guide. Instead of it being your doctor's responsibility to make you well, or your teacher's responsibility to teach you what you need to know, the doctor or teacher is recast as coach giving you guidance about how to get fit or pointing you in the right direction to discover how to learn. Though elements of this dynamic are already familiar, it is quite a big jump for both public servant and citizen to move to a world where your doctor declines to give you a pill and instead suggests exercise with a group of his other 'patients'.[51]

The paternalistic state does not necessarily imply, therefore, public servants telling patients, students and claimants what exactly to do, and certainly not doing it for them. A more plausible and mature relationship is one of partnership, even in the context of one side having more expertise (the parent) than the other.

Commitment devices – appointments, marriage

People aren't naive. Most of us know that we're subject to certain errors in our thought, even if we don't the detail. Alcoholics learn that having 'just one' drink is a bad idea; husbands and wives learn not to go out to dinner with flirtatious colleagues; and those struggling with their weight learn to avoid the cookie isle at the supermarket.

One of the kinds of devices we use to get a grip on our wayward selves are 'commitment devices'. The alcoholic joins AA and pledges to others and himself not to drink. Men and women get married committing themselves to each other and to hard sanctions if they break the bond. And those struggling with their weight choose to pay the up-front costs for a private gym and classes for a year, seeking to bind themselves into going.

It is clear that the state provides the framework for at least some of these commitment devices, notably marriage. The state effectively stands behind the bond that citizens voluntarily enter into. Thaler and Sunstein have a host of ideas for how citizens might create more such commitment devices for themselves. For example, two college professors might agree a mutual pact not to put on weight, with the sanction that either could demand a weigh-in within a given period. If either had failed, they would have to pay a given sum either to the other, or perhaps to a cause that they strongly dislike, such as a rival football team.

Many of these commitment devices don't require the state. An elegant example is 'pledgebank'. Citizens pre-commit to a pledge triggered when a number of other citizens sign up to the same pledge, such as creating a fund for good local cause.[52] Government can participate in such pledges too. For example, one local government in the UK agreed that if a certain number of residents signed up to look after small street gardens and flower boxes, they would provide the boxes, bulbs and plants.

Public services can use the dynamic of commitment and consistency as a way of improving outcomes, and reinforcing citizens' own efforts to improve outcomes for themselves. An increasingly familiar example is the use of school-parent-student 'contracts'. These involve each of the parties agreeing to undertake certain actions, and formally signing an agreement. These contracts are not normally legally binding, and are therefore better thought of as 'compacts', but can have considerable psychological power. Most people have a strong desire to be consistent with their former selves, so having made such an agreement they will try to keep it. They also have the effect of creating 'alignment' between the key individuals around the young person to ensure that all are pulling in the same direction.

Anti-social behaviour contracts have a similar structure. Although carrying no hard legal sanction, the explicit drawing out of what is and is not acceptable behaviour – with an agreement between the police, parents and young person – can be a highly effective way of changing behaviour. Patient–clinician 'contracts' are also under discussion and could have a similar effect, especially if they involve partners or other patients struggling with the same condition or issues.

It could be that such commitments could be strengthened further. For example, it could become widespread practice – though still optional – for parents, offenders, patients and their signatory partners to put up a bond of some kind to underwrite their word. In a simple form, this might be a small monetary bond – £10 or $20 – to be paid to a charity in the event of a breach. Or it could be a non-monetary bond, like an agreement to do community service. In some cases, it might be a positive pledge – the police officer might agree to wear a pink hat for a day if the child in the ABC stays out of trouble for six months.

The dynamic of commitment could be used in other ways too, such as helping to deal with the problem of DNAs ('Did not attend') in public services. One of my favourite examples from Cialdini is from a restaurant suffering from 30% DNAs – customers who didn't turn up for bookings leaving empty tables. When someone phoned to make a booking and a time was agreed, customers were asked 'Would you please let us know if you are unable to make the booking?' Staff were asked to make one seemingly tiny change to the booking procedure. After asking the question about letting the restaurant know if they couldn't make it, staff were told to pause long enough to allow the customer to respond. Faced with the pause, people would invariably respond along the lines, 'Yes, of course'. In this moment, the customer had made an explicit commitment. Almost overnight, DNAs fell from 30 to 10%. People like to be consistent and not to breach commitments.

Such micro-commitments could also be used in public services. Doctors surgeries might try the same trick as the restaurant and seek a verbal commitment or, a suggestion of Cialdini, patients might be asked to fill out their own appointment cards and give them to reception rather than the other way around.

Institutions: the role of collective responsibility

The rise of behavioural economics and a more paternalistic state takes us back full circle to reinforce the importance of reforms to the classic state. If the state is to make judgements on our behalf to nudge, commit and price us towards one behaviour and away from another, then we need a tight collective grip on what it is up to. In effect, we need to give permission to the state to manipulate or encourage us.

Given how wide ranging these subliminal and other tools can be in their application, we are not just going to give the state blanket permission to fiddle with any deep-seated behaviour, custom or institutional practice it feels like. Rather we are going to need to feel our way, giving the state permission to act on an issue by issue basis. Since we are also pretty busy, and not very keen on committees, this points strongly in the direction of the democratic innovations discussed in the first section. Indeed, I don't think it is a coincidence that the rise of interest and demand for using democratic innovations has coincided with the renewal of interest in more paternalistic forms of government.

Elsewhere I, Bob Putnam and others, have written on the extent to which effective government rests heavily on the 'virtue' of citizens,

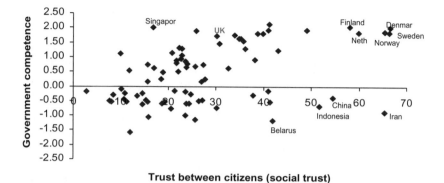

Figure 5.11 *The relationship between social trust and government competence. Data from the World Values Survey and from a composite measure based on World Bank data. The correlation is 0.42.*

and the strength of social capital and norms in society.[53] These webs of interconnection, everyday habits and institutional habits are what do most of the heavy lifting to keep our societies, economies and governments going (see Figure 5.11). Viewed from this perspective, the state is only a part-player in good government. When we talk about changing or nudging behaviour, we are actually talking about this massive reservoir and ecology of social habits, bonds and institutions – a form of 'hidden wealth'. The state can't just shove this great ecology of behaviour, nor should it try, not least because this same ecology flows through it in the habits and customs of its political leaders, public servants and a nation's political institutions.[54] Rather we have to create hot-houses – like the new generation of democratic innovations – to catalyse change within this ecology. Citizens need to negotiate with other citizens when social norms need to change, and to give the appropriately reluctant paternalistic state permission to act on matters that often bear directly on our personal and private everyday lives.

In short, the paternalistic model discussed here is one rooted in co-production and partnership, rather than the paternalism of previous ages. As was mentioned at the very start of the chapter, agency is not a zero sum game. More collective responsibility does not necessarily imply less personal responsibility. Well designed services and regulation, with collective permission, can clarify the architecture of choice to strengthen personal agency while reducing the problems associated with unmade or unintended 'choices'.

Box 5.3   *Scenarios, not prediction – a key tool of the paternalistic state*

Central governments used to spend a lot of effort predicting the future, then trying to plan for or shape it. From Stalin's grand plans of the 1940s to the widespread fashion for 'manpower planning' of the 1960s, these predictions and plans have a chequered history.

In recent years, domestic policy wonks have instead picked up lessons from their military colleagues and the private sector, and have learnt to test policy against scenarios rather than hard predictions of the future. Rather than try and work out exactly how many people there will be, what they will want, and what technology and pressures from elsewhere will allow, policymakers create a series of plausible and deliberately contrasting future worlds. The contrasts between these scenarios are envisaged as driven by exogenous factors (that is, external and out of our control). For example, one axis might be the extent to which the world economy becomes more and more integrated, versus a retreat into protectionism and a shrinking of world markets. Another contrast might be more value-based, such as public views moving towards collective solutions, versus towards more individualistic and market based solutions.

A simplified example of four scenarios, with implications for education and skills

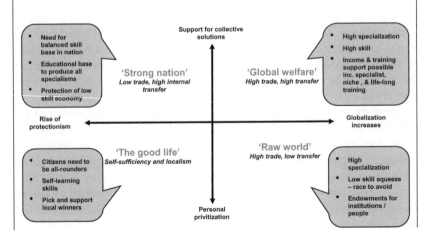

Using these underlying differences, several different future scenarios are worked out in detail, each with positive and negative aspects. Policy proposals are then tested against each of the scenarios. A long-range policy proposal that will only work in one of the scenarios may need revision or discarding. For example, an educational system that focuses state funding on high levels of specialism may be excellently suited to a world of high trade and high transfer welfare systems, but may leave smaller nations ill-prepared for a world that retreats into protectionism or more privatized provision.

It should be added that many government policymakers struggle with using scenarios, since unlike firms and local government, they think that they can choose the world they will end up in. Unlike traditional prediction, scenarios require a degree of humility about your ability to predict and shape the future. They are a tool for a wise state, not an arrogant state.

Conclusion: the paternalistic state revisited

The nature of the challenges that contemporary societies face has promoted a re-emergence of interest and activity around the 'paternalistic state'. Some aspects of behaviour change could easily have been swept up in the actions of a more traditional public service remit of the practical state. For example, there are clear economic and social reasons why the state should intervene to shape behaviour around the protection of true public goods, such as the environment, or around behaviours that have strong negative impacts on others, like anti-social behaviour.

However, it has become clear that the public appetite for action does not end with interventions around pure public goods. A new dimension of state action has emerged around behaviours that would previously have been regarded as substantially private in their causes and consequences. Obesity is perhaps the most high profile example at the current time, but it also concerns financial decisions; alcohol and drug use; and even the regulation of consumer markets. Though we want to retain our freedom and options, including sometimes to do things that others might regard as unwise, we also want the comfort of knowing that someone keeps a benevolent eye out, putting a few subtle safety rails around out actions to prevent us inadvertently spinning off down the side of a precipice that we did not see.

Twinned with behavioural – and traditional – economics, there is no doubt that governments can help us achieve better outcomes for ourselves and for the community. But the gulf between the rhetoric and interest in behaviour change and the practical expertise in government remains substantial. Consider health. The WHO estimates that more than half of all years of healthy life lost results from known behavioural factors, like smoking, diet and so on (Figure 5.9). Yet state spending on health-related behavioural change is marginal in comparison to that on conventional primary and secondary healthcare. Perhaps this is forgivable for a new area of understanding. But how do we excuse the fact that only around ½% of health-related research is aimed at behavioural factors, and much of this concerns how to increase compliance with conventional medicine (getting people to take their pills).[55]

What then, are the kind of headline conclusions that emerge from a resurgent interest in a gently paternalistic state?

- Research. We should invest more in research and pilots around behavioural and cultural change. At present, academic research is dominated by a relatively small group of North American economists and psychologists. Policy research on the subject is marginal and methodologically weak.
- 'Nudging' our habits. Behavioural economics is giving us powerful clues to address a number of contemporary problems, such as obesity. These tools include setting defaults that are in the interest of the busy citizen-consumer, such as around pension savings, organ donation, and how children get to school. They include insights into how we might better harness the power of social norms or 'social proof', such as by emphasizing the majority norm rather than focusing on the problematic exception; and into how to reshape conventional incentives to have greater impact, such as front-loading student grants or environmental taxes on cars.
- Strengthening our reflective selves. A complementary approach is to strengthen the reflective capacity of the citizen to resist behavioural predators and the traps in their own cognition. This includes recasting the public service provider as a guide and facilitator, and encouraging the co-production of public service outcomes. Education has a role to play, ensuring that citizens are more robust to predators and their own cognitive weaknesses. Finally, the approach may include the wider application of 'commitment devices' such as compacts between citizens and providers, possibly backed with financial or other contributory bonds.
- Re-drawing the lines of the state. Despite the claims of some proponents, the insights of behavioural economics often suggest a need to dust off conventional policy tools that have sometimes fallen out of fashion. For example, it can help us understand why people keep buying iridescent light bulbs and why some countries are having

to use regulation to ban them. Well-structured choice architecture, informed by new insights from behavioural economics may also allow us to back off some areas of state regulation, such as in relation to drug markets or the squeezing out of anti-social behaviour.

• A wise, co-owned state. The re-emergence of a more paternalistic state implies that government must up its game in a number of areas of institutional practice. It implies a state that is wise and competent enough to make good judgements about the future needs of citizens, such as through the use of sophisticated modelling and scenario testing. But perhaps more than anything, it cements the need to employ democratic innovations that allow representative samples of citizens to give the state permission to use such tools.

Paternalism is often caricatured as being authoritarian, or the 'nanny state'. But, as even a cursory reading of the literature on parenting reveals, there are a number of alternative forms of parenting styles apart from the authoritarian. Better outcomes are usually associated with 'authoritative' parenting rather than authoritarian or liberal parenting: putting a few key lines in the sand; explaining the reasoning behind the few rules you seek to enforce; but otherwise encouraging as much autonomy as you can.

Indeed, maybe we shouldn't even call this 'paternalism' at all. Perhaps the real model we're after is the relationship that follows parenting – a partnership between adults. Perhaps that is what the next generation will call it – the partner state.

Conclusion: The Partner State?

A key role of the modern state is to unlock and nurture the hidden wealth of its citizens. This chapter has explored three different notions of the state.

The first – the classic state – focused on arguably the most basic function of a democracy, which is to protect citizens from tyrannies of power. As such, much of the discussion concerned topics familiar to political scientists, such as the claimed falls in voter engagement, political interest and trust. Though many popular concerns prove to be myths, there are significant cracks in our political institutions and practices which need to be addressed, particularly around the slow death of political parties and the growing social and demographic skews in political engagement. These matter much more than headline movements in overall voter turnout, or the largely unchanging but low levels of political trust.

The second notion of the state – the practical state – is a relatively recent, primarily post-war invention. It covers many of the functions of government that today dominate its spending, such as health services, education and welfare benefits. Its raison dêtre lies in the provision of true public goods, and in the attenuation of bad brute luck effects, such as being born into poverty or suffering illness for reasons beyond your control. There has been considerable evolution and learning about how such public services can best be administered, but the underlying principles have not greatly changed.

Finally, we reflected on the re-emergence of an older notion of the state – the paternalistic state. This responds to the desire of citizens that the state should act in relation to challenges that have causes and outcomes that are substantially private, such as eating healthily, exercising or saving for our old age. This resurgent tradition owes much to the growing understanding of behavioural economics, and to the complex behavioural and cognitive ecology that explains why citizens sometimes appreciate a little help in the co-production of better outcomes.

In reality, these different conceptions have been overlaid one upon another, like a great snowman that citizens have periodically added to (see Figure 5.12). Sometimes a layer has partially melted away, and at other times a new layer has been added. Beneath the surface, the layers have melted together, but close examination can distinguish the hard ice of inner layers from the softer snow of more recent additions. And we can be sure that this process is not finished.

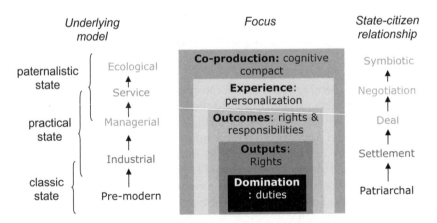

Figure 5.12 *The changing model of state-citizen relationship.*

Many of the same trends and dilemmas apply at the different levels of state, local through supra-national, and nations differ considerably in their within-state settlements, but a similar story can be discerned.

In final conclusion, the state is alive and well, though its boundaries are blurring and shifting. It is pretty clear that national states need to up their game in a number of areas, such as in relation to affecting behaviour change, and that we will need to strengthen our supranational state structures to bear the challenges of climate change, the democratization of war, and other new threats. But in general, we should be broadly pleased with the States and institutions that our predecessors have built. Our lives would be greatly poorer and more unsafe without them, and frankly, we don't stand a chance of getting through to the next century, or capitalizing on our hidden wealth, without them either.

6

Conclusion

It's time to draw this story together.

It is fashionable to front many current policy discussions with a roll-call of the great and unprecedented challenges that we face, and to emphasize the scale and rapidity of change that our societies, economies and governments are up against. The rise of China and India; the aging population; climate change; population diversity; the digital age, etc.

However, most of these 'challenges' have strong positive elements, and those that do not – like climate change – are highly tractable. Past generations would surely look at our problems with a mix of envy and puzzlement. Global terrorism is very frightening – and televisual – but the flu kills far more people every year.[1] Global warming has the potential to cause cataclysmic damage, but it is easily within our grasp to address it with, at most, a few per cent of GDP. Even the current recession, painful though it may be, is unlikely to slice more than a few per cent off world output. Compare these challenges to the terrors and sufferings of the generations who lived through the pandemics, world wars, and sheer everyday hardships of our Western grandparents, and they look like a 'walk in the park'.

Over the past century, we have shed the personal fatalism that walked hand in hand with the everyday life and death challenges that faced previous generations. Most of us take for granted that we will have materially comfortable and long lives, and express in our behaviour and attitudes a personal confidence that reflects this expectation in our dealings with other people and institutions. It is curious, then, that our collective lives are so dominated by the 'politics of deficit'. Political life is dominated by reducing 'bads' such as crime, unemployment, ill-health, low-skills, the risk from terrorism, and so on.

Keynes eloquently wondered what we, his affluent grandchildren would do with our unprecedented freedom from the endless struggle for personal survival (Chapter 1). We have the answer to his question now. We did not fall into the trap he feared from the idle wealthy of his own generation. We are certainly busy, though more on a hedonic treadmill largely of our own choosing. But, for the most part, people in the industrialized nations can make real personal choices about the balance of work and consumption in their everyday lives without fear of threat to their personal survival.

Yet there was another question that Keynes did not ask, and that we might ask of ourselves and for our own grandchildren. What are the collective positive challenges that we choose to take on with our wealth? It is striking that for decades, pollsters have asked the publics of affluent countries, 'what are the biggest problems facing the country?' The answers to these questions dominate the landscape within which elections are fought and policy is made. But polls almost never ask: what are the biggest positive challenges that we should take on?

Ironically, the current recession is starting to prompt such questions, at least at the margins. Some politicians and protesters are asking not just how will we get through the current crisis, but what is the better world that we will build beyond it. At a recent discussion in No. 10, someone made the parallel to the Beveridge report, a plan for a new welfare state written in some of the darkest hours of the Second World War. It offered a practical vision for a fairer and more supportive society, not just a return to the pre-war status quo. More than 600,000 copies of the report were published, and it was distributed not only to British troops but dropped behind German lines to make the case for what a democratic society could offer. The question today is, what is our equivalent – our vision for a better world in the post credit-crunch era?

Is this just semantics? After all, isn't to reduce ill-health to promote health; to reduce unemployment to increase employment; to reduce the number of children leaving school without qualifications to increase skills? We do spend collective resources on good things too: on museums and galleries; on transport systems to visit them; on science and academic inquiry; and on aid programmes to bring food, shelter and development. But the fact is the bread and butter of politics and policy remains dominated by reducing bads.

This pattern may have deep roots in who we are – in our humanity. Evolution has shaped us for struggle and survival. Social evolution too has shaped our psychology deeply. We claim successes for ourselves, and blame failures on others. When a task goes well, we attribute it to our hard work and skills. We claim credit for ourselves, for our family and for our group. When a task goes badly, it is because others disrupted us or our tools let us down. Perhaps this helps explain why we look to ourselves for the positive choices in life – the luxury we should choose or the project we should take on – but look to the community and the state to fix problems.

Of course, there are plenty of problems that do need fixing. But we can approach these 'challenges' with a reasonable degree of optimism. Most great problems of the past, including many seemingly intractable trends, have been addressed through much lesser tools and resources than we have today. We should also make a point to consider what positive challenges and collective projects that we might take on – our own letter to our grandchildren.

10 Things to Do If You're Prime Minister

There are lots of important things to do if you are Prime Minister, President, or a contemporary elected government. The vast majority of these involve carrying on doing what those before you were doing. The following list is therefore not at all comprehensive, but focuses on more novel actions that are relatively unlikely to be on the civil service's list of top priorities, but perhaps should be. It is also, of course, a relatively personal list – and inevitably biased towards the UK context – though rooted in the wider trends and analysis discussed throughout this book

1. Foster the 'economy of regard' – citizen to citizen support

If I had to choose one area that is in need of greater policy and public attention, it is the largely invisible web of exchange and affiliation that forms the scaffold on which both our economy and society is built – what I have called the hidden wealth of nations. We tend to view this 'economy of regard' as a soft and marginal shadow to the real economy, and to the business of government and life. But if anything, it is quite the reverse – it is the 'real economy' that is the shadow. The economy of regard takes up more time, more value, and has more impacts on our well-being than the conventional economy. Yet we hardly see that it is there.

If you even half buy this change of gestalt, it has big policy implications. It suggests a much more interesting and important space for a different kind of welfare state between the rational Weberian model of the left and the laissez-faire of the right that has dominated Anglo-Saxon thinking. It suggests a strong case for oiling the economy of regard with complementary currencies, banks and other institutional practices to encourage activity and exchange. And it suggests a whole new dimension to the exchange and obligations that exist between citizens, community and state.

This all sounds very grand, so let's put it in practical terms. What sort of things might this mean? It could mean much more active support and development around key human skills, such as parenting and relationships.[2] It could mean an expectation that every citizen should give a certain number of hours 'service' to non-kin other citizens over a given stage in life, and that this is an obligation that you could not buy yourself out of. For example, this might equate to 60 hours of 'citizen service' over a given ten-year period that could be discharged through activities such as mentoring or care. It could mean fostering large new margins of the welfare state based on reciprocity, notably around social care, but also in education, healthcare, and asset transfers. It could mean tax breaks to encourage people to bequeath their assets into descendents' trusts for their grandchildren and great-grandchildren, or social care substantially provided through reciprocal obligations. It could mean the state backing up mutual pledges between citizens, such as delivering tools and plants to groups of citizens who offer to maintain public spaces. And it would almost certainly mean the creation of a robust complementary currency, or currencies, to oil these exchanges. Essentially, you'd carry two currencies in your pocket and in your head, one for material things, and the other for your 'relational balance book' with your fellow citizens.

Of all the ideas here, this will be the most difficult for most people to get their head around. For this reason, it is rather 'brave' – as civil servants put it to Ministers or Prime Ministers when they come up with their nuttiest ideas – to put it first. But perhaps by doing so, the reader will pause for a moment longer before casting it aside. There are significant conceptual, political and technical issues in pursuing this agenda – such as around political acceptability, gaming and confusing extrinsic with intrinsic motivations. But these are addressable, and the prize of a more balanced, nurturing and pleasant society and economy is an important one.[3]

2. Support citizen-consumer information as a public good

Information, and particularly that generated through the everyday experiences of citizens, is a greatly neglected public good.

We should foster an explosion in the growth of 'Tripadvisor' or 'ebay'-style consumer generated information in every sector of business and public services. This will greatly empower citizen-consumers; will squeeze out poor providers; and will enhance returns to good providers. The sharper competitive pressures will also give that nation's firms, products and services a competitive edge in the world market. Similarly, the data from employee surveys using common questions can be used to drive up the quality of work.

In many areas, all the state needs to do is to apply pressure on trade associations or public service providers to ensure that there is in place a robust and independent method within which citizen-consumers can succinctly report their experiences of services and products, and where others can see these aggregated experiences. In more limited cases of informational failure, the state may need to become more involved in providing or facilitating this standardized framework, and sometimes in providing incentives for citizens to share their experiences.[4]

3. Environment – just do it

Honestly, I really think we shouldn't have to put this one down. We know what to do, it's not that expensive, and we should just get on and do it for environmental and security reasons.

Renewables, insulation, a bit of nuclear to tide us over, and so on. If you think the answer is wholesale lifestyle change, then we are doomed. An electric, or hydrogen fuel cell car doesn't have to struggle at 20 miles an hour, but can do 0–60 in 5 seconds. The deal has to be – and can be – we can keep our fast cars and big houses, but they are going to cost a bit more (for a while at least) and run on different technology. The excess power generated by renewables will charge our cars overnight; we'll need some state action and regulation to flip us over faster and solve some collective action problems in the market; and we'll be a bit smarter about the caps, collars and other incentives we place on energy producers and users to encourage them and us to squeeze out carbon.

We'll have a few bitter pills to swallow in international negotiations, but our kids will think that they were no big deal. But we'd also better develop some plausible plan Bs with our partners, such as the technology to increase global dimming through artificial cloud formation or carbon capture, because it's just to risky to rely on the strength of our collective action alone.

4. Sex, drugs and rock 'n' roll – applying evidence-based policy

OK – so this is here partly to spice things up. But it is also here to put down a marker about evidence-based policy, starting with the area where historically the gap between evidence and policy has been particularly large.

A huge swathe of acquisitive crime – up to 80% plus of certain common categories such as shop-lifting and burglary – is drug-related. We just have to square up to the fact that mature drug markets, such as around heroine, should be medicalized rather than handled through the criminal justice system. In contrast, new drug markets (such as around skunk) should be handled even more aggressively by the CJS. Alcohol, given its place in our culture, may be better handled through behavioural economic interventions.

Sex is a flag to note that the very substantial absolute differences and trends in teenage pregnancy across countries seem to have a lot to do with our cultural attitudes to talking about sex (and a bit of inequality in the mix). Anglo-Saxons have to loosen up a bit in the talking department.

Rock 'n' roll is just a reminder that we've been worried about disconnected kids and the generation gap for at least 50 years, and probably a lot longer.[5] Some countries and cities do seem better at providing structured activities for young people, ideally involving lots of contact with older adults. The results are also impressive from allowing young people to mentor and take responsibility for younger children, and this should routinely form a part of structured educational experiences. Such activities give young people an opportunity to put something back into society; improve their long-term outcomes; and are an order of magnitude more cost effective at reducing crime than the criminal justice based alternatives. We should be able to twin such schemes with ideas around complementary currencies and strengthening the economy of regard.

Where we do have good ideas, we should always try them out on a small scale and evaluate them. If they look promising, we should seek to replicate them in two or three other sites, and check it works. Only then should we move to national roll outs (see also innovation, below).

5. Reform the incentives in the planning system

This is a relatively UK-specific and urgent issue, given the severity of our house and land value fluctuations, capital inequalities and restrictive land use planning system.

The proposal is, in principle, relatively simple. We should reform the planning system to ensure that 'losers' in decisions can get financial compensation, or in more positive terms, that planning gains are more equitably divided. In other words, we would change the incentives away from the current system in which all rational players are incentivized to say 'no' to any development.

This could work through a number of different mechanisms. A simple form would be to allow local councils and communities to capture more of the gains from planning approvals, such as through auctioning land after granting permission for a change of use. The local community would then capture much of the gain to use either for lower local taxes or investment in the community.[6]

Apart from removing a substantial drag on the economy, including in relation to environmentally necessary development such as around renewables, this shift should lead to a gradual redistribution of capital to less advantaged sections of the public, helping to address a growing form of inequality.

6. Embrace behavioural economics

Behavioural economics provides a powerful new set of tools for policymakers and citizens to address the challenges of today and improve the quality of our lives. But even though many of the key insights are twenty to thirty years old, policymakers have been slow to apply them.

For example, we know that more than half of all years of healthy life lost are as a result of behavioural factors such as smoking, diet, alcohol or unsafe sex. Yet only a tiny fraction of health expenditure or health research is directed at behaviour change. Even in universities and the research councils, the importance of the development has yet to sink in.[7]

The application of behavioural economics could offer substantial gains in relation to the environment, crime, pro-social behaviour, education, welfare and health.

7. Broaden the attack on inequality

A number of the proposals here have a strong element of fairness about them. But the level of inequality in society is such a powerful and generally negative characteristic that it needs setting out as an objective in its own right.

Crude redistribution of income is rarely the answer, though it remains an important part of the answer. Fairness and equality are not interchangeable – some forms of inequality are more justifiable than others. Policy needs to span across the whole range of capitals that propagate disadvantage across generations, including not just access to income, but financial, social and cultural capitals. This implies a radical expansion – over time – in individual capital endowments, probably released at age 18. It implies addressing inequalities in social and cultural skills at school. It implies individual pupil premiums based partly on social background that are tied to the individual, not the school or service. And it implies the supplementing of differentials in the social networks and levels of trust across population segments.

Attention to the subtle growth of inequalities in power and engagement also need to feature in our strategies. Perhaps most of all, however, is a more open and robust public debate about the acceptability of current levels of inequality in incomes and resources. Current differentials have much more to do with public acceptability than economic rationale.

8. Devolve – including to democratic innovations and individual citizens

The UK is unusual in how limited the tax-raising and other powers are of its local government. A common devolutionary settlement across all local areas is difficult and unnecessary. We should embrace greater autonomy to high performing local areas, including over the provision of other local services such as policing and health (possibly subject to local referendum).

Perhaps more importantly, we should embrace other forms of 'devolution' and participation in government and public services. The new tools of 'libertarian paternalism', or behaviour change, will require the permission of the public for their use – and indeed their effectiveness may rest heavily on the messages that we receive from other citizens about them. This new generation of democratic innovations will include local referenda triggered by citizen petitions and the use of deliberative forums (of small random samples of citizens) where citizens can give a strong steer on how to address tricky policy dilemmas with a strong behavioural component.

Devolution comes in many shapes and sizes. It can be to neighbourhoods, non-geographically based patient or parent groups, and of course to individuals and families through personal budgets or lead-budget holders. This landscape of devolution also provides fertile soil for the co-production, or 'co-creation', of innovative public services, as well as the emergence of new types of cross-cutting providers. And it can help square the triple challenge of a public desire to be listened to;

the falling salience of politics; and the growing social and demographic skew in engagement.

Finally, there's a strong case for lowering the voting age to 16, or perhaps even younger. An even more radical twist would be to allow parents to cast votes in trust for their younger children. This would shift the emphasis of our politics to a greater focus on education and the future, and would boost long-term political engagement.

The key conceptual insight is that devolution of power and the use of democratic innovations is not a zero-sum game. Carefully done, it can simultaneously increase the agency of all involved.

9. Stimulate innovation and diversity in public service provision

It is always tempting to introduce or impose 'good practice' from the centre. But the single most important thing for central government to do in relation to public services such as health and education is to ensure that the overall dynamic of the system drives improvements in outcomes, productivity and fairness year after year. This involves at least three key areas for strategic intervention: 'market' structure, incentives and information.

On structure, perhaps the most important basic requirement is to ensure the existence of viable alternative providers who will themselves try out different approaches in an atmosphere of 'coopertition'. An early priority should be to remove the barriers to, and actively encourage, the development of large, non geographically based networks of public sector providers. For example, we might see a chain of Great Ormond St children's hospitals and a network of Thomas Telford schools. But we should also regulate to ensure that a single network cannot supply more than around a third of the 'market' in any given region and empower users to choose who should take over failing services.

On incentives, they matter and so does their detail. An early priority should be to introduce substantial 'public service improvement grants' within which a pot of money is distributed to the schools, hospitals, police forces and so on that show the largest improvement in performance in the previous year. This puts a 'bounty' on the heads of poor performers to improve themselves, form partnerships, or be taken over by more effective providers. It will also power the growth of the most effective public sector providers.

On information, oiling the exchange of information between citizens on their experiences and outcomes is a powerful start (see above). It empowers citizens, boosts effective providers, and provides a powerful drive for learning and improvement. It might also be usefully supplemented by better standardized information for public service commissioners – a sort of 'Which?' guide to effective providers and programmes.

10. Re-engineering government – boring but important

Fiddling with the internal workings of government is not of much interest to the public, and it is generally not of much interest to Ministers until it is too late for them to do anything about it. Changes to the machinery of government are disruptive, and to a Minister impatient to get things done, are a big distraction with a rather distant and uncertain pay-off. Where they do happen, such as the periodic reshuffling of the responsibilities of Departments, too often the only real underlying logic is that of the territorial interests of powerful Ministers or senior civil servants. Still, it is worth noting that key figures around Blair came to regret not seeking to reform the centre of government in his first term, and feel that he could have had far more impact in his 10 years in office had he taken the early hit and created a machine 'fit for purpose'.

Across countries, there seem to be some common emerging lessons about what structures work and that hint at what a well-functioning government might look like. At the very centre, though shrouded in political controversy, it makes sense to have a Prime Minister's, President's or Cabinet Office with enough flexible analytical resource to flush out a sensible sense of strategic direction. This doesn't mean the drafting of a grand plan that all must follow, but it does mean having the capacity to give an overall steer to the direction of travel so that Departments can in turn act more strategically within this – the worst kind of centre is one that flip-flops between political fashion, or that gets into too much detail and micro-management. Such units should also have a strong capacity in scenario building. Testing policies against alternative possible futures, rather than trusting any one analytical model, is a much better way of ensuring the robustness of policy. Surely this is a lesson that the credit crunch reminded us all.[8]

However you rearrange Departments, there is always a line or a break somewhere, and the chances are that this won't make much sense to the citizen whose life isn't organized around bureaucratic boxes. While the primary driver of service reform and improvement must revolve around re-engineering up from the 'bottom', it can be helpfully supplemented by a bit of joining up at the top. The UK is especially plagued with over-strong central government departments – over-centralized to Whitehall, and under-centralized within.[9] This is especially problematic during times of fiscal tightening, when Departments will tend to protect their core functions while cutting back on cross-cutting investments and innovations that often offer greatest promise, both at national and local level.

Some countries have sought to address this silo-based problem by creating objectives, or targets that cut-across Departments (such as the UK's latest Public Service Agreements). Others have done it by creating a senior group of Ministers with cross-cutting objectives, leaving Departments under the day-to-day control of junior Ministers (such as Finland and the Netherlands). And, of course, the dynamics of Cabinet and Parliament itself is intended to create a space within which a more holistic view can be reached, and conflicts resolved. Better still is to empower the individual citizen to have leverage over the budgets spent in their name, so that they can assemble provision that suits them.

The next step on this journey may be the creation of a clearer sense of a commissioner-'provider' split within government itself. This would mean the holding of resources around certain key themes administered by senior Ministers. These Ministers would have flexibility about how they used these resources, forcing contestability and cooperation between Departments over how best to address key cross-cutting questions. This effectively brings together the power of the Treasury or finance department with a more flexible and political process.[10]

Finally, there is a host of 'boring but important' things that governments can do to increase effectiveness. These include supporting Parliamentary committees' ability to conduct pre- and post-legislation scrutiny with support from regulatory and audit bodies; transparent and independent assessments of Departmental performance; and tougher regimes to remove underperforming senior civil servants and Ministers.

And finally ... well-being

It's often said that 'what gets measured gets done'. If much of the 'hidden wealth' of nations lies in the relationships between citizens, then the corresponding 'hidden measure' is our well-being.

Recent years have witnessed the gradual shift in the respectability, and robustness, of studying well-being. There is a much longer and more accepted tradition of studying unhappiness, but the study of positive well-being is starting to catch up. The measurement issues are a bit more complicated than some popular proponents make out, but they are perfectly tractable.

I am confident that within 10 to 15 years – that is before the end of this Kondratiev economic cycle – policymakers will routinely be using sophisticated psychological well-being measures in judgements about policies. This shift will subtly change the focus of policymakers, and probably of citizens too. Will it mean that we will sacrifice economic growth at the margins? Perhaps. But what it will certainly mean is far more focus on the currently hidden wealth around us – if we can increase the growth in this, then surely we shall have cause to celebrate.

Appendix: The PMSU

Building the Strategic Capacity of Government

During Blair's time in office, a number of new institutional structures appeared at the heart of British government. Some of these, such as the Office for Public Service Reform (OPSR), petered out leaving not much more than a footnote in history. But two central innovations stand out. One of these was the Prime Minister's Delivery Unit, strongly linked to the application of targets, the relentless rounds of one-to-one meetings between Secretaries of State and a Prime Minister impatient to see change on the ground, and the personal vision and style of its first Director, Michael Barber. The history and role of the PMDU is now well known, not least through Michael's own book, *Instruction to Deliver*. But the history, role and working style of Blair's other big central innovation – the Prime Minister's Strategy Unit – is much less well known.

1997–2001 The Performance and Innovation Unit

One of the innovations of the post-'97 UK administration was the creation of a within-government 'think-tank' called the Performance and Innovation Unit (PIU). The PIU was based in the Cabinet Office and was, in many ways, a simple strengthening of a very traditional Cabinet Office function – sorting out issues that fell between the responsibility of the big Departments.

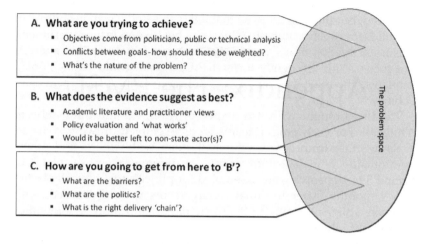

Figure A.1 *Strategy development rests on answering some basic questions.*

The basic idea of Cabinet system of government, unlike a more Presidential system, is that government is composed of a series of powerful and largely autonomous Departments, each headed by a Secretary of State with a place around the Cabinet table. The Departments get on and do their own things, with Ministers getting together once a week to discuss big issues and check that they are all going in the right overall direction. The Prime Minister chairs the Cabinet meetings and – assuming his position in the party is strong enough – can pick or sack who holds those Ministerial posts, and who sit around him at those weekly meetings. He (or she) has few people who work directly for him, and must rely on convincing or threatening his Cabinet colleagues to do want he thinks is right.

Of course, sometimes Departments and Ministers don't agree with each other. When this happens, the Cabinet Secretariat and, if necessary, the Cabinet Secretary (head of the Civil Service) springs into action to try and broker the conflict. But the reality is that the Cabinet Secretariat has relatively limited capacity to do analysis of its own, and indeed much of its time is spent simply organizing Cabinet meetings, circulating the relevant papers, and minuting the discussion.

The PIU created a substantial extra analytical resource that enabled the Cabinet Office to do more than just broker conversations between the Departments. This was particularly relevant for issues that were less a matter of conflict between Departments than simply falling between the cracks in between them. For example, there were concerns that the arrangements around adoption of children could be much improved, but this was an issue that fell between the responsibilities of several Departments, notably education, health and local government. This issue needed more than brokering – it needed detailed analysis and focus. With the newly formed PIU, a team could be assembled to analyse the issue and report back to the relevant Departments and Cabinet.

The PIU brought with it a degree of freshness and innovation to Whitehall. For each project, teams were assembled drawing civil servants together from across Whitehall along with experts and others from outside Whitehall with a range of different expertise. Teams of around 5 to 10 people were assembled for projects that typically lasted 6 to 9 months. After the final report, teams were disbanded, with members either returning to their original organization or sometimes moving onto the next project.

There were other contrasts with the traditions of Whitehall too. Under its young, civil servant head – Suma Chakrabarti – it adopted a highly open style. The PIU was open about what it was doing, often brought in outsiders to consult with and work on teams, and published its reports. It sought to look at new issues, and old issues afresh, like how to join-up Whitehall or how to better use ICT in government.

The PIU was like a small, institutional symbol of New Labour: new, fresh, open – but also a little suspicious of the dead-weight of Whitehall and the establishment, and fond of funky headlined reports.

By 2000, two factors had begun to lay the seeds of a marked change in the role of the PIU. First, the PIU was starting to run out of interesting and important issues that fell between the gaps of the big Departments. Second, and rather more privately, the Prime Minister was becoming frustrated with what he felt was the lack of vision and boldness of the proposals he was receiving from his fellow Cabinet members.

Within No. 10, the conclusion of two linked commissions by Blair was to persuade him of the need for a new kind of unit. He had asked John Birt, the former head of the BBC, to conduct an analysis and review of the way in which the whole criminal justice system worked. Birt set about analysing the issues from a 'cradle to grave' viewpoint, starting from long before an offender came into the criminal justice system, and then tracking their journey through this fragmented and unsatisfactory system, including how it interacted with services way beyond the remit of the Criminal Justice System itself, such as education, employment and housing. Blair liked the review, and in particular its style and breadth.

Blair had also asked a young political adviser, Ed Richards, to prepare a much broader and longer-range vision for the major public services so that he would have a more ambitious plan of his own with which to challenge his Ministers. After 18 months of trying, Ed, as he later put it, had to tell the PM that this was 'an impossible task' for one person and that his main conclusion was that the PM had to form a dedicated unit to perform the task. A list of names of potential staffers was given to the PM, and plans were drawn up in advance of the 2001 election for what was to become the 'Forward Strategy Unit'.

The hammering out of the new Unit fell to Geoff Mulgan, by then Director of the PIU; Jeremy Heywood, the PM's Principle Private Secretary; and Richard Wilson, the Cabinet Secretary.

2001–2002: The Forward Strategy Unit

Preparations began for the new Forward Strategy Unit (FSU), to be based within No. 10, were ready but not actioned until after Blair was returned to office in 2001. The election had returned Blair with yet another large majority, but with muted public support. The public verdict was that Labour needed to be given more time, but the public were also beginning to cast a more critical and impatient eye over progress so far.

As is usual in Whitehall, there was something of a battle about who should control the new unit, where it should sit, and how it should operate. The end result was that the FSU – a small group of around 15 people – would sit within No. 10 as a sister unit to the PIU which remained in Admiralty Arch as part of the Cabinet Office. Both Units would come under Geoff Mulgan who would in turn report to the Prime Minister via the Cabinet Secretary (at that time, Richard Wilson).

However, despite their similar reporting lines, the FSU was a very different animal to the PIU, and with some real tensions between the two. Where the PIU was open, the FSU was secretive and its reports confidential.[1] Where the PIU looked at issues that fell between the responsibilities of Departments, the FSU looked square at big policy issues that overlapped directly with the big Departments. And whereas the ideas for PIU projects could come from a number of sources, including other Departments or even bright ideas from within the Unit, the FSU was focused squarely on the key priorities of the PM, notably education, health and transport.

Suffice to say, Departments – particularly the Permanent Secretaries (the most senior civil servant and head of a Department) – were not too happy about No10's new 'tank' being parked on their front lawns. As a result, part of the deal with No. 10 was that FSU reviews would be headed by civil servants loaned to the FSU from the relevant

Department, and could therefore also keep the Permanent Secretary in the loop. But there was a further complication. Partly in the light of the Birt review on crime, the PM was keen to bring in senior figures from outside government who would help guide and provide a critical, and typically private sector, steer to the reviews. John Birt himself was retained to keep an eye on the reviews overall. But Geoff and others were also keen that the reviews did not just go Department-native, and wanted to retain some of the freshness associated with the PIU, so a new structure of Deputies was also created to keep an eye on each of the reviews.

Confused? You should be. It was a very complex and contested governance structure. I had been brought in to provide intellectual rigour and thought leadership to the work of the FSU. I had known Geoff before, though not terribly well, as a result of *Options for Britain* (1996) and the activities of Nexus, the policy network. Before 2001, I had sent at his request a list of interesting projects that I thought the PIU might engage in, and we had also spoken about the need for a more strategic unit at the heart of government (indeed, this was one of the proposals suggested by *Options*).

There was an uncomfortable relationship between those in the FSU and PIU. This was illustrated with humour at a joint away-day for the two units with a mock sketch involving a conversation between a PIU and an FSU team member trying to make conversation during a chance meeting. The PIU would talk about all the interesting work they were doing and who they were working with, but all the FSU person could say was 'I can't tell you'.

The governance problems of the FSU projects will be familiar to anyone who has ever worked in No. 10, the White House, or indeed any leader's office. The essential issue is that normal formal hierarchies tend to break down in a context where power and influence rests less on your formal position than on your relationship with the leader. In crude terms, whoever can claim most authoritatively to know the mind of the leader, whether because they were the most recent to speak to him or her or because they are known to be most trusted on the subject, effectively gets to pull rank. Of course, often this isn't completely clear, especially since people will sometimes bluster and bluff, so it is a recipe for endless arguments and much confusion. It's a court.

Despite the governance problems, the FSU did ultimately write a series of very wide-ranging and ambitious reports, broadly themed around a blueprint for what each of the major public services should look like in 2010, and how we would get there.[2] But though the FSU did deliver these reports, it did not necessarily deliver the goodwill and sense of ownership necessary to turn the reports from paper to change on the ground. The secrecy meant that key stakeholders were often not brought along with the process, so that when they finally got to see the conclusions these could seem a giant – even impossible – leap from where they were now. This was aggravated by the inevitable hostility of 'not invented here', and sometimes by personal or ideological dislikes of some of the figures involved.

In fact, Ministers and their Permanent Secretaries who didn't like the final conclusions of the FSU reports had several strategies they could use to slow them down or block them. The first was simply to say no or disagree with specific conclusions. This did happen, but rarely directly with the PM. Second – and something of a classic – was to agree '110 per cent' with the analysis and its conclusions in the meeting with the PM, but then either 'reinterpret' it to make it line up with what the Department wanted to do anyway, or just ignore it after the meeting. Prime Ministers are very busy, and in many cases they won't follow up on matters that seem to be agreed. A third strategy was for a Department to agree to feed the conclusions into its own work programme or reviews. This was tricky because it could indicate a sincere attempt to operationalize the proposals, but could also be death through a thousand cuts.

The personal animosity, and sometimes overt hostility between senior Ministers and John Birt undoubtedly became a major problem, and one that also picked up on the well-known – but sometimes creative – tensions between No. 10 and the Treasury under Gordon Brown.

Yet the practical trigger for the reconstitution of the FSU and the PIU into something new was not any internal battle, but the ramifications of a very public event – the attacks on the World Trade Centre in September 2001. In the weeks that followed, not only did the FSU begin to look at security issues, but new assessments were conducted about the safety of No. 10 itself. It turned out that there was real concern that a severe bomb blast would cause the upper part of No. 10 to collapse. Though we were in the lower half and therefore thought to be safe, some rearrangement of staff across the building was felt prudent. More generally, it seemed wise to move out as many functions and staff as was possible anyway, not least to reduce the numbers of visitors coming and going.[3]

To cut a long story short, the FSU moved back to Admiralty Arch and in with our sister unit the PIU. The two Units retained their separate identities and work programmes for a while. But in the open-plan atmosphere of Arch and in the light of lessons we were learning about what did and didn't work in relation to our working style and reports, a new and hybrid style of working began to emerge, and eventually a combined unit was born.

2002-today: The Prime Minister's Strategy Unit

In essence, the Strategy Unit came to combine the approaches of its two parent units in a way that was ultimately more effective than either. Like the FSU, the PMSU retained a clear focus on the PM's priorities and the big issues of the day. A formal commissioning board developed that had on it the key players at the centre – including from Gordon Brown's Treasury – but an unmistakable focus on the PM's concerns. The commissioning board acted as a short-circuit to deal with different interpretations of the PM's concerns on an issue and to ensure that work by the Unit meshed with other linked activities such as forthcoming legislation.[4] On the other hand, much of the more open working style of the PIU was retained. The analytical background of PMSU reports was typically published in full, though policy advice to the PM generally remained private. Publication of analytical work, helped to prepare the way for subsequent action, allowed opportunity for public challenge, and generally secured agreement within and outside government on the nature of the problem to be addressed.

We took a project by project view on working arrangements with the Departments most affected, but generally favoured close working arrangements. Often PMSU teams would physically locate in the Department most likely to be responsible for acting on the conclusions, so that they felt ownership and up to speed with the work. Indeed, concluding reports were often effectively in the form of Green or White papers from the host Department, not as separate PMSU reports.

One innovation or project – the 'Strategic Audit' – merits a particular mention. One weakness of our project based approach is that it did not allow us to stand back and assess the overall challenges and opportunities that we faced. The idea arose, in the wake of the big FSU reviews, to conduct our own version of *Options for Britain* – a strategic review of the UK's strengths and weaknesses in an international and historical perspective, covering all areas of policy. Geoff Mulgan, then Head of Strategy, felt we should call it an 'audit' partly to deliberately make it sound a little dull and less politically sensitive. Unsurprisingly, it was the largest project we had ever conducted, taking more than half of all our staff.[5] We triangulated across all the data we could get our hands on, including segmentation work within the UK population on who was doing well or badly within the overall trends. We also undertook interviews with every member of Cabinet, Permanent Secretaries (heads of Departments) and thought leaders outside of government about what they thought had gone well or badly since 1997 and what they thought the key challenges were that we faced. For the latter, we even got our interviewees to rate what they thought the Government's future priorities should be on a two-dimensional grid, with the primary

Figure A.2 *The Prime Minister's Strategy Unit having a rare group drink in 2006. Stephen Aldridge, previously Chief Economist and then Director is to the far right (but one); David Bennett, Director of Strategy and policy in No. 10 is to the far left; and Prime Minister Tony Blair stands in the centre. I am perched in front having just gone down to the lobby to rescue a new member of staff stuck at the gate, and not wanting to obscure those standing behind.[6]*

axis being how important they thought the issue was, and the secondary axis was how much impact they thought government could have on it. The conclusion of the audit was relayed back to the Cabinet and Permanent Secretaries, as well as helping to shape the agenda of the Unit for the coming years.[7]

With the passage of time, and the maturity of the Administration, the PMSU moved away from project by project team working, and evolved into partially fixed teams each of which shadowed the big Departments and PM concerns. In particular, we had semi-permanent teams covering Home Affairs (crime, policing and immigration); education; and health. This helped build and maintain relationships with key Departments and stakeholders and avoided the problem of reinventing the wheel for every project. At the same time, much of our resources remained fluid so that we could reconfigure around important issues and projects that didn't fit in these boxes, such as the 'strategic audits', local and neighbourhood government reform, energy, and social exclusion.

By 2005, aided by a set of senior people within the Unit with good access to the PM and a Director, Stephen Aldridge, with the quiet confidence to let us get on with the job, the PMSU had managed to pull off the trick of focusing on the PM's priorities but also working closely and effectively with the Departments. As a Permanent Secretary said at the time, it is much easier for a Department to act strategically and effectively when the centre of government itself acts this way.

The Strategy Unit name: fact and fiction

A few years before the Strategy Unit was created, the author Michael Frayn wrote a novel – *A Landing on the Sun* – featuring just such a named unit created by a fictional British Prime Minister conducting an inquiry into the causes of happiness and what government could do to promote it.

As it turned out, in late 2002, one of the projects we were working on was a paper on happiness and life satisfaction.[8] At this time we were still loosely split into the PIU and FSU. I had a bright young civil servant working with me on the Life Satisfaction paper, called Nick Donovan. As some light reading, he took Frayn's novel on holiday, partly because the story centred on such a similar topic.[9] As Nick read on, he began to find the book rather disturbing. The story revolved around the civil servant (like him) and the Oxbridge academic (like me) wrestling with some of the same big issues that we were looking at, albeit with us using rather more statistical and empirical methods. Unfortunately for Nick's opposite number in the story, the civil servant ended up going somewhat insane, crawling around on the roof and falling to a slow and painful death in one of the courtyards below. It also happened that Frayn had set the story and the location of his Unit up in a high floor of Whitehall almost exactly where we were based.

When Nick came back from holiday, the story was still raw in his mind. You can imagine his disbelief, and then genuine shock, when he discovered that while he was away the FSU had merged with the PIU and was now going to be called the 'Strategy Unit' from then on. I'm sure he thought it was a joke, but was genuinely a little freaked out when he realized it was for real.

I'm pleased to say that we did publish the *Life Satisfaction* paper, and Nick didn't kill himself. In fact, we sent a copy to Frayn who wrote back, kindly congratulating us on making a better job of the paper and the Strategy Unit than the characters in his book. Though Nick has since moved on from the Strategy Unit, I'm sure he still has the letter on his wall.

The spreading of a strategic approach to government

One of the side effects of the Strategy Unit work was that it created a demand from other Ministers for a similar style of work from within their own Departments. Suddenly the trademark style of PMSU power-point presentations – dense in graphs and data, but easy to flip through at pace – became common across Whitehall. John Birt's endless hours of pushing us to boil down our complex analyses to a headline that could be understood in a few seconds began to push out the long and wordy Ministerial briefs of old. The constant and revolving loan of economically and analytically literate staff to other Whitehall Departments, as well as the secondments into the Unit, also had an impact.

By 2008, most Whitehall Departments had created their own Strategy Units. Like their parent, the ones that are working most effectively have direct lines to the Minister within their Department. They were often headed by people who had learnt their trade in the PMSU, or in close association with it, such as Paul Maltby in the Home Office, Sarah Healey in Education, Jonathan Brearley in the Office of Climate Change, Will Cavendish in the Department of Health and Cat Tully in the Foreign Office. This created a new network of relationships across Whitehall of people who shared a common history and, more importantly, an empirically rigorous, long-term and politically attuned approach to policy-making.

In my view, power is not just a zero sum game (see Chapter 5 on government). The increased analytical and strategic capability of Departments doesn't just generate a new tug-of-war or analytical arms race. Rather it increases the capacity of government as a whole to function more effectively, more like the components of a tuned machine rather than a clunky old banger.

Other countries have also developed equivalents of the Strategy Unit, though their success has been variable. The Canadian PRU, which was slightly more analysis and less strategy, got moved away from the Prime Minister's Office and killed off. The Australians are currently transitioning between a PIU-style group around the Cabinet Secretary to something more like the PMSU. The French under Sarkozy were also in the process of creating a Strategy Unit in 2008–9. Several developing countries have sought to replicate the PMSU, down to cutting and pasting directly from the PMSU website onto their own. But as Jonathan Powell of No. 10 was apt to point out, plagiarism is to be welcomed in our game.

A key lesson, both within the UK and across countries, is that high quality analysis and able people are a necessary but not sufficient condition for an effective Strategy Unit. The details of the governance and commissioning arrangements are pivotal. Strategy Units that report through long loops of the civil service rapidly have their creativity and room for manoeuvre squeezed out: direct commissioning from, and a line to, the Prime Minister, President or Minister is critical to success.

Effective strategic policymaking brings together three points of a triangle. Good government requires a capability to analyse the past in order to understand the present, and shape the future. This requires a blend of quantitative and qualitative skills, that inevitably gives the work of strategy units a relatively technocratic feel. A second point of the triangle is a sensitivity to, and engagement with, the current and likely future concerns of the public. If the public are worried about increasing diversity, for example, then it is a problem even if your econometric models tell you the concern is 'misplaced'. Finally, there must be a focus on the distinctive objectives of the elected government, be this to reduce poverty, make a more cohesive society, or prioritize economic competitiveness. Without this focus, such units rapidly become just another voice adding to the cacophony of problems and special interest pleas thrown at political leaders on an everyday basis.

The Future

The Conservative manifesto in 2005 stated an intent to scrap the PMSU, had the then Opposition won the election. Similarly Gordon Brown indicated privately that he intended to strip down the PMSU before taking over as Prime Minister. Even the Cabinet Secretary, Gus

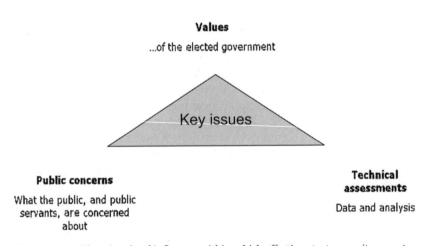

Values

...of the elected government

Key issues

Public concerns

What the public, and public servants, are concerned about

Technical assessments

Data and analysis

Figure A.3   *The triangle of influence within which effective strategy units operate.*

O'Donnell, was sceptical about keeping the PMSU before he took up his role (having previously been head of the Treasury). But Brown, the Cabinet Secretary, and other newly arrived figures at No. 10 soon came to realize how invaluable it was to have a strong analytical and policy-making capacity at the heart of government.

Similarly, the Opposition in 2009 have expressed a desire to get rid of the PMSU and slim down the centre of government. Yet while it is correct that the UK is highly centralized to Whitehall, it is at the same time highly decentralized within Whitehall. UK Department Ministers have the highest levels of budgetary discretion of all OECD countries, largely reflecting the constitutional position that they formally answer to the Queen, not the PM. Similarly, the size of the UK centre (including Treasury) is roughly a half to a third of the size of most comparator nations in proportionate terms. The chances are that an incoming Cameron administration will soon rediscover Blair's surprise: 'where are my people?' Ironically, if an incoming Government want to reduce the size of Whitehall, they may need to increase the size of the very centre, expanding a flexible pool of talented individuals drawn from across the Departments and beyond to help develop policy and sharpen deliver. In this sense, the PMSU looks a lot like the future of government, whether the name sticks or not.

In April 2009, the latest head of the PMSU, Gareth Davies was appointed. Though he also spent time serving in No. 10 (as an adviser on welfare policy), Gareth was appointed by civil servants not by politicians according to the civil service code. The interview panel will have probed his suitability to serve an administration of left or right. We shall see whether he is the last head of the PMSU. The chances are, he will not be.

Notes

Preface

1 Nikolai Kondratiev was a Russian economist who identified long wave movements in prices, wages and interest rates. New innovations – such as the steam engine and mass production of textiles, railways and steel, and the development of electrical devices – drive an economic 'spring' of about 25 years. This is then followed by a brief 'summer' of about 5 years where excess production leads to falling profits and growth. An 'autumn' of mild recession, flat growth and rising debt follows. Finally, a protracted recession triggered by the need to repay debt triggers the 'winter', with a period of a further 15 years of sluggish growth until the next innovation kicks in.

1 Prosperity and Well-being

1 The Cambridge–London (Kings Cross) trains were found to be the most crowded commuter train in the UK, along with Woking–Waterloo. A spot survey found 870 passengers on the eight carriage 7.15 train designed to carry 495 people – 76% above capacity. *Passenger Focus Survey*, 2008. In early 2009, peak Cambridge–London trains were extended to 12 carriages.
2 Ipsos-Mori monthly tracker poll.
3 F. Hirsch (1976), *Social Limits to Growth* (Cambridge: Harvard University Press).

4   N. Donovan and D. S. Halpern (2002), 'Life satisfaction: the state of knowledge and implications for government', London, Cabinet Office.

5   Alois Stutzer and Bruno S. Frey (2008), 'Stress that doesn't pay: the commuting paradox', *Scandinavian Journal of Economics*, 110 (2), 339–66.

6   See the work of Danny Kahneman; and the accessible book by Daniel Gilbert (2007), *Stumbling on Happiness* (HarperPerennial: new edn).

7   Some researchers and economists, such as Richard Layard, have become especially excited about brain scan experiments that show that certain areas of the cortex 'light up' when people are happy. Since the gold standard of well-being is how you feel, not what a scan is showing, these experiments seem to add relatively little at present, though I've nothing against them.

8   In a study of 28 nations, respondents consistently rated happiness as more important than wealth, and marginally more important than health. Ed Diener (2007). 'Happiness accounts for policy use', Presentation to the OECD, Rome.

9   Danner, Snowden and Friesen (2001), 'Positive emotions in early life and longevity: findings from the nun study', *Journal of Personality and Social Psychology*, 80(5), 804–13. An accessible summary of these studies can also be found in Seligman (2003), *Authentic Happiness* (London: Nicholas Brealey Publishing).

10 E. Diener, C. Nickerson, R. E. Lucas and E. Sandvik (2002), 'Dispositional affect and job outcomes', *Social Indicators Research* 59, 229–59.

11 F. Huppert (2009), 'Psychological well-being: evidence regarding its causes and consequences', *Applied Psychology: Health and Well-Being* 1, 137–64.

12 Carlos A. Estrada, Alice M. Isen and Mark J. Young (1997), 'Positive affect facilitates integration of information and decreases anchoring in reasoning among physicians', *Organizational Behavior and Human Decision Processes* 72 (1), 117–35.

13 The most recent of these reviews is by Ed Diener and his son Robert (2008), *Happiness: Unlocking the Mysteries of Psychological Wealth* (Oxford: WileyBlackwell).

14 Diener compared individuals' life satisfaction ratings over a seventeen-year period, and found a correlation of 0.51 between the first 5 years and the last 5 years. F. Fujita and E. Diener (2005), 'Life satisfaction set point: Stability and change', *Journal of Personality and Social Psychology* 88, 158–64.

15 National Accounts of Well-being. New Economics Foundation, 2009.

16 Diener and Seligman found the correlation to be 0.08 among countries with incomes over US$10,000. E. Diener and M. E. P. Seligman (2004), 'Beyond money: toward an economy of well-being', *Psychological Science in the Public Interest* 5, 1–31.

17 M. Haller and M. Hadler (2006), 'How social relations and structures can produce happiness and unhappiness: an international comparative analysis', *Social Indicators Research* 75, 169–216.

18   P. Brickman, D. Coates and R. Janoff-Bulman (1978), 'Lottery winners and accident victims: is happiness relative?', *Journal of Personality and Social Psychology* 36(8), 917–27.

19   Green, Doherty and Gerber (2003), 'Estimating the effects of an exogenous shock to personal income: a study of lottery winners,' unpublished paper.

20   Eckblad and von der Lippe (1994), 'Norwegian lottery winners: cautious realists', *Journal of Gambling Studies* 10 (4), 305–22. Also reported in Christoph Lau and Ludwig Kramer (2005), *Die Relativitätstheorie des Glücks. Uber das Leben von Lottomillionaren* (The Relativity of Luck. About the Life of Lottery Millionaires, Herbolzheim).

21   Jonathan Gardner and Andrew J. Oswald (2007), 'Money and mental wellbeing: a longitudinal study of medium-sized lottery wins', *Journal of Health Economics* 26 (1), 49–60. I'm not sure if some of the delayed positive effects result from the decay of other negative events associated with windfalls in this panel data, e.g. damage and repairs to a house associated with an insurance claim, or death associated with inheritance.

22   B. Heady, R. Muffels and M. Wooden (2004), *Money Doesn't Buy Happiness . . . Or Does It? A Reconsideration Based on the Combined Effects of Wealth, Income and Consumption.* IZA DP No. 1218.

23   V. K. Borooah (2006), 'How much happiness is there in the world? A cross-country study', *Applied Economics Letters* 13, 483–8.

24   C. Kenny (1999), 'Does growth cause happiness, or does happiness cause growth?' KYKLOS 52(1), 3–26.

25   E. F. P. Luttmer (2004), 'Neighbors as negatives: relative earnings and well-being', National Bureau of Economic Research Working Paper No. 10667. D. G. Blanchflower and A. J. Oswald (2004), 'Money, sex and happiness: an empirical study,' *Scand. J. of Economics*, 106(3), 393–415.

26   C. Bjørnskov, N. Gupta and P. Pedersen (2008), 'Analysing trends in subjective well-being in 15 European countries, 1973–2002', *Journal of Happiness Studies* 9, 317–30.

27   See Layard for an accessible model of these scale effects. R. Layard (2005), *Happiness. Lessons from a New Science.* (Allen Lane: Penguin Books).

28   www.oprah.com/article/omagazine/200810_omag_happiness_plan

29   D. Halpern (2005), *Social Capital* (Cambridge: Polity).

30   Halpern (2005), *Social Capital*, ch. 2. Whiteley found that social trust was as, or more powerful a predictor of economic growth than investment in human or physical capital.

31   Andrew Oswald's calculation. The large figure partly reflects the relatively small impact of income *per se* on subjective well-being. See table and discussion in Halpern and Donovan (2002), 'Life satisfaction: a review of the evidence and policy implications', www.strategy.gov.uk.

32   See the work of Brendan Burchell.

33   S. Meier and A. Stutzer (2008), 'Is volunteering rewarding in itself?', *Economica* 75(297), 39–59.

34   J. Geirland (1996), 'Go With The Flow', *Wired* magazine, September, Issue 4.09.

35 M. Csikszentmihalyi (1975), *Beyond Boredom and Anxiety* (San Francisco: Jossey-Bass).

36 Halpern, D. 2005. *Social Capital*. Cambridge: Polity. See Chapter 3 on health.

37 M. E. P. Seligman (2003), *Authentic Happiness* (London: Nicholas Brealey Publishing).

38 G. W. Brown and T. Harris (1978), *Social Origins of Depression* (London: Tavistock).

39 For example, see John Helliwell's cross-national analysis of the World Values Surveys. J. F. Helliwell (2002), 'How's life? Combining individual and national variables to explain subjective well-being', National Bureau of Economic Research Working Paper No. 9065.

40 E. Diener (2007), 'Happiness Accounts for Policy Use', Presentation to the OECD, Rome.

41 M. Rose (2007), 'Profile of Information Technology Professionals', Economic and Social Research Council, Award RES-341-25-0015. University of Bath.

42 J. H. Fowler and N. A. Christakis (2008), 'Dynamic spread of happiness in a large social network: longitudinal analysis over 20 years in the Framingham Heart Study', *British Medical Journal* 337, a2338.

43 R. Veenhoven (2007), 'Measures of gross national happiness', Presentation to OECD conference, Rome.

44 Bruno Frey found a strong association between numbers of referenda across Swiss Cantons and life satisfaction, with a weaker effect among immigrants who were not able to vote. However, follow-up studies have struggled to replicate the effect. Bruno S. Frey and Alois Stutzer (2001), *Happiness and Economics: How the Economy and Institutions Affect Human Well-Being* (Princeton: Princeton University Press).

45 For example, one UK poll found that 81% felt that the government's prime objective should be 'the greatest happiness' rather than 'the greatest wealth' (NOP poll for the BBC, 2006).

46 New Economics Foundation NEF, 2009.

47 There is an inverse correlation between countries' level of prison and forensic psychiatric provision.

48 See, for example, J. F. Helliwell (2002), 'How's life? Combining individual and national variables to explain subjective well-being', National Bureau of Economic Research Working Paper No. 9065.

49 George Loewenstein, pers. comm. See also L. Babcock, X. Wang and G. Loewenstein (1996), 'Choosing the wrong pond: social comparisons that reflect a self-serving bias', *Quarterly Journal of Economics* 111, 1–19.

50 See Daniel Kahneman, Ed Diener and Norbert Schwarz (2003), *Well-being: The Foundations of Hedonic Psychology* (New York: Russell Sage Foundation), pp. 16–17.

51 Ipsos MORI analysis on the drivers of public servants' satisfaction.

52 See the *Sainsbury Review of Science and Innovation: The Race to the Top*. HMT, October 2007.

53   David Cameron has repeatedly referred in speeches from 2007–9 to the need to move into a 'post-bureaucratic' age.

54   Avner Offer – see the next chapter for more detail. 'Between the gift and the market: the economy of regard', *Economic History Review*, L3 3(1997), 450–76.

55   This phrase was coined by Iain McClean in *Options for a New Britain*, 2009.

56   It is estimated that 95% of all life was wiped out by the temperature rises associated with this geological period, with a series of environmental triggers that look alarmingly familiar.

57   J. Gershunny, Presentation to the Prime Minister's Strategy Unit (see also Chapter 3).

58   From Keynes (1963), *Essays in Persuasion* (New York: W.W. Norton and Co.), pp. 358–73.

2   Not Getting Along

1   Pew data. The question asks which issues are 'a top priority', and in this case 'reducing crime'.

2   The British Crime survey now asks 40,000 people a year whether they have been a victim of crime over the last year. This means it picks up crimes that they may not have reported to the police, or that the police may not have recorded for some reason.

3   Controversially, it has been argued that the fall in 'unwanted' young people has especially reduced crime across US states as a result of the wider availability of birth control and abortion – a theory popularized in S. Levitt and S. Dubner (2005), *Freakonomics* (New York: William Morrow).

4   Similarly, a key predictor of crime at the very local level is the number of young people as a proportion of the local population.

5   The figures for EU countries from the ICVS are averages across the countries sampled in each year. This means that the 1992 data is drawn from a smaller sample of countries, so the absolute size of the differences should be treated with caution.

6   It seems that we are hard-wired to learn fast and long remember negative events. Rats made to feel sick after drinking flavoured water will learn to avoid that taste after a single trial.

7   The figures for the UK were that 34% thought they would be burgled next year, while 3.3% were burgled the previous year.

8   Levels of urbanization are also sometimes found to help to explain some of the variability – see Halpern 2001 and van Dyke 2007, but was non-significant in these data. This regression updates previous analyses as reported in D. Halpern (2001), 'Morals, social trust and inequality: can values explain crime?' *British Journal of Criminology* 41(2), 236–51.

9   For a fuller discussion of the relationship between social trust and crime, see Halpern, *Social Capital*, Chapter 4.

10   See, for example, Interpol trend data on homicides.

11 J. Braithwaite (1989), *Crime, Shame and Reintegration* (Oxford: Oxford University Press).

12 It has been estimated that even if we could shut down the growing of heroin in Afghanistan tomorrow, there would still be around seven years of supply left in the supply chain (compare this with supplies of petrol or natural gas!) The other problem with seeking to cut supply is that it puts up street prices, meaning that addicts have to commit more crime to pay for each fix.

13 'The economic case for and against prison', Matrix, 2007, www.matrixknowledge.co.uk/wp-content/uploads/economic-case-for-and-against-prison.pdf.

14 'A question of conviction: juries should have the option to find a defendant "probably guilty"', *New Statesman*, 28 February 1997, p. 14.

15 Ipsos-MORI monthly poll.

16 The correlation is 0.01 – i.e. there is no linear relationship at all. Of course, it is possible that the data on the percentage of foreign born understates the actual level of immigration, though this alone would not explain the lack of a relationship. However, there could theoretically be an interaction that could conceal a relationship, such as if immigrants were systematically less likely to show up in the figures in countries where there was higher levels of hostility to immigration.

17 William Brown (Cambridge and Low Pay Commission), pers. comm.

18 Some of this effect is also due to the shrinking numbers without any skills, leaving behind an increasingly tough to employ group.

19 Robert J. Sampson, Jeffrey D. Morenoff and Stephen Raudenbush (2005), 'Social anatomy of racial and ethnic disparities in violence', *American Journal of Public Health* 95, 224–32.

20 Bob Putnam; for a summary see Halpern (2005).

21 Y. Esmer and Thorleif Pettersson (2007), *Measuring and Mapping Cultures: 25 Years of Comparative Value Surveys* (Boston: Brill Academic Publishers).

22 Eurobarometer data (2007): correlation = −0.45; prob. < 0.05.

23 1999 Mori socio-mapping data.

24 MORI analysis of UK data.

25 This table is based loosely on the figures compiled by *Wired* magazine by Ryan Singel, supplemented by other statistics from the National Center for Health Statistics and elsewhere.

26 This was seen most clearly in Walthamstow, London, in the wake of the 7/7 and subsequent bombings.

27 I.e. the logo of Department for International Development.

3 The Politics of Virtue

1 'Unleashing our Hidden Wealth', published in *Yes!* magazine, www.yesmagazine.org/article.asp?ID=524. For a fuller exposition of Cahn's

views and work, see E. Cahn (2000), *No More Throwaway People, The Co-Production Imperative* (Washington: Essential Books).

2 The Home Office was the Department responsible for policing and law enforcement. Louise Casey, who was the dynamic and irrepressible face of the Anti-Social Behaviour Unit and then Head of the Respect Action Team, kept a log of the press reports, the vast majority of which were positive.

3 Pakistan 74.2%; Indonesia 64.7%; Morocco 44.2%; Jordan 44.1%; Egypt 42.2%; Iraq 32.8%; Saudi 29.2%; and Iran 27.4%.

4 Some scholars regard the Ten Commandments as being a particularly important societal development because they reflect a moment when religion and ethics were 'democratized'. Previously, religions had tended to rely on priests or holy men to express the word of God, but with the Ten Commandments they are communicated directly for all to follow – particularly important for a 'nation' of escaped slaves with very different origins trying to get along together.

5 The exception is keeping the Sabbath. This may reflect the widespread practice of limited Sunday trading and activity in most European countries at the time.

6 N. Nevitte and C. Cochrane (2007), 'Individualization in Europe and America: connecting religious and moral values', in Esmer and Pettersson (eds.), *Measuring and Mapping Cultures: 25 Years of Comparative Value Surveys* (Leiden and Boston: Brill), pp. 99–126.

7 In general, the pattern of change – though not the absolute levels of acceptability – is very similar across Western regions, but there are a few differences. For example, attitudes to abortion hardened very slightly in North America, while softening in Scandinavia, Northern and Southern Europe. Attitudes to prostitution hardened slightly in Northern Europe, while softening elsewhere, perhaps reflecting a growing understanding and focus on the role played by people trafficking.

8 Avner Offer has pushed the latter term, both in an early article in 1997, and his more recent book, *The Challenge of Affluence: Self-control and Well-being in the United States and Britain since 1950* (Oxford: Oxford University Press, 2006).

9 See the work of Jonathan Geshunny, now at Oxford.

10 F. Hirsch (1977), *Social Limits to Growth* (London: Routledge).

11 Baum and Vallins (1977), *Architecture and Social Behaviour: Psychosocial Studies of Social Density* (Hillsdale, New Jersey); or see Halpern (1995), *Mental Health and the Built Environment* (Oxford: Taylor and Francis), pp. 133–8, for a summary. Student accommodation is of particular interest because, at least in their first year, students are generally randomly assigned to their rooms. In normal housing, lots of other factors such as wealth and personal preference also affect who ends up living where, making it much harder to identify the effects of housing and the physical environment *per se.*

12 These were studies of US student dorms, so there would normally be three students sharing a room together in the first year.

13 M. Bulmer (1986), *Neighbours: The Work of Philip Abrams* (Cambridge: Cambridge University Press).

14 W. Yancy (1971), 'Architecture, interaction and social control: the case of a large scale housing project', *Environment and Behaviour* 3: 3–21.

15 O. Newman (1973), *Defensible Space* (London: Architectural Press); details reproduced in Halpern (1995), pp. 125–7.

16 See re-analysis of SCPR dataset, originally gathered by Morton-Williams, in chs. 2 and 3 of Halpern (1995). There is some evidence that roads that are curved, instead of straight, can also provide some of these positive effects by virtue of creating a visual enclosure of a smaller number of dwellings than a long straight road (Gordon Thompson, pers. comm.).

17 An elegant example comes from Festinger's post-war studies of married student villages, again with the benefit of random assignment but in this case to houses. L. Festinger *et al.* (1950), *Social Pressures in Informal Groups: A Study of Human Factors in Housing* (New York: Harper Brothers Publishing).

18 Taking back the streets, *Panorama*, BBC One, 3 March 2008, http://news.bbc.co.uk/1/hi/programmes/panorama/7267418.stm.

19 A Radburn layout is where the roads run around the back of the houses, while the fronts of the houses open onto green pedestrianized areas. This study is reported in detail in ch. 7 of Halpern (1995).

20 M. Eisner (2001), 'Modernization, self-control and lethal violence: the long-term dynamics of European homicide rates in theoretical perspective', *British Journal of Criminology* 41(4), 618–38.

21 Of course, occasionally – notably under the rare condition of deflation, such as in Japan in the 1990s – this may be exactly what you want: to get people to stop saving and start spending.

22 Mark R. Lepper, David Greene and Richard E. Nisbett (1973), 'Undermining children's intrinsic interest with extrinsic reward: A test of the "overjustification" hypothesis', *Journal of Personality and Social Psychology* 28(1), 129–37.

23 Kathleen D. Vohs, Nicole L. Mead and Miranda R. Goode (2006), 'The psychological consequences of money', *Science* 314, 1154–6.

24 See reviews by David Boyle, www.david-boyle.co.uk/funnymoney/london.html.

25 The EU has now funded several other experimental schemes, including the Scottish Organizational Currency System (SOCS).

26 For more, see Edgar Cahn and Jonathan Rowe (1992), *Time Dollars* (Emmaus: Rodale Press).

27 Bernard Lietaer (2003), *Access to Human Wealth: Money beyond Greed and Scarcity* (Access Books).

28 N. Folbre and J. A. Nelson (2000), 'For love or money – or both?' *Journal of Economic Perspectives*, 14(4), 123–40.

29 Over the same period, 'homemakers' expressed as a percentage of all workers fell from 36 to 16%.

30 These data are from the cross-European SHARE project survey conducted in 2004, which includes data from Denmark, Sweden, Austria, France, Germany, Netherlands, Switzerland, Greece, Italy and Spain. See M. Albertini, M. Kohli and C. Vogel (2007), 'Intergenerational transfers of time and money in European families: common patterns different regimes?', *Journal of European Social Policy* 17, 319.

31 In Southern European countries, the figures are particularly high, with typically around 1,500 hours given by the older generation, and around 1,000 received.

32 B. Frey (1998), 'Institutions and morale: the crowding out effect', in Ben-Ner and Putterman (eds.) *Economics, Values and Organisation* (Cambridge: Cambridge University Press), pp. 437–60.

33 Tony Health, Nuffield College, Oxford: analysis prepared for the PMSU.

34 H. Tajfel (1981), *Human Groups and Social Categories: Studies in Social Psychology* (Cambridge: Cambridge University Press).

35 It is interesting to note that the 'respect for parents' is also the most resilient of the Ten Commandments.

36 P. Collier, V. L. Elliott, H. Hegre, A. Hoeffler, M. Reynal-Querol and N. Sambanis (2003), *Breaking the Conflict Trap: Civil War and Development Policy* (Washington, DC: World Bank and Oxford University Press).

37 Bo Rothstein provides an interesting example. Around two-thirds of Swedes report high levels of social trust – that is, they say most other people can be trusted. Rothstein found that a key explanation for the low trust of the remaining third was exposure to means-tested benefits. He concluded that the need to assume that the claimant might be cheating was strongly corrosive of trust of both claimant and public servant. Studies of tax systems provide complementary evidence – aggressive checking by tax collectors creates a climate of distrust and, ironically often fails to increase the tax take compared with systems based on trust and self-report. Pers. comm. and B. Rothstein (2001), 'Social capital in the democratic welfare state', *Politics and Society* 29(2), 207–41.

38 What should the exchange rate be between a community credit and a pound, euro or dollar? If you take a hard line on fungibility, you might ban all such exchange, saying for example that it is impossible for an adult to buy their way out of their obligation. I think a more practical but acceptable compromise would be to allow people to buy their way out of the obligation, but I would set the rate to punitively high, signalling the unacceptability of buying yourself out and the high value we place on the contribution of others.

39 I sent an early draft of this chapter to a friend and colleague at No. 10 for comment – partly in response to an interesting lecture he had given himself. He emailed back: 'Enjoyed the chapter – especially the early bits. I felt you were not convinced that the policy solutions you pointed to – a bit of LETS, vouchers for volunteering, etc – were 'big enough' given the potential prizes on offer. Could you not go deeper and say we need a different conception of the state/capitalism/regulation/localism etc?'

I've had a bit of a go at it, but it's such a big question, let me extend his challenge to you, the reader, too.

40 See the work of Robert Cialdini (and also Chapter 5 in this book). A 'declarative norm' is that which people deduce from what seems to be the behaviour of those around them, as opposed to what they know is supposed to be the way to behave. For example, litter on the floor makes us more likely to drop litter ourselves, even if we think it's wrong, because that's what everyone else is doing.

4 Fairness and Inclusion

1 Speech to launch the Social Exclusion Action Plan: 'Our Nation's Future – Social Exclusion', York, www.number10.gov.uk/Page10037. Many of the phrases in the speech came from Phil Collins, Tony's speechwriter at the time.

2 There are issues around measurement. Surveys of income are thought to be less reliable at the top and bottom of the income scales which may lead to underestimates of inequality. The most common technical measure of inequality is the gini coefficient, though there are more refined measures such as developed by Tony Atkinson. In the figures in this chapter, I have used the ratio of high to low incomes. Gini coefficients are considered better technical measures because they use information from the whole distribution – not just the ends – and they produce a tighter distribution across countries (e.g. so that high inequality countries don't look like massive outliers). The latter is important if you are running lots of statistical models like regressions. But the basic ranking and story is much the same using ratio measures which most readers find much easier to understand. For a recent discussion on measurement issues, see A. B. Atkinson and A. Brandolini (2009), 'On data: a case study of the evolution of income inequality across time and across countries', *Cambridge Journal of Economics* 33(3), 381–404.

3 G. A. Cornia (ed.) (2004), *Inequality, Growth and Poverty in an Era of Liberalisation and Globalization* (Oxford: Oxford University Press).

4 This is confirmed by a negative correlation between income per capita (PPP) and the ratio of top 20 to bottom 20 per cent incomes of –0.26, or –0.37 with the Gini coefficient.

5 See R. Wilkinson and K. Pickett (2009), *The Spirit Level: Why More Equal Societies Almost Always Do Better* (London: Allen Lane).

6 Richard Wilkinson's work has powerfully made the case – perhaps modestly overstated – for the effects of inequality *per se*. I also reviewed the balance of the evidence in *Social Capital* (Halpern, 2005).

7 Interestingly, nations such as China (not surveyed in the early sweeps) have even higher levels of agreement than the Americans that it is fair that the secretaries should be paid at different rates.

8 Notice published in the official newspaper *Granma*, and reported in *The Week*, 21 June 2008.

9 There's actually some evidence that *occupational* mobility – workers' children becoming professionals and service workers etc. – may have

increased over the last few decades in the USA. However, this has not translated into increased income mobility. It would seem that the children of the rich get to be a different kind of, and better paid, lawyer and manager than the children of the poor.

10 Paul Gregg analysis, June 2008. Presentation to the PMSU.

11 Analysis of BCS 1970 by Halpern and Myers, see www. instituteforgovernment.org.uk.

12 A non-IQ illustration of this effect is that in rich countries, where everyone basically gets enough to eat, variations in height are dominated by genes (i.e. high heritability), whereas in poor countries, how tall you are is dominated by environmental and social factors (i.e. heritability estimates are lower).

13 Professor Robert Plomin, pers. comm., comparing the IQs of an artificially selected sample of parents with similar IQs and that of their children using the Colorado data set.

14 Analyses of the OECD PISA data on educational attainment at age 14 show that the link between social class and educational attainment is especially strong in the UK.

15 Anthony B. Atkinson, 'Increased income inequality in OECD countries and the redistributive impact of the Government budget', in G. A. Cornia (ed.) (2004), *Inequality, Growth and Poverty in an Era of Liberalisation and Globalization* (Oxford: Oxford University Press), ch. 10.

16 See Tim Leunig's analysis, accessibly presented in 'A fall in property prices that kick away the ladder', *Financial Times* op-ed column, 9 April 2008.

17 Paul Johnson, now at the Institute for Fiscal Studies, pers. comm.

18 Halpern (2005), *Social Capital*.

19 Analyses by Leon Feinstein, of the Institute for Education, were very influential in making this case.

20 These figures were released in 'Reaching Out: Social Exclusion Action Plan' (2006), Cabinet Office. The statistics were based on calculations by Leon Feinstein using data from the UK longitudinal surveys, particularly the 1970 cohort.

21 The correlation between attitudes to the income gap and the Gini coefficient is slightly higher at 0.15 – but curiously in the same direction. In other words, if anything, the higher the level of objective income inequality, the more people say that the gap should be bigger still!

22 The correlation is –0.25.

23 Peter Taylor-Gooby, pers. comm.

24 Taylor-Gooby and Martin (2008), Trends in sympathy for the poor in *British Social Attitudes: the 24th report* (London: Sage).

25 This story is confirmed in the World Values Survey data for the UK. At the end of the 1990s during a period of objective inequality growth, public sympathy lay towards greater inequality (av. = 6.45 on the 10-point scale). By 1995, opinions had swung towards reducing the gap (av. = 5.1), and by 2000 had eased back (av. = 5.6).

26 The programme was developed by David Olds. With nearly three decades of follow-up data, and replication on at least three sites, the NFP has

now attracted mainstream interest across a number of countries including Germany, NZ and the UK.

27 Blair was careful to later revisit the 'FASBO' myth and to offer a more nuanced account in his speech later that month, but the underlying sentiment – albeit about support rather than punishment – remained.

28 T. H. Marshall (1950), *Citizenship and Social Class* (Cambridge: Cambridge University Press).

29 In contrast, questions that just ask about development in general tend to get a majority against.

30 Readers will note the similarity to the trust funds proposed by Bruce Akerman and Julian Le Grand. Unlike Julian, I propose financing the endowments mainly from existing educational spending, not from increased death duties.

31 Some Local Authorities are already offering generous financial support to children in care to go to university (e.g. Hertfordshire), but still stop well short of the more flexible endowment proposed here.

32 Current estimates are that around 6 per cent of children who were in care in the UK go onto university compared with over 30 per cent of other young people. In Finland, children who were in care are if anything more likely to go on to university. In terms of prison, around 0.5 per cent of children are in care, though more than this pass through the care system. In contrast, it is estimated that around a quarter of the prison population were in care as children.

33 As an aside, there was a period when the capital distribution in the UK flattened in the twentieth century due to tax laws encouraging the very wealthy to pass on assets to their children while still alive. This scheme would have a similar but larger flattening effect, albeit it would take a generation to see its most progressive effects work through.

34 Leon Feinstein, an expert educationalist who has done many of the most interesting analyses of the cohort studies, has become an advocate of cross-age teaching.

35 This effect has been elegantly illustrated in a study of Harvard students: R. L. Zweigenhaft (1993), 'Prep school and public school graduates of Harvard: a longitudinal study of the accumulation of social and cultural capital', *Journal of Higher Education* 64(2), 211–25.

36 The big evaluations of socially mixed housing, notably in the USA, tend to find that while the adults enjoy living in their new environments it does not greatly change their life prospects – but it does seem to help their kids.

37 The overall effect on educational performance of having such selective schools in an area is essentially neutral, once population characteristics are controlled for – though those who go to the selective schools do a bit better and those who don't do slightly worse. It is an interesting question whether if such schools were more genuinely meritocratic, that is that they took the most able regardless of background, whether areas with more selection would then do marginally better.

38 See work of John Ermisch, e.g. M. Brynin and J. Ermisch (eds.) (2009), *Changing Relationships* (London: Routledge).

39 There's fascinating evidence that even small gender imbalances, such as those caused by lots of males being locked up in prison in one area, undermine the bargaining power of the over-represented gender in relationships making them more likely to fail.

5 Power and Governance

1 Jan van Deth has expounded this position. As an aside, ratings of the importance of religion in European countries fell even more markedly than ratings of the importance of politics – though it still ranked higher than politics overall. J. Van Deth (2000), 'Interesting but irrelevant: social capital and the saliency of politics in Western Europe', *European Journal of Political Research* 37, 115–47.

2 Based on Edison National Exit Polls.

3 Turnout fell from 39 to 37% among 18–24 year olds, but rose from 69 to 71% among the 55–64 age group and 70 to 75% among the 65+. The only other age group to see a fall was the 45–54 year olds, among whom turnout fell slightly from 65 to 64%.

4 A lowering of the voting age to 16 was put to a Commons vote in 1999 and massively defeated by 434 to 36 votes. But more recently, the idea has been re-floated in the 2007 Governance of Britain Green Paper and the Prime Minister Gordon Brown has indicated support for the idea.

5 The Cambridge historian, Simon Szreter, was an early advocate of this novel idea.

6 Eurobarometer data.

7 Both cross-sectional and longitudinal data show the same pattern of increasing voter volatility or de-alignment. For a careful analysis across more than 20 mature democracies, see R. J. Dalton and M. P. Wattenberg (2000), *Parties without Partisans* (Oxford: Oxford University Press).

8 Eurobarometer data.

9 It is no coincidence that the Minister responsible at the time, Patricia Hewitt, had herself advocated the use of citizens' juries a decade before when at the think-tank, the Institute for Public Policy Research.

10 Indeed, to quote a friend in No.10, 'I can't bear to hear about Porto Alegre one more time . . .'

11 British Social Attitudes data.

12 There is a case for asking a sub-sample of each Forum to participate in a second event, so that some of the participants in each Forum are already up to speed with the procedure and could act as guides to their fellow citizens.

13 There are some issues that have an impact that falls disproportionately on only a sub-section of the population, such as sexual health on young adults or domestic abuse on women. In these cases, consideration should be given to skewing the sample to the population most affected.

14 Singapore is also not without a form of accountability in that it has vigorously pursued anti-corruption measures within government. Though effectively a one-party state, it does allow some debate and criticism within the party, though not much from outside.

15 Nick Barr, of the LSE, wrote an excellent paper on the subject in 1998, and his work was a loose inspiration for the question. See also N. Barr (2004), *The Economics of the Welfare State* (Oxford: Oxford University Press).

16 P. John and M. Johnson (2008), 'Is there still a public service ethos?', in Park *et al.* (eds.), *British Social Attitudes, 24th report* (London: Sage).

17 See Uberoi, Coutts, McLean and Halpern (2009), *Options for a New Britain* (Basingstoke: Palgrave Macmillan).

18 See reviews by Julian LeGrand: (2006), 'Equality and choice in public services', *Social Research* 73(2), 695–710; (2007) *The Other Invisible Hand: Delivering Public Services through Choice and Competition.* (Princeton: Princeton University Press).

19 See, for example, research by S. Burgess, B. McConnell and C. Propper (2007), 'The impact of school choice on sorting by ability and socio-economic factors in English secondary education', in P. Peterson and L. Woessman (eds.), *Schools and the Equal Opportunity Problem* (MIT Press).

20 David Varney, Head of Transformational Government.

21 Mary Tatlow, in the Office of Public Sector Reform (now disbanded), was early to draw attention to the Canadian Citizen First experience in the UK.

22 The police in the UK are the only public service for which citizen satisfaction is lower if they have actually had contact with the service. In a rare example of being slightly out of touch, the PM was clearly shocked, in a television discussion in 2005, to discover the reality of how slow police responses to public reporting of crime could be, and often that they would not investigate at all.

23 Faculty of Social and Political Sciences, 1995–2001. I gave up my tenured post in 2003.

24 The New Local Government Network has been particularly optimistic.

25 T. Gash *et al.* (2008), *Performance Art* (London: Institute for Government).

26 Ed Miliband, as Cabinet Minister and long-time advisor to Gordon Brown, often bemoaned the 'letterbox' model.

27 I am grateful to Tom Gash for detail. See also Webster, Adrian, Society of IT managers (2006), 'Report on 2005 Socitm Conference', www. socitm.gov.uk/socitm/Events/Annual+Conference/Past+Conferences/ Socitm+2005/Conference+reports.htm. Other US cities have also introduced a 311 number, such as Chicago and San Antonio. Within the UK, the need for such a number was illustrated in pilot work for the 'NHS-Direct' which found that people often confront problems where it is not obvious which service should be responsible. For example, if one saw a figure lying on the pavement, the chances are that this is not a police matter (though they often get called), but it might be a health issue, a drugs issue, social services, or perhaps not something for public services at all. So who should you call? But cross-agency boundaries have substantially thwarted moves to make the single non-emergency number work in the UK.

28 Mark Moore (1995), *Creating Public Value: Strategic Management in Government* (Cambridge: Harvard University Press).
29 Nauru, the Cook Islands, Micronesia, and Tonga top the world obesity tables, all coming in with rates from 60 to nearly 85% of adults with BMIs over 30. Some Middle Eastern nations are also beating the USA in the obesity tables, such as Kuwait with more than 50% of women with BMI's over 30.
30 WHO estimate that around 2 to 6% of healthcare costs currently result from obesity-related illness. In the UK, it is estimated that the cost to the National Health Service of obesity is currently around 2.5% of the NHS cost (around £7bn in 2002). Welfare payments have been recently estimated at £1–6bn, excluding social care (Foresight (2007), 'Tackling Obesities: Future Choices' project; see also PMSU (2008) Food matters).
31 Halpern and Bates (2004), *Personal Responsibility and Changing Behaviour: The State of Knowledge and its Implications for Public Policy*, www.strategy. gov.uk, PMSU discussion paper.
32 Ipsos MORI, UK data.
33 A classic UK example was the game show 'Mastermind', where participants had to answer a series of questions about general knowledge and about a chosen specialist subject. The show's host, Magnus Magnusson, seemed very clever and was used to market various brain-testing games. But of course, he had the answers on a bit of card.
34 A. Tversky and D. Kahneman (1974), 'Judgment under uncertainty: heuristics and biases', *Science* 185, 1124–31.
35 Halpern and Bates (2004), 'Personal responsibility and behaviour change', PMSU, Cabinet Office.
36 Effective popularizations include R. Cialdini (2001), *Influence: Science and Practice* (Allyn and Bacon), which is especially good on decision making in the moment; Gilbert (2006), *Stumbling on Happiness*, which is stronger on distortions in memory; and Thaler and Sunstein (2008), *Nudge*, which is arguably stronger on errors in future prediction and policy implications. Another recent addition is Dan Ariely (2008), *Predictably Irrational* (New York: Harper Collins).
37 In a strict sense, the lower brain is often taken to refer to the brain stem, which keeps a lot of the 'boring but important' stuff going, like breathing, walking and going to the toilet. I just mean the less conscious stuff and mental heuristics, more mid and lower-upper brain.
38 Avner Offer has a good account of commitment devices. Offer (2006), *The Challenge of Affluence: Self-Control and Well-Being in the United States and Britain since 1950* (Oxford: Oxford University Press).
39 Some economists feel that concerns about the 'pension crisis' may have been overstated as many people die with significant assets, notably their homes. There is a case that we could liquidize more of our assets later in life (i.e. re-mortgage the house, and not leave so much to the kids). This critique changes the quantum for the necessary savings rate, but not the underlying principles discussed here.

40　Thaler and Benartzi (2004), 'Save more tomorrow: using behavioural economics to increase employee saving', *Journal of Political Economy* 112, S1.

41　Sunstein and Thaler (2003), 'Libertarian paternalism is not an oxymoron', AEI-Brookings Joint Center for Regulatory Studies, Working Paper 03–2.

42　This greater political project is expressed in Thaler and Sunstein (2008), *Nudge*, and is strikingly bolder than that expressed in earlier papers.

43　Halpern and Bates (2004). Also picked up by Gordon Brown once he became PM, encouraged by Greg Beales who helped on the PMSU paper and went on to become Brown's advisor on health in No.10.

44　The normal trigger power would still remain whereby say 5% of the local population could trigger the referendum – you could not only have a blocking power that a small minority could use to stop referenda.

45　There are two exceptions. If the litter has been swept up into neat piles, then people become less likely to drop. Also, it has been found that people are marginally less likely to drop a piece of litter in an otherwise immaculate environment but with just one piece of litter. See Cialdini's early experimental work.

46　See abandoned car experiments by Zimbardo; smoke filled room and other 'diffusion of responsibility' experiments by Latene and Daley; and compliance experiments by Asch, Muscovisi and, of course, Milgram.

47　Cialdini claims to have markedly increased recycling in a local area through a public service advert designed along these lines.

48　C. Abraham, B. Krahé, R. Dominic and I. Fritsche (2002), 'Does research into the social cognitive antecedents of action contribute to health promotion? A content analysis of safer-sex promotion leaflets', *British Journal of Health Psychology* 7, 227–46; reported in Halpern and Bates (2004).

49　The most famous illustration being Zimbardo's Stanford Prison Cell Experiment, 1971. C. Haney, W. C. Banks and P. G. Zimbardo (1973), 'Interpersonal dynamics in a simulated prison', *International Journal of Criminology and Penology* 1, 69–97.

50　www.theonion.com/content/node/39192, 5 November 2003.

51　The Peckham project tried this out in the 1930s, but it has taken more than seventy years to revisit the idea in a serious way.

52　www.pledgebank.com

53　Halpern (2005), *Social Capital* (Cambridge: Polity); R. Putnam (1993), *Making Democracy Work* (Princeton: Princeton University Press); R. Putnam and L. Feldstein (2003), *Better Together* (New York: Simon and Schuster).

54　See David Willett's Oakshot lecture for an interesting reflection on this issue from the reflective British right. D. Willetts (2008), *Renewing Civic Conservatism* (London School of Economics).

55　UK figures identified by the Department of Health, during the Darzi review (2008).

6 Conclusion

1   Around 500,000 die a year from flu, 90 per cent of whom are over 65. This still leaves 'only' 50,000 a year of children and relatively young adults dying from the disease. Of course, there have also been major pandemics including the 1918 outbreak which is thought to have killed 40–50 million, but also in 1957 and 1968 and possibly in 2009 (which killed roughly 2 and 1 million respectively).

2   The landscape has already changed dramatically over the last decade around the preparedness of governments and communities to intervene in relation to families. For example, in the UK, see *Reaching Out – Think Family*, Social Exclusion Task Force (2007).

3   There is also a case that the state or third sector could facilitate more direct financial support and exchange directly between citizens, such as the fostering of credit unions where citizens lend to each other without using a traditional bank as an intermediary. Similarly, Local Economic Trading Schemes, that facilitate economic exchanges in the real local economy (as opposed to the economy of regard) are particularly relevant where capital and credit is short, such as applies in the current credit crisis.

4   This idea is picked up on in the UK government's most recent thinking on public service improvement: 'Working together – public services on your side', Cabinet Office, 2009.

5   In 1963, only 38 per cent of Northern European countries had 'mainly favourable' attitudes to young people. This rose to 44 per cent by 1969, and to 56 per cent by 1990.

6   See Steve Nickell's chapter in, Uberoi, Coutts, McClean and Halpern (eds.) (2009), *Options for a New Britain*.

7   One of Britain's most senior policy-makers – an economist by background – just commented how he advised his daughter to take a degree that enabled her to cover both economics and psychology. She was unable to find any such course, and instead just started on a degree in economics and history.

8   Peter Hennesey has recently, and forcibly made the arguement for expanding the non-military use of future methods in government.

9   OECD analysis (forthcoming) shows that Department Ministers in the UK have the highest levels of budgetary discretion of any OECD country.

10 The UK's most senior civil servant recently backed this idea – in the form of Public Service Agreements with linked budgets – at his speech of the launch of the Institute for Government (June, 2009).

Appendix

1   'Confidential' had a very particular meaning in the Civil Service. A confidential document meant one that had the potential to cause serious

damage to the nation and Government if public. In practice this meant that it should not be left out on a desk overnight (even within No. 10); that it should be kept in a locked cabinet and a note left if it was removed overnight; that if sent to another Department it had to go inside a double envelope to ensure it was not opened by the wrong person; and its circulation was highly restricted, preferably with numbered and named recipients.

2   There was also a sort of FSU 'pilot project' which was focused on Higher Education and research, that preceded the other big reviews.

3   It seems remarkable now, but pre-9/11 No. 10 had a remarkably relaxed approach to security compared with many government Departments, and relied very heavily on the police and doormen simply recognizing the faces of the regulars. There was no screening of the bags of visitors; and people were often let in even though their names were not on the list at the gate. On one occasion, a Canadian Ph.D. student who I supervised from Cambridge came for a discussion of her work on her way to the airport, two huge suitcases in tow. I only realized this as I walked her out after the meeting, seeing these two huge and unchecked bags sitting in the lobby where everyone passed through. Even after 9/11, I recall a meeting called by Jeremy Heywood bringing everyone together to discuss the situation and explaining that there were still people coming to meetings at No. 10 without their names on the gate. He explained that this wasn't good enough, and he was inclined to tell the police on the gate that from two weeks hence not to let anyone in whose name wasn't on the list. I think it's fair to say that a few of us expressed our surprise that this wasn't already the case.

4   There were times when the Commissioning Board fell into disuse, but mainly because the channels to the PM were so direct anyway.

5   The overall size of the PMSU fluctuated from about 50 to 80 people, though at one time peaked at around 120 people, following our temporary, absorbtion and breakings of the Office of Public Management (OPSR).

6   I actually picked up an armchair for the PM to sit in but, as was Tony's style, he didn't want to sit while others stood – though to the slight disadvantage of our shorter policy analysts.

7   See www.strategy.gov.uk for a published version of the 2003 Strategic Audit. The exercise was repeated with a more domestic focus before the 2005 election, and again shortly after Gordon Brown became Prime Minister (the latter published under the title of 'Strategic Challenges'). This Second Audit formed the Foundation of the 'Third term plan', led by me and Clive Bates.

8   Donovan and Halpern (2002), 'Life Satisfaction: the state of knowledge and policy implications', www.strategy.gov.uk

9   Michael Frayn (1991), *A Landing on the Sun* (London: Faber and Faber).

Index

Page numbers in *italics* denotes figure/table